Letters Home to Sarah

Guy Carlton Taylor (courtesy of Monroe County Local History Room, Sparta, Wisconsin)

Letters Home to Sarah

The Civil War Letters of Guy C. Taylor,
Thirty-Sixth Wisconsin Volunteers

GUY C. TAYLOR

Edited by Kevin Alderson and Patsy Alderson

THE UNIVERSITY OF WISCONSIN PRESS

The University of Wisconsin Press
1930 Monroe Street, 3rd Floor
Madison, Wisconsin 53711-2059
uwpress.wisc.edu

3 Henrietta Street
London WC2E 8LU, England
eurospanbookstore.com

Printed in the United States of America

Library of Congress Cataloging-in-Publication Data
Taylor, Guy C., b. 1840.
Letters home to Sarah : the Civil War letters of Guy C. Taylor, Thirty-sixth Wisconsin
Volunteers / Guy C. Taylor ; edited by Kevin Alderson and Patsy Alderson.
p. cm.
Includes bibliographical references and index.
ISBN 978-0-299-29120-4 (cloth : alk. paper) — ISBN 978-0-299-29123-5 (e-book)
1. Taylor, Guy C., b. 1840—Correspondence. 2. Soldiers—Wisconsin—
Correspondence. 3. United States. Army. Wisconsin Infantry Regiment,
36th (1864–1865) 4. United States—History—Civil War, 1861–1865—Personal
narratives. 5. Wisconsin—History—Civil War, 1861–1865—Personal narratives.
6. United States—History—Civil War, 1861–1865—Regimental histories.
7. Wisconsin—History—Civil War, 1861–1865—Regimental histories.
I. Alderson, Kevin L. II. Alderson, Patsy. III. Title.
E537.536th .T39 2012
973.7′475—dc23
2012015329

To our children and grandchildren with all our love.

Joseph Alderson; Jeremy, Angela, Carson, Brantley, and Landry Biermeier; Ryan, Nichole, Katherine, Brayden, and Ashlyn Alderson; Bryan, Christin, Rylee, and Blake Biermeier; Greg, Dana (Biermeier), and Ella LaBansky.

To all other family members, past, present, and future.

To all of America's veterans and their families, past, present, and future.

Contents

Illustrations

Preface

Going once . . . going twice . . . gone!! Sold to bidder number 80. The date was Saturday, April 29, 1995.

My wife Patsy and I were attending a household auction in Cashton, Wisconsin. Auctions had become one of our favorite pastimes, and we especially enjoyed collecting antiques to display in our folk Victorian home. At that auction, we were not intending to buy anything in particular but were willing, nevertheless, to bid if the right object caught our attention. Earlier in the day, we had executed our pre-auction ritual. We arrived about an hour before the sale and methodically inspected the items to be sold. We had learned from experience that once the selling started, there was little time to look things over. As I explored inside the garage of the residence, I spotted an old cardboard box. Upon examining its contents, I found a large quantity of envelopes. Most of the envelopes were blank, but on a few I noticed some printing along their top. I looked closer and read the words *U.S. Sanitary Commission*; on others, I read *U.S. Christian Commission*. Being a U.S. history teacher, I knew that during the Civil War both organizations had made significant contributions to the Union cause. None of the envelopes were sealed, so I picked one up and carefully peeked inside. I discovered a letter dated 1864. I thought to myself, "These are not just any old letters. They are, or at least I believe they are, Civil War letters."

I was excited, to say the least, but I was also an auction veteran. So I tried not to bring too much attention to myself. I made every effort to act normal, at least normal for me. I quietly shared the news of my discovery with Patsy. She humored me and, at least on the surface, seemed to validate my excitement with her own. Her enthusiasm was, however, somewhat more tempered than mine, and she quickly helped me arrive at my bidding limit.

Then I waited . . . and waited . . . and waited some more. Often thousands of items are sold at auctions, and I knew I needed to maintain my focus on the proceedings. I tried to be sociable and not be rude, but I also made every effort to keep from being distracted.

After what seemed like an eternity, I began to panic. Had the letters already sold? Did I somehow miss them? Where were they? I shared my concerns with Patsy. She advised that I should exhibit more patience. Finally, I saw the box! The time for the sale of the letters had come.

The bidding began. In our experience, auctioneers usually start by seeking a high bid before bringing the price down to secure a first bid. Sometimes auction rookies, being overzealous, bite at the high price. When that happens, the opening bid is often higher than my limit, and I end up getting in no bid at all.

This time, however, the price came down. I bid early, but not too early. I did not want to appear too interested in buying the box. I also waited to see if family members of the auction household were bidding. I had made it a practice not to compete against a family trying to maintain ownership of one of its heirlooms. But I was relieved and surprised to find that no family descendants were bidding. As the price increased, prospective buyers gradually weeded themselves out. Then, only a local antique dealer and I remained. The price was rapidly approaching my limit. I glanced at Patsy and saw a somewhat troubled look on her face. I knew that my participation would soon need to end. I thought I would have to accept the old adage: you can't always have what you want.

Suddenly my competitor stopped bidding. At least for the moment, I held the high bid. I waited. I knew that a late bidder or some crafty auction attendant might still get into the action and push the price beyond my reach. Meanwhile, the auctioneer worked the crowd in an attempt to get one last offer. I waited some more. After what seemed to be a long pause, it was over. The box and its contents were mine. Applause arose from the crowd, and I stepped forward to claim my prize. I gripped that box of letters like a running back grips a football at the goal line: tight! Very tight!! For $95 I was the proud and happy owner of an old cardboard box and the contents within it. I assumed many would consider my investment to be a small one, but to a husband and wife with five children and a tight budget, the purchase bordered on being extravagant.

I really had very little knowledge of exactly what Patsy and I now owned, but I was anxious to find out.

Upon returning home, I eagerly, yet apprehensively, searched through the contents of the box. I was certain I would find some Civil War letters, but I had no way of knowing their number, condition, or quality. For all I knew, most of the envelopes could be empty or have nothing to do with the Civil War or be in poor condition or illegible. I knew that I had taken a chance at the auction, and now I could hope only for the best.

I began opening each envelope. Inside, I found letters from Guy C. Taylor to his wife Sarah. They were indeed Civil War letters from a Union soldier. At first, I didn't take time to read them because I simply wanted to see how many there were. I was pleased to observe all but a few of the letters carried a heading that included a date and a location. I enjoyed placing each letter in chronological order. I felt as a prospector must have felt after discovering gold. I was ecstatic! This time my modest monetary investment had paid large historical dividends.

Eventually, I placed each letter in an acid-free plastic sleeve, and I purchased a Union-blue notebook in which to store them. At the Wisconsin Veterans Museum, I bought a short summary of Taylor's service record with the Thirty-Sixth Wisconsin Volunteer Infantry and used it for the cover of the notebook.

Now that the letters were properly cared for, I was ready to read and transcribe their contents. As a Civil War enthusiast, I was filled with anticipation.

As I initiated my project, I was impressed by Taylor's penmanship; however, his original spelling considerably slowed my pace. With the use of a magnifying glass, I continued to read. I transcribed the letters from his writing into my printing and found that by printing each word, I could better internalize the information in his correspondence. Steadily I proceeded. I had finished approximately forty letters when basketball season arrived. At that time, I was teaching social studies at Cashton High School and was the head boys' basketball coach. After the season began, I had no spare time to continue my project. Reluctantly I put Taylor's letters in safe storage. Except for occasions when I brought them out for display or to extract content to use in my classes, they remained untouched for the next fifteen years.

Although Taylor's letters were usually out of sight, they were not out of mind. It became a dream of mine to someday have them published. However, with family and career responsibilities, it became evident that my dream could best be realized after retirement.

After the 2007 school year, I retired from teaching. I assumed ample time would be available to continue my letter transcriptions. Had I heeded the advice of my busy retired colleagues, I would have had a more realistic expectation of what was to come.

Patsy and I decided to sell our house in Cashton and build a retirement home on land we owned near LaFarge, Wisconsin. Over the next two years, the selling, building, and moving process took much of our time. In addition, we established our new business, Kickapoo Valley Heritage–Art & Tours. Along with the Vernon County Historical Society, we self-published our first book, *Barns without Corners: Round Barns of Vernon County, Wisconsin*. Our book proved to be very successful, and we looked forward to further publications.

After considering other projects, we turned our attention to Taylor's letters. Since 2011 to 2015 were the sesquicentennial years of the Civil War, we determined that time period would be an excellent choice for the letters' publication.

At long last I brought the letters out of storage and continued their transcription. As I proceeded, I began to realize how informative and historically valuable they were. Taylor had been a keen observer of everything he experienced. In his letter dated January 6, 1865, he wrote, "It is natral for me to want to see evrything that is agoine on." In addition to seeing everything, it appeared he wanted to share much of what he saw with Sarah. Fortunately, his writing skills allowed him to provide detailed descriptions of what he witnessed. Taylor transformed his visual observations into vivid verbal images for her to view. What's more, several of his letters contained summaries of historic events for her examination. It also became evident that, as the war continued, Taylor's letters to Sarah became more engaging and reflective.

I was quite certain the content of these letters would appeal to teachers, scholars, and Civil War buffs. I also believed that most people could empathize with Taylor and his wife Sarah, who, despite their separation, struggled to function as a family. Their attempts to comfort each other from afar and their mutual efforts to raise their son, Charley, served as touching examples of their family commitment.

Eventually, Patsy and I began to question whether we would be able to distribute our new book on a wide enough scale to reach potential readers. Therefore, we decided to seek a publisher with a solid reputation and access to national and international markets. Since Taylor had been a Wisconsin

Civil War soldier who had trained at Madison's Camp Randall, we decided
to contact the University of Wisconsin Press. We received a prompt response. They expressed a strong interest in the letters, and a meeting was
scheduled. We were impressed by their cordiality and professionalism. We
were also pleased with their enthusiasm for our project. Patsy and I together
with the University of Wisconsin Press reached a mutual agreement for the
publication of Taylor's letters.

In hindsight, it was probable that Guy and Sarah Taylor had no idea their
letters would someday be published. Sarah did, however, preserve them
during her lifetime. After her death, the letters remained in the attic of
what was once Guy's Cashton, Wisconsin, home. Nearly 100 years later,
they were discovered and sold at an auction. By chance, Patsy and I became
their owners. We have since considered them to be a treasure and have
felt honored to be their stewards. We are pleased they have become acces-
sible to others and we know they can enhance our understanding of the
Civil War. And, perhaps, that was the reason for their survival—so that we
can view the war, as Guy Taylor saw it, through the eyes of a soldier.

Acknowledgments

Thank you to Kathryn Shively Meier for contributing her outstanding introduction. Also, thanks to our highly skilled copyeditor, Barbara Lund, Lakeshore Editing Services.

We would especially like to thank Park Rangers Tracy Chernault, Elizabeth Dinger, and Emmanuel Dabney from the Petersburg, Virginia, National Battlefield staff. Elizabeth was extremely helpful in connecting us with Tracy, who gave us a tour of the Petersburg Battlefield on March 21, 2011. The tour was tremendously informative and inspirational. Emmanuel, on the following day, provided us with information concerning City Point. Tracy, Elizabeth, and Emmanuel are truly representative of the incredibly valuable role public employees perform on a daily basis for their fellow Americans.

To Jack Davison, thank you for the wonderful tour of Sun Prairie and the town of Bristol.

Thanks to Lucy Vaaler for her expertise and input in the preparation of our manuscript.

We would also like to thank the following individuals and groups for their part in preparing the Guy Carlton Taylor Civil War letters for publication: the University of Wisconsin Press; Peter Michael Klein, Sun Prairie Historical Society; author Jerry Apps; Bonnie and Mike Schmitz, residents of the town of Clinton, Vernon County, Wisconsin; Beth and Jerry Hemmersbach and the Cashton Village office; Kristen Parrot and Carol Krogan, Vernon County Historical Museum; Jarrod Roll, Monroe County, Wisconsin History Room; Wisconsin Historical Society library staff; Kristine Zickuhr,

Wisconsin Veterans Museum; Vernon County Register of Deeds staff; Don and Sharon Copper, our Petersburg traveling companions; Janet Chapiewsky, resident of the town of Clinton; Jeremy Mosely, history teacher, Cashton High School, Cashton, Wisconsin; Nadia Lau; and our family, Joseph Alderson, Jeremy and Angela Biermeier, Ryan and Nichole Alderson, Bryan and Christin Biermeier, and Greg and Dana (Biermeier) LaBansky, for your love and support.

Visiting the Petersburg National Battlefield, Petersburg, Virginia (*left to right*): Ranger Elizabeth Dinger, Patsy Alderson, Kevin Alderson, and Ranger Tracy Chernault

Editors' Note

In preparing Guy Taylor's letters for publication, we considered correcting his spelling errors. In the end we decided to leave most of his spelling in its original form. Our advice to the reader is "when in doubt, sound it out." We did, however, find it necessary to correct the following words: *of* to *off*, *now* to *know*, and *one* to *own*. With these corrections, we felt the letters were much easier to understand. We also kept other kinds of changes to a minimum. For example, we did not make major changes to his grammar or punctuation but did insert an occasional comma or period and capitalize the beginning of his next sentence. We did not put his writing into paragraphs nor, although tempted, shorten his often lengthy sentences. In several instances Taylor incorrectly used ellipsis, which we let stand. We felt too much editing would alter the authentic structure and tone of his letters. Other considerations involved what material to include. We did want readers to be able to view the quality of Taylor's penmanship and the overall appearance of his correspondence, so we provided illustrations of some of his original letters. We also provided some notes to enhance the information in Taylor's letters. We kept the notes as brief as possible because we wanted the reader's primary focus to remain on Taylor's writing. Rather than write one lengthy introduction, we felt it was better to write one general prologue and then include previews of each section of letters. Our sections are based on time periods related to Taylor's various situations during his military service. Whenever possible, we identified the people who Taylor mentioned in his letters; however, there were some individuals who we were unable to identify. We have included the rosters of the Thirty-Sixth Wisconsin Regiment's officers and staff as well as Taylor's Company F in Appendixes A and B.

Introduction

KATHRYN SHIVELY MEIER

Guy C. Taylor was a typical Civil War soldier in some respects. A farmer and a Christian, he was nearly twenty-four when he joined the ranks of the Thirty-Sixth Wisconsin Infantry as a private. He wrote often to his wife, Sarah, in Bristol, Wisconsin, consumed as he was by thoughts of home and the welfare of their one-year-old son, Charley. Unfortunately for Taylor, he also shared in the omnipresent illness that characterized the life of the Civil War soldier. He was repeatedly, and at times severely, debilitated by disease to the point that he may never have fired his weapon in combat. Yet surviving sickness, as much as combat, was part of becoming a seasoned soldier. In that sense, though Taylor served just one year in Virginia, he was truly a veteran.

Yet the ways in which Taylor's letters contrast with the average published collection are what make them noteworthy. First, by being near but not engaged in the action, he was able to almost daily describe the major events of the last year of war and, unlike many comrades, analyze them in detail. The Thirty-Sixth was among a select group of Wisconsin units that served in the eastern theater of war, so as a midwesterner Taylor brought a unique perspective to such topics as geography and race relations while offering frequent glimpses into life back home. Second, the reason he avoided combat is itself interesting. Taylor enlisted late and was often sick, but so were many other soldiers; Taylor, however, parlayed his skills, as well as his relationships with medical personnel, to secure noncombatant jobs. Because Taylor's collection paints the world of soldier experience *behind* the frontlines, it provides an interesting counterpoint to previously published accounts of the final Virginia campaigns, such as Frank Wilke-son's *Recollections of a Private Soldier in the Army of the Potomac.*

The soldiers of the Thirty-Sixth were latecomers to the war, joining just after Ulysses S. Grant's appointment as general-in-chief of all US military forces in March 1864. On February 1, 1864, President Abraham Lincoln had put out a call for 500,000 additional troops, which would be satisfied by volunteers and conscripts. Taylor took pride in the fact that he chose to receive the bounty, a cash bonus paid to entice enlistees into service, instead of incurring the stigma of being a draftee. Even so, the veterans of the Army of the Potomac, who had faced years of fighting in Virginia, Mary-land, and Pennsylvania, regarded new recruits with suspicion and distaste, fearing their quick extermination by disease or bullet. In the spring of 1864, the outcome of the war remained entirely uncertain, and Grant's new strategy of exhaustion—which would involve a seemingly interminable ero-sion of Robert E. Lee's army in Virginia—would convince many Americans that the war was far from over. Considering that upwards of 45 percent of Grant's troops and 50 percent of Lee's would become casualties in the Overland Campaign of May through June 1864, the odds were not in favor of new recruits returning home.[1]

Taylor's first foray into a crowded army camp proved poisonous to his rural constitution, and he succumbed to measles before even leaving Wis-consin.[2] Upon reaching Virginia, he was hospitalized in Belle Plain and then moved to Mount Pleasant Hospital in Washington, DC, while his reg-iment endured tremendous slaughter at North Anna, Bethesda Church, Cold Harbor, and Petersburg. Taylor, meanwhile, battled first his meas-les, then pneumonia, lameness, and rheumatic pain. Yet when he was well enough to explore his new environs, he did. During his stay in the nation's capital, he displayed an outsider's knack for capturing the foreign sights that caught his eye. He described the capitol building as "a splended bild-ing it is all made of granic stone" (33), while a visit to the grandiose Smith-sonian humbled the farmer.[3] He wrote that the museum's hall "is about 100 feat long and fifty wide and their is glass cases on each side which is about 12 feet by 8 reaching from flore to flore." The cases were filled with "birds of all kinds from the humingbird to the conder" and other exotic curiosities, from crocodiles to period weapons (38). During his sojourn, Taylor exemplified the process by which rural soldiers enlarged their for-merly narrow worlds of experience.

Miles from the front, Taylor's most pressing concern in his first months of deployment was coordinating finances with Sarah to manage the family farm, rather than facing down the enemy. Soldiers endured inordinately long gaps between paychecks, and Taylor feared for Sarah's survival in the interim. When he did receive pay, he mailed it home in small increments, not only to safeguard against theft along the mail routes, but also to remind Sarah not to overspend. Taylor had to admit that he himself lacked financial restraint, as he grew bored in Washington with little else to do but fritter away his meager funds.

When Taylor did rejoin the Army of the Potomac in late July, it was already engaged in the nine-month siege of Petersburg. He vividly rendered the first sounds a green soldier heard of battle, not all of them unfamiliar. "[Y]ou can hear the boys talk, the dogs howl, the cats mew, the pigs a squealing, the calf a blating, and the chickens a squacing." That made "fine music," especially "when the bellow of the canons & the rattle of the muskets are intermingle with the rest." Wistfully, Taylor admitted, "if that was all that we cood see or hear war wood not seam to be such a horable thing, but when you [. . .] hear the shreeks and grones of the wounded, it is a diffrence thing alltogeather" (146). Novel sensory experience aside, Taylor was not immune to the crushing tedium and melancholy trench warfare engendered. "The boys say that if they do not moove prety soon that they will be so fat they cant walk at all" (87). Some men deserted when the opportunity was presented, as Taylor had learned when steaming back to Virginia aboard a transport ship. He observed, "We have got about 8 or 9 hundred of men on board that has deserted." A group of these deserters grew so desperate that "last nite their was som 18 or 20 that gump overboard and one of them was struct by the corner of the wheal house and went to the bottom" (50). But most soldiers did acclimate to the strange juxtaposition of clamor and paralysis along the Petersburg lines. At times a true philosopher, Taylor explained, "While som of our men are geting blown to atoms, others are laying (rite in hearing) as though their was nothing goine on at all. The men can lay rite by the side of a foart and sleap gust as well as so they was at home while the guns are makeing a deafing roar" (110). Such men had long since pushed aside fear to carve out temporary homes in the trenches.

Boredom for Taylor meant more time spent being homesick for Wisconsin. He kept up a daily subscription to his local newspaper, frequently igniting a mad scramble in his regiment for news of the familiar. "When I get my Madison paper the hole company and good meny others are runing after it so I cannot hardly read untill it goes the rounds," he complained (79). For news particular to Bristol, Taylor turned to his wife's letters. A topic of continued negotiation was how to manage the family farm. When Sarah sent word of poor agricultural conditions, Taylor fretted not just for his own fortunes but for those of his entire home state: "I am sorrous to hear that the crops are so poor for it is hard time anough their now and if the crops faile it will be a vary hard thing for Wis." (67).

While Taylor's private fortunes were bound up in news from home, he could hardly miss the political excitement electrifying the nation in the fall of 1864. Sick again, this time with malaria, Taylor observed the impending presidential election from behind the lines. The Army of the Potomac was in an odd predicament. The election pitted their beloved former commander, George B. McClellan, against the well-respected incumbent, Lincoln. In Taylor's estimation, the conflict at the heart of the political contest remained over slavery. "Their is a sturing times now in Camp [. . .] on the next election," he explained. "It beats all about the old army of G. B. McClenon, the most of them are strong slavery men. It is no wender that they have had hard times in this army hear before for it is slave men against slavemen, it is like a man trying to fite himself" (48). Yet with a tone of critical detachment, Taylor had little sympathy for their predicament: "[S]om boys that cant tell one letter from another, will talk as though they new evrything that is agoine on in the war department, when in reality they do not know what is don in their own company" (116).

As the election approached with no military progress in Petersburg, it appeared that Lincoln might fail; however, last minute triumphs from William T. Sherman in Atlanta and Philip Sheridan in the Shenandoah Valley secured Lincoln the win. This emboldened Taylor to predict the impending Union victory, his rising morale paralleling that of the Northern populace. Taylor penned expectantly, "[O]ur armey is now runing over the best part of the south, that is Georga. Shurmen is a striping evrything slick and clean, and Georga, had bin the vary mainstay of rebeldom." Taylor noted the scores of Rebel troops wandering into Union lines requesting the bounty for volunteering for United States military service. He attributed their defection to increasing Confederate poverty: "[I]t must be vary hard for poor people to live in the South" (146).

As Taylor contemplated the dissolution of the Confederate States of America, he regarded with interest the fate of black Americans. Lincoln considered his election a sign of popular support for a Thirteenth Amendment abolishing slavery, and by January 31 Congress passed this amendment to await ratification. Of equal interest to Taylor was the Confederacy's eleventh-hour debate to arm the enslaved, which the private termed "a bad egg." He predicted the "south will find out that Coten is not King of America," its underpinning system of slavery defunct (225).

Indeed, Taylor provided a midwestern perspective on the complex and shifting dynamic between white Union soldiers, the United States Colored Troops (USCT), and the enslaved he encountered. Taylor admired the black soldiers' eagerness to fight, an enthusiasm that had long since waned among white veterans. According to Taylor, "[T]he Negroes pickets keepe up a roar of Musketrey, while the whites [. . .] dont want to bring on a fite untill they are ablidge to, but the negro dont care how much they are a fiteing" (79). By the time Taylor encountered black soldiers, the USCT had worked for almost two years to curry favor with a Northern public skeptical of their ability to perform like white troops. An avid newspaper consumer, Taylor no doubt learned of such valiant USCT performances as those at Fort Wagner in July 1863 or at the Battle of Nashville in December 1864. Most Wisconsinites had had little contact with African Americans prior to the war, and certainly not enslaved people. Taylor appeared favorably impressed by those in bondage that he encountered. Indeed, he told Sarah, "Folks may say what they have amine to about the negro rase. They are grate deal more inteligant class of people then I had any fear, and if they had their freedom for a few years they wood be more able to take care of themself then their masters are" (79).

For all of the captivating details Taylor's letters provide about the final events of the Civil War, his most interesting contribution to the body of published eyewitness accounts pertains to his health. Managing various and protracted illnesses dominated the soldier's wartime experience, and yet he appears to have made the most of a bad situation. Because of his various skills, he was able to secure a series of noncombatant positions. He could tend to horses and was a decent launderer and good cook—a vital talent among men whose poor cooking often triggered diarrhea.[4] Furthermore, he befriended medical personnel, particularly his regimental assistant surgeon, Elijah A. Woodward, who employed him as an aide and later as a hospital nurse. On July 29, 1864, the doctor had Taylor sign over his gun and prepare for noncombatant service. With no love lost, Taylor wrote, "I do not think that I shell cary a gun again while I am in the armey" (79). He was well aware of what this meant for his prospects of surviving the war. He told Sarah, "The doc says that I can go to the hospital any time I want to, but he wants me to stay with them, so you must not worey about my being shot for in a few days I shell be in the hospital or with the dockers" (79).

While Taylor surrounded himself with medical staff, he also took his health care into his own hands. Two-thirds of soldier mortalities were from disease rather than combat, not because the men had no access to care, but because disease and treatment were poorly understood. Civil War physicians occupied a transitional intellectual space, where old beliefs in bodily humors persisted and competed with alternative theories, such as topographical medicine or homeopathy. Thus, some treatments required purging, while others suggested relocating to healthier climes further north or consuming herbs. Most field surgeons had to rely on quick treatments in their medical kits, generally mercury- or opium-based medications, which did little to cure underlying conditions and could even compound suffering. Besides quinine for malaria and fresh fruits and vegetables for scurvy, few effective medical treatments were understood. Yet some soldiers, such as Taylor, adopted self-care regimens that proved surprisingly effective at managing health.[5]

Taylor explained to his wife that his peculiar position behind the lines afforded him considerable health benefits. He enjoyed free time and flexibility that his fellow soldiers in the Thirty-Sixth did not. For instance, Taylor practiced good sanitation, in particular frequent bathing. As he told Sarah, soldiering was a filthy endeavor: "We lay down in the dust and swet and the wind will blow dust on ous so when we get up we look like a dust stack. You wood not know any of ous" (57). Most of Taylor's comrades could not bathe and grew desperate: "[S]om of the boys has bin 3 days without washing, but you may bet they wash in urnest when they get a chance to" (57). Taylor, however, could locate fresh water at will, for bathing and even more important, for drinking.

The private also commented that building adequate shelter from Virginia's mercurial elements improved his comfort and well-being. He wrote, "You may think that others can fix up beds as well as I, but it is not so, they do not have the chance that I do, you see the orders are not to cut a stick for anything but I can go and get stuff" (32). Furthermore, Taylor meticulously managed his own diet. He was attentive to his intake of fruits and vegetables, which helped him avoid scurvy and kept his spirits up by improving upon the monotonous army rations. He wrote, "The woods are full of huckelbarys [. . .] I got a pint yesterday and made me som sauce and it went nice now I tell you" (62). Despite his generally sickly countenance,

Taylor succeeded in keeping himself well enough to return home alive—an achievement indeed.

One common treatment for illness, both prescribed by doctors and self-administered by soldiers, was alcohol. Taylor usually avoided the remedy, as he carried the unique mantle of Wisconsin temperance to the warfront.[6] A fiery battle over the regulation of alcohol had been raging in his home state since the 1830s, with the Sons of Temperance and the Good Templars on one side and the anti-Prohibition Germans on the other.[7] Both Taylor and his wife were members of a temperance order, and Sarah frequently reported progress on their quarrelsome home lodge. Taylor hoped the brothers and sisters could work it out, writing, "I expect to be back there again in the course of time and I want to see that Lodge and all of the Lodges in good running order" (166). In the ranks, Taylor lambasted alcohol consumption. He expected army chaplains to preach abstinence and chided officers for failing to police the vice or even participating in it. In a particularly vitriolic manner, Taylor tells how "one lieutenet got so drunk last nite that he cood not get to his tent and layed out all nite and sombody was good anough to go and cut off his sholder straps." Taylor spat, "[I]t is a great pity they did not cut his head off, then he would not be a torment to himself nor to anybody eles" (85). Thus, Taylor attempted to avoid what he considered a crude treatment for the illness and loneliness rampant in the ranks.

Taylor's open recognition of the benefits of noncombatant work along with his late enlistment date and frequent complaints of illness beg the question: Was Taylor a shirker? If so, his letters become all the more significant, as identifying such accounts has proven incredibly challenging for the scholar. By 1864, the Union and Confederate medical departments had warned surgeons to be on the lookout for feigned symptoms of invisible ailments, such as rheumatic pains. Yet Taylor began the war with a clear case of measles, which can produce a string of secondary ailments. Furthermore, contracting multiple diseases per year was in no way extraordinary for a Civil War soldier.[8] At the very least, if Taylor exaggerated his illnesses to continue to avail himself of life behind the frontlines, then his friends among the medical staff did not object.

For Taylor and his comrades, the war dragged on until April 1865 when Grant and Sherman finally wore down the major Rebel armies. At that point, Taylor's letters began to meditate on one thought: going home. Even his April 19 letter addressing the president's assassination was more concerned with demobilization than politics, though he did hope to see John Wilkes

Booth "hang dingling in the air" (250). When participating in the May 23 and 24 Grand Review of the Armies in Washington, he could barely contain his impatience to be home. "[T]he Cry of the Soldier is let ous go home [. . .] we do not like to be lead around (like wild beasts) for a mear show" (263–64). Nor could Sarah Taylor understand her husband's continued absence, apparently pushing for him to procure a discharge. After all, the soldier had been sick for the entire war. But Taylor took an almost perverse pride in sticking to his service till the end: "I have stood the test untill the war is over and pease once more raigns over our land, and now to have a discharge that says that I am not fit for a soldier, I do not want" (276). He reassured his wife that he would probably be home sometime over the summer. "I had reather stay 3 months longer and go out with the reg then to go out on a sick discharge," he declared (276).

Despite Taylor's lack of combat experience, he eventually developed a deep grasp of war, perhaps more incisive than the men in combat who did not have as much occasion to reflect on it. In his early months in uniform Taylor had expressed discontent with his subservient role: "We are like a dog go wheirever our master goes" (56). But over time he conveyed respect and awe for the soldier experience. "It is a good school for a man to be in the army that is if he is a mind to make it so. He can lurn human nature rite along" (34). Part of Taylor's education was watching so many friends in the Thirty-Sixth Wisconsin fall—a ghastly 57 percent casualty rate—and part was grappling with his own homesickness and mortality. While Taylor pored over his wife's letters and occasionally peeked at her photograph, he recognized that there had to be a divide between soldier and civilian in order to retain his sanity. As he succinctly put it, "Why if I should sit down and let my mind run on things at home I should bin ded long ago" (72). In the end, it did not matter that Taylor wore the blue uniform for only a little over a year. He had become a veteran, just like the rest of the men who had the good fortune of making it home.

NOTES

1. For casualty estimates, see Rhea, *Cold Harbor*, 393.

2. Approximately 50 percent of new recruits succumbed to contagious diseases in their first months in camp (Steiner, *Disease in the Civil War*, 12–13).

3. Taylor's colorful spelling is a sign of the lack of standardization at the time rather than a lack of education. More than ninety 90 percent of Union soldiers were literate (McPherson, *For Cause and Comrades*, 11).

4. Diarrhea was no trifling ailment in the Civil War; it carried with it a 10 percent mortality rate (Calcutt, *Richmond's Wartime Hospitals*, 25).

5. For details regarding soldier self-care, see Kathryn S. Meier, "'This Is No Place for the Sick': Nature's War on Civil War Soldier Mental and Physical Health in the 1862 Peninsula and Shenandoah Valley Campaigns," *The Journal of the Civil War Era* 1 (June 2011).

6. Taylor did, however, write of taking bitters and gin on May 14, 1864.

7. See Joseph Schafer, "Prohibition in Early Wisconsin," *The Wisconsin Magazine of History* 8 (March 1925): 282.

8. See Steiner, *Disease in the Civil War*, 104.

RECOMMENDED READING

Adams, George Worthington. *Doctors in Blue: The Medical History of the Union Army in the Civil War*. Baton Rouge: Louisiana State University Press, 1996. First printed 1952 by Schuman.

Calcutt, Rebecca Barbour. *Richmond's Wartime Hospitals*. Gretna, LA: Pelican Publishing.

Clarke, Frances M. *War Stories: Suffering and Sacrifice in the Civil War North*. Chicago: University of Chicago Press, 2011.

Glatthaar, Joseph T. *Forged in Battle: The Civil War Alliance of Black Soldiers and White Officers*. New York: Free Press, 1990.

Hess, Earl J. *The Union Soldier in Battle: Enduring the Ordeal of Combat*. Lawrence: University Press of Kansas, 1997.

Linderman, Gerald F. *Embattled Courage: The Experience of Combat in the American Civil War*. New York: Free Press, 1987.

Lonn, Ella. *Desertion during the Civil War*. Lincoln: University of Nebraska Press, 1998. First printed 1928 by the American Historical Association.

McPherson, James M. *For Cause and Comrades: Why Men Fought in the Civil War*. New York: Oxford University Press, 1997.

Mitchell, Reid. *Civil War Soldiers: Their Expectations and Their Experiences*. New York: Viking, 1988.

Rhea, Gordon C. *Cold Harbor: Grant and Lee, May 26–June 3, 1864*. Baton Rouge: Louisiana State University Press, 2002.

Rutkow, Ira. *Bleeding Blue and Gray: Civil War Surgery and the Evolution of American Medicine*. New York: Random House, 2005.

Sheehan-Dean, Aaron, ed. *The View from the Ground: Experiences of Civil War Soldiers*. Lexington: University Press of Kentucky, 2007.

Steiner, Paul E. *Disease in the Civil War: Natural Biological Warfare in 1861–1865*. Springfield, IL: Charles C. Thomas, 1968.

Valencius, Conevery Bolton. *The Health of the Country: How American Settlers Understood Themselves and Their Land*. New York: Basic Books, 2002.

Wilkeson, Frank, *Recollections of a Private Soldier in the Army of the Potomac*. New York: Putnam, 1886.

Letters Home to Sarah

Prologue

G uy Carlton Taylor was born April 7, 1840, in the town of Ripton, Addison County, Vermont. His parents were George and Axchsa (Russel) Taylor. In 1855 the Taylor family, consisting of seven members, moved to a farm in the town of Bristol, Dane County, Wisconsin. In 1861 Guy married Sarah J. Thompson, daughter of John and Elizabeth Thompson, who also farmed in the town of Bristol. Sarah's family consisted of nine members.[1]

On February 1, 1864, President Abraham Lincoln called for 500,000 additional Union soldiers. The Civil War was about to enter its fourth year. When the call came, Guy was twenty-three years old, Sarah was twenty, and they had a one-year-old son, Charley. They lived on a farm in the town of Bristol. In response to Lincoln's request, Guy volunteered his service to the Northern cause. In his letters, it became evident that financial enticements (bounties) as well as patriotism were factors in his decision to enlist.

More than 160 letters are in the Guy Carlton Taylor collection, with several of those letters being written over multiple days. During his military service, Taylor wrote, on average, more than twice a week to his wife Sarah. His first dated letter was written from Camp Randall on March 25, 1864—only four days after he had enlisted. His last letter was written from Jeffersonville, Indiana, on July 9, 1865—just three days before his unit was mustered out.[2] The only gaps between letters were the result of Taylor's illnesses, his travel to and from the front, his being on the march, or his involvement in battles. Each time there was a significant lapse between letters, Taylor offered a complete accounting for each missing segment of time.

From his letters, Taylor soon emerged as a devoted husband, father, and family man. He was very interested in and concerned about the physical and emotional well-being of everyone at home. He loved getting mail from home and encouraged family members to write often. References to family members other than Sarah and Charley included those to his father George, sixty-six; mother Axchsa, sixty-one; brothers William, thirty-eight, and George, twenty-nine; sisters Martha, thirty-one, and Amanda, twenty-six;[3] father-in-law John, forty-three; mother-in-law Elizabeth, forty-one; sisters-in-law Frances, sixteen, Henrietta, fourteen, Harriet, ten, and Mary, seven; and brothers-in-law William, twelve, and John, nine.[4]

In his letters, Taylor provided detailed descriptions of casualties, fortifications, weapons, camp organization, weather, and terrain. Entire pages were devoted to passages concerning battles, strategies, and troop movements. His correspondence regarding camp life created an interesting account of a soldier's diet, housing, amusements, and punishments for misconduct. He wrote about picket duty and the fraternization that frequently occurred between Yankee and Rebel soldiers. Taylor's letters clearly revealed the ambivalence he felt toward his enemy. He despised the Southern cause and its leaders, but he felt a certain camaraderie with Rebel soldiers in the ranks.[5]

The most outstanding feature of Taylor's letters was the evolving depth of his idealism and reflections as the war progressed. Early on, his letters were often focused on logistical items, such as bounties, allotments, finances, and general pleasantries. As time passed, his letters gradually turned to more complex subjects, such as race, duty, politics, and war.

Taylor entered the army shortly after Ulysses S. Grant received his commission as lieutenant general. In his new position, Grant commanded all of the Union armies. He left the western theater of the war with William Tecumseh Sherman in charge. Grant moved to the eastern theater, where George Meade continued to be the ranking general of the Army of the Potomac; however, Grant's military role was dominant. When Grant left the West, he brought General Philip Sheridan to the Army of the Potomac and placed him in command of the cavalry.

As I sought to put Taylor's service in perspective in relation to the Army of the Potomac, I found General Grant's memoirs to be a valuable source. Grant summarized conditions in the East in March of 1864 as follows:

The eastern theatre of the Civil War found the opposing forces in substantially the same relationship to each other as when the war began in 1861. The

Union Army of the Potomac and Confederate Army of Northern Virginia were both located between the federal capitol Washington, D.C. and Confederate capitol Richmond, Virginia. Battles had been fought with as great a severity as had ever been known to war. Fighting had occurred over ground from the James River and Chickahominy near Richmond to Gettysburg and Chambersburg in Pennsylvania with indecisive results. While a portion of the Army of the Potomac was engaged in guarding lines of communications the rest of the army was located on the northern bank of the Rapidan. The Army of Northern Virginia was on the opposite bank of the Rapidan strongly entrenched and commanded by the acknowledged ablest general in the Confederate service Robert E. Lee. The country back to the James River was cut up with many streams which were generally narrow, deep and difficult to cross except where bridged. The region was heavily timbered and the roads narrow and in poor condition after the least amount of rain. The enemy had prepared adequate fortifications at convenient intervals all the way to Richmond so that when they were driven from one fortified position they would always have another to the rear to fall back into.[6]

It is apparent from this passage that Grant understood the difficulty of the struggle at hand. He knew that defeating the Army of Northern Virginia and their brilliant commander General Lee would be a formidable task; however, unlike Union generals before him, Grant also understood that only the destruction of Lee's army would bring an end to the Confederacy. At long last, Lincoln had found a general who would achieve on the battlefield his primary goal of saving the Union. From the beginning of Grant's Overland Campaign in the spring of 1864 until the final Union offensive culminating with Lee's surrender at Appomattox in the spring of 1865, the Army of the Potomac and the Army of Northern Virginia were in constant contact. During this period, I believe Grant can best be described as relentless. Nothing deterred him from his military objective of not only defeating but in fact destroying the legendary Army of Northern Virginia.

The time has now come to turn to Taylor's letters to continue this story. Collectively, they reveal an exciting, although tragic, account of one soldier's adventures of a lifetime, during the bloodiest year of America's Civil War.

NOTES

1. "1850 United States Federal Census," www.ancestry.com; accessed September 15, 2010.

2. The regimental roster included in James M. Aubery's history of the Thirty-Sixth Wisconsin indicates Taylor was mustered out July 12, 1866, but he was in fact mustered out July 12, 1865 (Aubery, *Thirty-Sixth Wisconsin Volunteer Infantry*, 309; see also Appendix B).

3. "1850 U.S. Federal Census." To arrive at the ages of the Taylor family members, I added fourteen years to their ages listed in the 1850 census.

4. "1860 United States Federal Census," www.ancestry.com; accessed September 15, 2010. To arrive at the ages of the Thompson family members, I added four years to their ages listed in the 1860 census.

5. See Taylor's letters dated January 14, February 23, and April 14, 1865.

6. Grant, *Personal Memoirs*, 364.

CHAPTER I

In Training

March 25 to May 16, 1864

I n March of 1864, Guy Taylor, along with his fellow recruits, reported to
Camp Randall in Madison, Wisconsin. There they were formed into the
Thirty-Sixth Wisconsin Volunteer Infantry Regiment. Taylor was assigned
to Company F. The unit was organized under the command of Colonel
Frank A. Haskell. Colonel Haskell was a veteran of the Sixth Wisconsin
Regiment, which belonged to the famous "Iron Brigade." In July of 1863,
he had distinguished himself at the Battle of Gettysburg and earned the
reputation of being a soldier's soldier. He was known for his courage under
fire, his discipline, and his sense of duty.

James M. Aubery in his history of the Thirty-Sixth Wisconsin reported
his impressions of Camp Randall in this way:

> Camp Randall was located near the State University, a short distance from the
> beautiful capital city, Madison, and when first made must have been a beau-
> tiful camp. When we arrived there grass was badly cut up, the spring rains
> had made it muddy and wet, and we could hardly reach headquarters without
> getting over our shoes in mud. Barracks had been built especially for the
> Thirty-sixth, consisting of ten long, narrow, rough-board buildings. . . . Madi-
> son and vicinity was patrolled by the provost guard to pick up any soldier who
> had no pass, and they had their hands full, for there were, at one time, while
> we were there, seven thousand men.[1]

As Guy Taylor trained to be a soldier at Camp Randall, Sarah and Charley
moved into the farm home of her parents, located in the town of Bristol,
Dane County, Wisconsin. There they would live for the duration of the war.

In March and April of 1864, General Grant developed plans for what became known as his Overland Campaign. At that same time, the Thirty-Sixth Wisconsin continued its training at Camp Randall.

Then in a letter written on April 5, Taylor told Sarah that "the docter says that I am acoming down with the measles." Eventually Taylor recovered his health enough to rejoin the Thirty-Sixth and complete his training, but he would continue to be plagued by illness throughout the rest of his service.

On the third and fourth of May 1864, the Army of the Potomac crossed the Rapidan River. Its primary objective was to destroy the Army of Northern Virginia. The war was about to enter a new phase, and in his memoirs, Grant stated that he knew "the losses inflicted, and endured, were destined to be severe."[2] His prediction proved to be true as his Overland Campaign resulted in heavier losses to both armies than had been experienced in previous campaigns of equal duration. It appeared that this Civil War was to be a total war, a war of attrition, a proverbial fight to the finish.

The first major confrontation in the spring campaign of 1864 occurred on the fifth and sixth of May. It came to be known as the Battle of the Wilderness. According to official war records, the Union suffered nearly 18,000 casualties compared to an estimated 11,200 for the Confederates. To make matters even more tragic, many of the wounded burned to death as they attempted to escape fires started during the engagement. After the battle was over, Grant, unlike his predecessors, continued south. As the battle raged, the Thirty-Sixth Wisconsin finished their training and waited for the order to board railroad cars at the Madison depot.

The next major battle of the campaign was fought from May 8 to May 21. This engagement took place in the vicinity of Spotsylvania, Virginia. Again the fighting was furious, with losses reaching 18,400 for the North and an estimated 12,400 for the South. On May 11 during the battle, Grant sent a letter to Major General Halleck, chief of staff of the army. In the letter, Grant declared, "I . . . [propose] to fight it out on this line if it takes all summer."[3] Grant knew he had advantages in manpower and provisions over Lee, and he intended to put his advantages to good use. Meanwhile, Lee held on to the hope that inflicting enough casualties on the North would lead to Lincoln's defeat in the upcoming 1864 presidential election—and perhaps if that happened, the new administration might negotiate a settlement to the conflict.

On the tenth of May, during the Battle of Spotsylvania, the Thirty-Sixth Wisconsin (after losing 26 men, who had died from disease) left Camp Randall by rail. They arrived in Washington, D.C., on May 14.[4] Taylor wrote an account of their journey. He also revealed that he became very ill along the route from lack of sleep and exposure to the elements. On May 17, the Thirty-Sixth Wisconsin left Washington, D.C., and headed for the front. That same day they reached Belle Plain, Virginia, which had become the major supply depot for Grant's campaign.

NOTES

1. Aubery, *Thirty-Sixth Wisconsin Volunteer Infantry*, 34–35.
2. Grant, *Personal Memoirs*, 391.
3. Ibid., 419.
4. Aubery, *Thirty-Sixth Wisconsin Volunteer Infantry*, 36–37.

[Note: *Taylor's first letter—no date.*]

Dear Wife

I suppose that you hav given me up as a lost child, but it is not so, for I am in Camp Randel[1] and it is garded all around by men so I cant get strayed nor lost I am well and at work in the cooks room. We have about 90 men

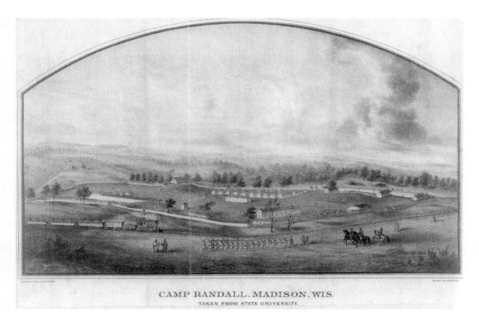

Camp Randall, Madison, Wisconsin, taken from state university, c. March 7, 1864 (courtesy Library of Congress Prints and Photographs Division; Louis Kurz, lithographer)

to cook for and it makes som work I thank you, Mr. Marr[2] is my bunk mate. We have one blanket apease so we can sleep as well as so we ware at home. I think now that I shell be to home in 2 or 3 days but may not in 2 or 3 weaks I wish that you would tell Moses[3] or George[4] to sell the chance on that . . . [illegible] for what they can and George had better take the cow and sell the oxen if he can. Tell George I want him to com out to camp on a mondy or teusday if he can and tell Mose that I can let him hav som money in 2 or 3 days if he wants som, if he does he had better come to camp and get it in case I am not at home by Wenesday next. Pleas write so I may know how you and Charley is getten along and all the rest.

G.C. Taylor.

Derrect Madison Camp randel 36 Reg Co. F

I will inclose a invelop with the derrections on so you can see. I have inclosed 10 dollars for you to use for what you wish.

NOTES

1. Camp Randall was a training camp located in Madison, Wisconsin. It was named for Governor Alexander W. Randall. In excess of seventy thousand soldiers were trained at Camp Randall during the Civil War.

2. Pvt John B. Marr, age 41, farmer, Bristol, Dane County, Wisconsin, Co. F, Thirty-Sixth Wisconsin Infantry (*Roster, 36th Wisconsin Infantry Regiment of Volunteers and Draftees*, 135).

3. Moses McKinney was married to Taylor's sister Amanda (Vernon County Historical Society, Genealogy Collection, Taylor family file).

4. George was a brother to Guy Taylor.

∾

March 25, 1864
Camp Randell
Madison, Wisconsin

My dear wife,

I write to let you know that I am well and I hope that you and Charley and all the rest of the folks are injoying the same blessing, but I had rather go home and tell you that I am well then to write to you but I am under Unkell Sams orders and cannot do as I want to but must obay orders I do not know when I can get home but I can write and so can you and I hope that you will write often and tell me all about how you are ageting along.

You had better let eather george or moses take the cattle and sell them and you had better go and stay with moses untill I do get home and do not woury about me for I am in good quarters wheir I have agood place to sleep and have anough to eat. We have got our uniform so we have plenty of clothing for rain or shine. Tell moses or George that I want to see one of them or both wright away and tell them to com so that they can stay all nite with me, som of the boys just com in and says that we are orded to Racein[1] to camp for drill. It is said to be the best camp in the state but we shell not go for a weak or so, if any of you com out inquir CoF 36 Reg it is in barrect 24. When you write derrect to Camp Randell CoF 36 Reg Madison Dane Co Wis.

Guy C. Taylor

NOTE
   1. Camp Utley was a Civil War camp located in Racine, Wisconsin.

∽

Camp Randell
March 31, 1864

Dear wife

   I was glad to hear from you and to know that you and Charly is well. I have bin a little unwell for a few days but I feal furst rate today but the Capttion[1] sed that I had better not go out to drill, so it gives me a chance to write so I thought that I wood write to Amanda[2] and to you. I received a letter from Amanda last nite and they are all well. I am sorry that Moses shood get mad about our affair, but I dont no as I can help it. I think that we must look out for ourself before we can for others, I suppose that you want to go to Farther Thompsons[3] to live, while I am gorn. I think that he has made you a good offer and if you want to go their I am purfetly willing for you to go and I will build a snug warm house for you but I wood like to see Father Thompson before I do anything about bilding. I wish that I cood go home and see you and Charley, but I must wait untill the time coms for a furlow without murmering and you must waite with pasiant and hope for the best. We had a Temperance meating[4] in our barreck last nite and we had a good speaker now I tell you if I am any judge of speakers. I am agoing to send this letter up to town to be mailed by John Slinglan[5] and he is a waitting for it. I thought that I would write to Farther on the other page of this sheat but I must close so good by.

G. C. Taylor

NOTES

1. Capt Prescott B. Burwell, age 33, cabinetmaker, Sun Prairie, Wisconsin, Co. F, Thirty-Sixth Wisconsin Infantry (*Roster, 36th Wisconsin Infantry Regiment of Volunteers and Draftees*, 124).

2. Amanda McKinney, sister of Guy Taylor.

3. Father Thompson, Guy Taylor's father-in-law.

4. The temperance movement was a social movement against the use of alcoholic beverages. Guy Taylor was a strong advocate for Prohibition.

5. Pvt John Slingerland, age 33, butcher, Sun Prairie, Wisconsin, Co. F, Thirty-Sixth Wisconsin Infantry (*Roster, 36th Wisconsin Infantry Regiment of Volunteers and Draftees*, 141).

Camp Randell
Apr 5, 1864

Dear wife

I take my pen in hand to let you know how I am. When I wrote to you last I was well, but I can not say I am real well at the preasent time. The docter says that I am acoming down with the measles. I suppose that you will want to com and see me but I think that you had not better com for you wood have to bring Charley with you and it wood expose him and you cood not help me much. I will write to you ever other day if I am able to so you can tell how I am a getting along. Most likely by my being carfull I shell be well again in a few days. You must write often. It has bin four or five days since I have received any letters and I have written as meney as one a day since I have bin in Camp. You must not worrey about me for the boys will take as good care of me as can be.

I must close

Guy C. Taylor

∾

Camp Randall
Madison, April 8th/64

Mrs. Guy Taylor,

At your husband's request I take my pen to inform you that he is now down with the measles and under my care attended by a regular Physician. The measles came out first rate yesterday, I attended him faithfully in bunk last night and am happy to write that he is now five minutes to eleven alright, and having a good nap. I have just read two letters to him one from his bro William Taylor[1] the other from his sister McKenney all well. One boy in barrack has had the measles and got about alright. We intend to keep our boys from the Hospital if possible, others have been in the Hospital and come out safe. Our company are as well as any I know of in camp. We have a first rate ordily. At nine o'clock eve all is quiet and prayers attended to. We have one Methodist Preacher, two Class Leaders, one Recording Steward and four other church members in our company. Your husband thinks you had not better try to come out here as he is doing so well. I will write again if necessary, keep up good courage your husband is my brother.
    Resptfly yours,

J. B. Marr for Guy Taylor

PS: Your husband has awoke and tells me your letter was rec last eve. We expect a furlow soon, will be glad when it arrives we want to see home once more
    Good noon,

J. B. Marr

NOTE
    1. William Taylor, Guy Taylor's oldest brother.

∾

Camp Randall
Saturday AM April 9th/64

Mrs. Taylor,

Having a chance to send a line by Mr. Murdaugh of Sun Prairie, your husband wishes me to write that he is on the gaining hand. The Dr. was in this a.m. and told me he was doing finely and would be out in a day or two. He told me I might now give him cold water. He has often told me he wished he could have some but the Doctor's orders were warm drinks and that he has had, also baked apples all he has called for. I shall still have an eye to him that he takes no cold but the order has come for drill and I must close. We drill six hours a day. If you have a chance send word to my family all is well.

In haste

J. B. Marr

For Guy Taylor

◠

Camp Randell
May 5, 1864

My dear wife

I thought I wood write and let you know what we have bin aboute today. This fornoone we drill as useal and this afternoone we was led out through the gate and drill on the commons in frunt of camp awhile and we ware led upon the hill north of camp and we had a nice green place, for drill, we had just got up the hill when we saw a fire up town and the Curnol[1] gave the command about faice, place rest, and we run for stumps and stons to get seats so we cood look and see the fire and we did not sit but a few minuts when we see another fire and we cood see the men arunning with the fire engine and in a few minuts the fire was plaid upon by the engine and the flaims was stopt and a black cloud of smoke arose, but the buildens that was on fire was burnt to ruan. Their was one house one barn and one granery. The house belongs to a widow, and it is most all she is worth, but about the drill, we fell into line again and we march in line of battle down the other side of the hill, and it is covard part of the way with brush and one of the boys fell down and struct rite on his face and it made his nose blead in good urness. We march to the bank of the forth lake[2] and stood on prarade dress and the boy that got hurt went and put watter on his head and we waited about 15 minuts for him, and the Cournel said that we wood have to leave him on the enemy ground for we had no wagons to cary him on, but when we got to camp he was their. Our guns have got hear to the depot. I have not hurd anything new about our going away. The Capt wife came in camp tonite and we had for our supper a good peace of blackbary pey and some pickled bets. After a few remarks from our ordely we fell in for supper. We sind the alotment[3] roll today so we have no more to do with the bounty[4] nor what we alot. When you come out again if you get your papers made out I will go with you to get your money, in case you have to com aloan. Tell Hen[5] she must send me hur picture for I hurd she had som taken. Tell Bub to com out to camp and see me, in case that George Chipman[6] pays you for the plowing you had better buy you and Charley some close with it for most likely they will be hire instid of lower.

I must close.

Guy C. Taylor

NOTES

1. Col Frank A. Haskell, Madison, Wisconsin, Thirty-Sixth Wisconsin (Aubery, *Thirty-Sixth Wisconsin Volunteer Infantry*, 327–30).

2. Madison is sometimes described as the City of Four Lakes. The fourth lake refers to Lake Mendota.

3. Payments made from soldiers' pay to spouses, parents, creditors, or other individuals.

4. A program of paid bonuses to entice enlistees into the army.

5. Henrietta Thompson, a sister-in-law to Guy Taylor.

6. George Chipman, married to Guy Taylor's sister Martha (Vernon County Historical Society, Genealogy Collection, Taylor family file).

◡

Camp Randell
May 7, 1864

My dear wife

I thought that you would like to know how I are a getting along. I am a getting along first rate. Chipman and Mart[1] and father and mother was out hear last thirsday. I got a letter from Amanda a few days ago and they are all well. She said she thought she wood com and see me in to or three days. We have head agood rain, but the boys that was out on gard last night thought it was pretty ruff. They come in this morning wet to their vary hide and their was som loud talk. Our cook is sick and I have taken his place and Henry Vroman[2] is helpen and we have a good time of it. The boys get eggs and want ous to cook them and we take anough to pay ous for our truble of cooking them, we have got our guns, and the report is now that we are to leave next tuesday for somewheir but we do not know wheir but the cars are at the depot awaiteing for ous. Some think that we are agoing to be sent to Minasota but I do not know and dont care much onely to get out of Camp Randel. We may not see one another again for a long time, but after the time has pased to look back it will look short. You must not get downharted but hope for the best. Mr. Marr is well and he seems to injoy himself first rate he is getting as fat as a hog. If we do not go now you must try and come out again before long. I understand that Jovy has bort that forty off Mr. Seaver I think that he had better get somebody to tell him what he wants (if he has not all ready). We have got vary good guns they are the Springfield Rifle.[3] Tell the girls that they must write and the boys to and let me know what Faneys adress is and as soon as you find out wheir John is I want you to write to me. I must close and go to work.

Guy C. Taylor

NOTES

1. "Mart" is Martha Chipman, Guy Taylor's sister (Vernon County Historical Society, Genealogy Collection, Taylor family file).

2. Pvt Henry Vroman, age 33, farmer, Sun Prairie, Wisconsin, Co. F, Thirty-Sixth Wisconsin Infantry (*Roster, 36th Wisconsin Infantry Regiment of Volunteers and Draftees*, 143).

3. The Springfield rifle was a 58-caliber percussion musket that was the most widely used shoulder arm of the Civil War (Garrison, *Webb Garrison's Civil War Dictionary*).

Washington
May 14, 1864

My dear wife,

We have just landed in the great city all saft and sound. I am not vary well but I feel a good deal better today then I have for the two past days. I got up and cook the rations the last night I was in Camp Randel and I work vary hard and I haven no sleap and then getten on the cars and then the boys make such a noys nobody cood sleap and being without sleap so long it was to much for me, and then we wrode in cars that the raine went threw from overheade and the sids and it rained for 3 days and nites and we ware a nice looking set of felows now I can tell you, but the worst nite I got into the baggage car and I kept dry but it was not a vary easey place to sleap. I had no apatite to eate. I did not eate as much from Madison to Maryaland as I would have eaten to one meal when I feal allrite, but one of the boys run the gards that stood at the dore and went to a drugs store and got me a bottle of bitters and sum gin and I tooke the bitters for 4 or 5 times only when I began to eate again and I begain to feal better again. I think by the time I get my bottle yoused up I shell be allrite again but the docker says that he would till I get strong again. I am thinking that will be a good many days for I am vary weake now but I feal vary well. We are agoin to leave hear tomorry morning for the frunt, but we do not know wheather we are agoing into some fortification or to take the field.

May 15

I feel little better this morning by being carfull I will get my strenth again in the corse of 2 weeks but I shall not be fit for duty before then, so if you hear of battles for a while you may know I am not in it. You will worrey and think that I am vary sick but it is not so, for I feal well as I ever did except being weak. You may derrect to the 36 Reg CoF Wis. Vol. via Washington.

I will write in a few days again.

G. C. Taylor

May 16, 1864

My dear wife,

I take my pen in hand to let you know how I am and wheir I am, I am a gaining slowley but I think by being cairful I will soon be fit for duty but you may rest asuared that I will not try to do duty again untill I am as strong as ever. Ive tryed it once and it was anough fore me to learn to do better I begin to think that my health is worthe more to me then the worke that I can do is to the company but a child never dreds the fire untill it gets burnt. We started from our quorters in Washington this morning at 7 o'clock and pass up by the Capital and down threw the sitty and took the boat to go to the frunt. We do not know yet whether we will go rite on the frunt or go into some place our men have laitely taken. We are now going down the river[1] we just pass Alaxander.[2] I should think that it was about as large as

Madison, the capital at Washington is a splendid thing. As I am tiard after walken too miles and the gain of the heat so I will not try to write any more this time but I will again when we stop so I can so good by to all of you.

G. C. Taylor

Dir to 36 Reg Co. F Wis. Vol. via Washington D.C.

NOTES
   1. The Potomac River.
   2. Alexandria, Virginia, at the time of the Civil War, was a busy Potomac River port and the terminus of three Virginia railroads. The city is separated from Washington, D.C., by the Potomac River. Alexandria was occupied by Federal forces from May 24, 1861, to the end of the war. The city was well fortified and served as a Union camp, supply depot, naval base, and hospital center.

CHAPTER 2

Hospitalization

May 17 to June 23, 1864

On May 18, the Thirty-Sixth marched to Spotslyvania and joined the
Army of the Potomac. They were assigned to the First Brigade, Second Division, Second Army Corps. Their corps commander, General Winfield Scott Hancock, was regarded as one of the Union's finest officers. The
regiment, although being held in reserve, came under fire for the first time
on May 19. When the Thirty-Sixth arrived at the front, Guy Taylor was
not with them. The sick and the lame had been sent back to the hospital at
Belle Plain, Virginia. Taylor's illness on the train may have been a com-
plication of his earlier case of measles. He was hospitalized at Belle Plain
until May 22, and by May 24 he had been sent back to Mount Pleasant Hospital in Washington, D.C. He did not rejoin his regiment until June 25. By
that time, the Thirty-Sixth had fought at North Anna, Bethesda Church,
Cold Harbor, and in the assault on Petersburg. In his history of the Thirty-
Sixth Wisconsin, Lieutenant James M. Aubery of Co. G stated that on June
1, 1864, 240 soldiers from Companies B, E, F, and G of the Thirty-Sixth
made a dashing charge on the enemy. During the assault, 166 men were
killed or wounded. With a casualty rate of 69 percent, the Thirty-Sixth
endured one of the highest casualty rates of any Union regiment in any
battle of the war.[1]

In a second frontal attack on June 3 at Cold Harbor, the Thirty-Sixth's
losses were 73 men killed or wounded. One of those killed was Colonel
Frank Haskell. Haskell received a Rebel ball to the temple.[2] Total Union
losses in the attack were approximately 7,000 for the North and 1,500 for
the South. In his memoirs, Grant noted it was the only assault he ever

regretted having ordered.[3] Total losses for the Army of the Potomac at Cold Harbor from June 1 to June 12 were nearly 15,000. Lee's total losses were approximately 4,900.[4]

Assaults on Lee's lines at Petersburg from June 15 to June 30 brought another estimated 16,500 Union casualties. From May 5 to June 30, during the Overland Campaign, the Army of the Potomac experienced more than 60,000 casualties.[5] Despite the Union losses, Lee's army was still firmly entrenched, and the war was evolving into a siege.

While the slaughter at the front was taking place, Taylor remained hospitalized. Ironically, his serious illnesses might well have saved his life. But despite his having missed the battles, he witnessed the carnage caused by the fighting.

During his lengthy hospitalization, Taylor developed a realistic expectation of the effects of war. His fellow soldiers of the Thirty-Sixth had been rushed directly into the meat grinder, probably before they understood what was to come. Taylor was blessed, or perhaps cursed, with ample time to observe the agony of the wounded, ponder his own situation, and contemplate his uncertain future. His realizations must have been chilling indeed.

On June 17 Taylor was ordered to headquarters to be examined and was selected to go to the front.

At sundown on June 25, 1864, Guy Taylor arrived at the front. There he found himself embroiled in the siege of Petersburg.

NOTES

1. Battle of Bethesda Church, June 1, 1864 (Aubery, *Thirty-Sixth Wisconsin Volunteer Infantry*, 264).

2. Ibid., 68–69.

3. Grant, *Personal Memoirs*, 444.

4. Trudeau, *Bloody Roads South*, 315.

5. "The Price in Blood: Casualties in the Civil War," http://www.civilwarhome.com/casualties.htm.

∽

Belles Plains Landing
May 17, 1864

My dear wife,

When I wrote to you last I said that we ware a going to the frunt. We left Washington and at the Plains[1] and marched about 1½ miles and camped

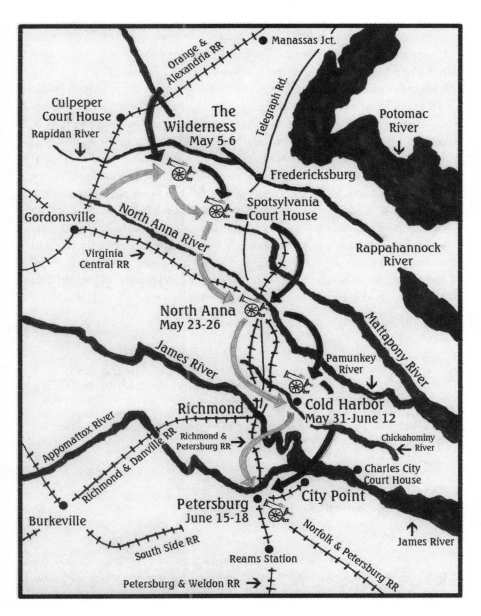

The Overland Campaign, 1864 (map by Patsy Alderson)

for the nite, and I found that I cood not travle so in the morning the sick and the lame went back to the landing again and I was one of them. We struck our tents on a side hill so we have a fine vew of the boats and men, by being sick I have lost my napsack and everything that was in it so I have not a shurt to put on. I have got another napsack I found and a blanket so all that I miss is my tent and my paper and invellops and my undercloaths but I can get what I want in clothing in a day or 2 for the boys are a throwing them away by wagon lods.[2] I see in one plaice as much as two lods of coats & blankets. I do not know how long we will stay hear but it will be till we can go to our reg. again but that wont be long if we dont have no pull back[3] for mose of us can walk 3 or 4 miles vary well with our napsacks but we cannot stand it for all day. I have got so I can eate my reglar ration now so I think that I will be allrite again in 2 or 3 days. I espect that we will be wheir I cannot get a letter threw so you must waite with patiance untill time so I can write. I have not written to any of the rest for want of paper and pen but you must send them word and as soon as I can write I shell. Pleas write often for your letters will come to me if I cannot write to you but I do not know for surtain but I can write to you reglar.

Guy Taylor

NOTES

    1. Belle Plain, Virginia, located on the Potomac River, was a base of supplies for Gen Grant's Army of the Potomac. The base was constructed specifically for the Civil War and was constantly crowded with transports and naval vessels that received and uploaded stores and troops.

    2. Union soldiers would lighten their load for marching by discarding gear they felt they did not need at the time of the march.

    3. Retreat.

U.S. Sanitary Commission[1]

May 17, 1864[2]

    Bells Plains, my dear wife as I have nothing to do I think that I can write to you pretty oftain. I am on the gain evryday. I can travel pretty well now, but I do not intend to starte for my company untill I am still better then I now am for I do not think that I cood travel to keepe up with the rgt. and cary a napsack but then I suppose I cood follow the regt by going as gard over the baggage wagons but I do not yet propose to do so. I have lurnt to be as independant as any of them and I have got threw runing at evrybodys say so. Now as we are hear and it is our place to report to the dock, but as shure as one gets so he can walk atawl the doc puts them on gard of some wagon that is going to the frunt and sends them to their regt. so I think that I do not know whair the doc lives or elce I do not want to know. I expect that our regt. has gorn rite on the frunt[3] and most likely they will be in a batle in a few days but may not. Their is about six hundred wounded men

Belle Plain, Virginia, Army wagons and transports at the lower landing, 1864 (courtesy Library of Congress Prints and Photographs Division; Timothy H. O'Sullivan, photographer)

hear today that has just come frome the frunt[4] and they look pretty bad are some of them ware shot rite threw the head and still aliven. I see one die and their was 3 or 4 more that died. The boys that are wounded so to loose a arm or a legg says they are better off then the rebs are that are a marching by them between gards, for they say they can ride and are well fed while the prisners have to walk. Write to the 36 Reg. Co F Wis. Vol. via Washington. I cannot write long letters for I cannot get the paper but I hope to get some prety soon.

Guy C. Taylor

NOTES

1. The U.S. Sanitary Commission was organized by civilians in June 1861 to assist the army in caring for its sick and wounded soldiers and to protect their dependent families. The commission's programs ranged from those using field ambulances and nursing and hospital services to those that cared for and protected discharged soldiers. The personnel maintained soldiers' rest and convalescent camps, which offered soldiers special diets, attention, and even supplies that included paper, envelopes, and stamps (Faust, *Historical Times Illustrated Encyclopedia of the Civil War*, 199). It was one of the Sanitary Commission–furnished envelopes that attracted my attention at the auction.

2. Either Guy Taylor wrote two letters to his wife on May 17 or one of the letters was misdated.

3. His regiment arrived at the front during the Battle of Spotsylvania Courthouse, May 8–21, 1864.

4. Guy Taylor was encountering casualties from Grant's Overland Campaign, May 5–7.

❧

Bells Plains, Vergina
May 19, 1864

My dear wife,

As we are about redy to go to the frunt I thought that it mite be a good while before I cood send you another letter but I do not know but the mail runs regorly to the frunt. I am a getting real smart again but not quite as strong but we mite as well be with the regiment as be hear for we have tent liven and have to camp the same but the camping and liven is good anough for a well man but a man that is vary sick had better be somewheir elces. You must not wory about me but try and injoy yourself the best you can and I will do the same. I suppose you wood like to know what kind of country I am in. Well we are on a side hill and it is a hill (not a Wisconsin bluff) and

Belle Plain Landing, Virginia, view of the tents of the Sanitary Commission, 1864 (courtesy Library of Congress Prints and Photographs Division)

the river[1] is on one side of ous. The lay of the land is hills and rivers and the land is covard with bushes for all the large treas have bin cut off. When we left Madison we pass threw Jansville then to Checargo, Ill. and we hade a nice supper their. The land threw Ill. is vary low and wet allso threw Indiana. The next time we stopt it was at Pitsburg in Penn. And we got some supper their. Pensilvany is vary hilley in deed. We did not stop again untill we got to Maryaland and we stop at Baltermore for a few hours. I was so sick that I cood not get out of the cars but I cood looke from the car and see some of the sitty. We then went to Washington and we got their a Saterday about fore o'clock in the afternoon and we staid their untill on moundy morning and then we started for the frunt and we landed at Bells Plains 20 mils below Washington and hear I am yet but the reg. has gorn to the frunt.[2] Their is about 20 of ous that is left behind but we will soon be with the other boys at least some of ous. We may go into a fite and we cannot tell who may be hurt but you must try and hold up good currage and be pre-paired for the worst and then all will be rite. I wish I cood see you and Charley but I cannot and it will be a long time before I can but time flies on and when this war is over if I am premited to return home again I can injoy myself so can my famley. I shell have to close you must write often if you do not get any frome me.

Direct to the 36 Reg. Co F via Washington, D.C.

Guy C. Taylor

NOTES
    1. The Potomac River.
    2. The Thirty-Sixth Wisconsin reached the Army of the Potomac on May 18, 1864, at Spotsylvania, Virginia.

∾

Bells Plains
May 21, 1864

My dear wife,

We are still hear and I do not know how long we may stay. I am still gain-ing in strenth but I am not able to go to the Reg. to think of going on duty for I cannot cary a napsack two mils I do not belive to save my live but I feal first rate except being weak. I suppose that you and Charley is well at least I hope so. I wish I cood hear from you but it is so I cannot untill I get back to my company for we do not know when we shell be taken to the frunt but I hope it will be before long for the sake of some of the boys for their is no dockers hear to take care of them. As for my part I do not cair for I do not want no docker for I do not want any medison. All I want is time to get my strenth and I had as live be hear as neir the frunt if I was onely able to stand it I would like to go to the frunt of the line of battle with the rest of the boys but I am not and it will be many days before I shell be able. I have gust come from getting my Breakfast and I see one boy that had two of his fin-gers shot off. He just come from the frunt and he said that we drove Lee fore mils with a hevry lost. Our lost in all the fites has bin about 50,000 kill and wounded[1] but Grant is receiveng reinforcements faster than he losses men while Lee dos not receive any reinforcements atall so we have the advantage of them on men but they are on their own ground and we have to attack them so we loose more men then they do but we have taken a good many prisners. Their has bin some 7,000 sent threw hear and they say that their is a mess more that has not bin sent hear yet but are garded in the rear of the armey. I went over on a point yesterday wheir I supposed their was a Suttlers tent[2] and when I got over their I hurd that the quertermaster[3] of our Reg was their laying in a boat, and I went out to the boats and I found that all our rations and findly evrything that belongs to our regment was their and I found Mr. Marr was their on gard. I went in the morning and I staid till the midle of the afternoon. It is about one mile and I was nearly tiard out when I got their I found my napsack their and Mr. Marr came back with me and brot it over for me so we are well supplied for a tent and for blan-kets so we are in as good a place as we cood ask for. Their was a man fell from a Steamer as it came up to the whorf and the poor fellow was drowned to death before they cood get him out. I must close for this time but I will write again tomorrow or next day if we are not taken nire the frunt and if we are I can not write anymore untill after this battle is over and I hope that wont be meny more days but we do not know. Good by for this time.

Guy Taylor

You must hold up good chear and hope for the best. Write often to the reg for I shell get them some time or another. You must not get downcast but keepe up good chear and injoy yourself the best you can. You must not let it disstroy your happerniss becaus of me gorn from you.

Direct to the Company via Washington D.C.

NOTES

1. The 50,000 killed and wounded refers to losses during Grant's Overland Cam-paign in 1864.

2. A *sutler* was a civilian licensed, or permitted, to operate a shop at a military camp or post.

3. A *quartermaster* was an officer whose primary duty was to provide quarters, food, clothing, and transportation for troops and forage for their animals. Charles B. Peck from Edgerton, Wisconsin, was the quartermaster to whom Guy Taylor was referring (Aubery, *Thirty-Sixth Wisconsin Volunteer Infantry*, 293).

Washington D.C.
Mount Pleasant Hospertol[1]
May 24, 1864

My dear wife,

    When I wrote to you last I said that we wair agoing to leave. The next morning we went and see the dock and he sent 13 of our reg to Washington. We started on the boat at about ten oclock and we got to Washington at half pas foar. Then we got into wagons and got at the hospertol about sunset. The hospertol is in a pleasant place and it is neat and clean around the tents. We have cloth tents but they are hevy canvas cloth and the ruff is double so it is as dri as any hous and their is a good flore laid so their is no dampness from the ground. We have vary good beds each man has his own bed so he cannot croud upon his naighbor. I do not know how long we will be hear but we will not leave untill we are fit for duty, and I do not think that will be for some time with me at any rate. I am about the sam as I have bin. It is the effects of my taken coal after the measels. I feal vary well but I am vary weak and my legs are same as they was when I was at home last. I think that now I have got hear that by being careful I shell get along now in the cors of time but it will take time to fetch me allrite again. Their is one thing surtain as long as I am laim so I cannot do duty, their is no danger of being shot, so you may rest asured that their is no ball run for me yet, but I am in hopes that I shell get well anough to go to my company again for if I do not in a month or so they will put me in the invalid core,[2] and I had rather go to the frunt then to stand gard around camp, but if I do not get well anough to get to the frunt, wone thing surtain I shell be out of danger, and I shell not have to march and lug my napsack, so if I have lost a good deal in loosing my health I have gain a little. The old saying is, "their is no great lost without some small gain," but I think my gain is vary small, but then if a man dos not know anough to take cair of his own health he must bair the quanciquancs of his ignrance. We have a plenty to eat hear and I do not have to lug stuf up hill to keepe the other men alive. The same men are hear in the next tent to me so we can see one another as oftan as we have a mind to for the tents are not more than twenty feat apart. They are a getting along pretty well but it will be a long time before they are fit for duty. You must write as soon as you get this and write all about how you

Mt. Pleasant Hospital, Washington, D.C., view of buildings and grounds, between 1861 and 1869 (courtesy Library of Congress Prints and Photographs Division)

get along and write all the news. I must close for this time but I will write in a day or two again so good by for this time.

Guy C. Taylor

Direct to Guy C. Taylor, Mount Pleasant Hospertol, Washington, D.C.

Be carful in derrecting your letter I have written on hear all that is wanted on to have it come hear.

NOTES

1. Mount Pleasant Hospital opened in March 1862. It was one of many military hospitals located in Washington, D.C. It closed in August 1865.

2. As the war dragged on, disabled soldiers were reassigned to noncombat duty so that others could fight. In April 1863, the Union War Department created the Invalid Corps, which consisted of two battalions of disabled men. The first battalion was assigned garrison duty, and the second performed hospital duties. In the spring of 1864, the corps was renamed the Veteran Reserve Corps. An estimated 60,000 men filled its ranks during the war (Garrison, *Webb Garrison's Civil War Dictionary*, 158).

Mount Pleasant Hospertol
Washington D.C.
May 26, 1864

My dear wife,

   I take my pen in hand to let you know how I am a getting along I am a gaining vary well now. I can see that I am considable stronger then I was 3 days ago but I have got some coff yet but the dock has given me some medison this morning for it. It is not vary bad but I think I had better stop it before it gets to be bad. I am getting so I can walk better but it will be some time before I shell be fit for duty. They do not send men from hear untill they are well so they can go to work. The other two men that camp with me at Bells Plains are hear but I have not sean one of them since the first day we got hear the other is now sitting on my bed, by the side of me. He is a getting a long first rate but I think it doutful if he is evry fit for duty, his back is worse than no back. He is one of our company and we shell stay togeather as long as we can. I suppose that you are injoying yourself first rate and Charly to at least I hope you are. I wish I cood just step in their some of theas eaveins and have a chat with the folks, but it will be some time yet before that can be, but time is on the wing and as we look back it seams vary short. I am injoying my self first rate and I like camp life first rate if I was able to folow the company I shood be as contented as a lamb in a clover field but I cannot go yet so I content myself hear. We can get out around hear and not get stuck in the mud as we did at Camp Randel. It is sand around hear and if it rains evry so hard it is dry in a hour after it stops, so it is good walking and then their is a nice grove of timber gust outside of the tents so we can go and sit in the shade. It is vary warm weather hear, it is not like Wis. I do not know when we shell get our pay but I think not untill this battle is over.[1] You have bin in the habet of getting letters in my name but I shell not write them so any more for the letters that the govermant writes will be in your name so I shell write them so and then it will not bother the Postmaster any. I expect that you are getting pretty short for money, if so; you must go to Chipman and tell him to let you have som. You must take good cair of Charly but dont pet him to much for a pet lamb is a poor thing but make him mind when you speak to him. I wish I cood see him and you to but I must wait untill Unkel Sam says I may go home and I am willin to wait for the more I see of the effects of the war the more I want to be in it. You do not know nothing about the war in Wis. if you cood come hear and see the men it would make your blod run cold in your vanes. In this little place 2500 men wounded in this hospertal, some with one leg & some with one arm some shot threw the head and evry place you can think of. Their is 16 wounded in the tent that I am in but this is nothing what it was at Bells Plains, but I must close for this time. You may not write any letters to come hear for I do not know when we may be sent away. They are sendin them away as fast as they can to other places to give room for others that are wounded vary bad.

Good by, Guy Taylor

NOTE

1. Taylor was referring to the Overland Campaign, specifically the battles of the Wilderness, Spotsylvania, and North Anna.

∼

In camp near Washington D.C.
May the 27, 1864

My dear wife,

As it is a weet rany day and time seams to drag sloaly away I thought that I cood not spend a part of the day any better way then by writing to you and let you know that I am well and full of misschief, as you well know I wood be if I am well. Well it is natral for me to be rather wild but then I guess that I will get over it somwhat in course of 50 years or such a matter. Well I cannot tell you any nuse this time for we are hear likee so many dogs shut up. We cannot go a mile from camp for anything whatever unlesswe run the pickets and of coarse we dair not do that for fear of being shot with a empty gun. We have laid around in the rain and mud untill their has about one six of the men got sick. They are not hard sick but are not fit to do anything and if we lay hear for 4 or 5 weaks longer and keep such damp weather as it has bin for the last 2 weaks their will be ⅓ of the men sick. They have to lay rite on the ground and they have no blanket to put over them but they say that the things we sent away last spring will be hear in 2 or 3 days. You must not think that I have to lay on the ground, for I do not I have got a good bed, and I did have 2 vary large blankets besides my over coat & ruber,[1] but one of our co. boys was not well and I gave him one of the blankets but I have a plenty, and have a big tent to stur into. You may think that others can fix up beds as well as I, but it is not so, they do not have the chance that I do, you see the orders are not to cut a stick for anything but I can go and get stuff and their is no officer to com and ask any quastion about my bed for the same officers that have charge over me wants a bed of the same kind so we agree first rate and have no growling about it. Well I have sed that I had not got anything new to tell you, but I have got one thing that will be nothing new though for you to hear, that is that I got mad today but I did not hurt anyone. Well perhapes you wood like to know what I got mad at. Well you see I port som beans to soak last nite and today I thought that I wood have a nice dish of beans and I hade got them all cook and they was nice to and I sat them down on som wood and down com the wood and down com the dish of beans all in the dirt (den I was mad) but I guess I will feal better by morning if I do not have to get up to meny times to stake down the tent to keep it from blowing away. Their has one of our officers gust got his discharge papers Capt Potter[2] is his name. I wood have don the same as he has if I was in his plais. At any rate I never wood have bin in camp when the reg was discharged, for I shood not expect nothing less than a crack head and think myself luckey if I cood get off as easy as that. Well how is our little boy a getting along, if he has not got so to walk on his foot yet you had better send for som other docter. You cannot take too much pains with him their will be cripples anough at the best and it may be his luck but if we do our best we shell not feal as though we was to blam. Well how dos the baby and all of the little famley at father Thompsons house get along, and how do they get along about their work. Well sis[3] I sent you 10 dollars in confed. money[4] and you have not sed anything about getting it. I have got 5 dollars more but I do not think that I will send it untill I know wheather you have got that or not. Well Sis I must close for this time so I will bid you good by from you husband

Guy C. Taylor

　　To his wife & child
　　Sarah J. and Charley G. Taylor

NOTES

　　1. Union soldiers were issued a waterproof rubber blanket for use as a groundcover or a covering.

　　2. Capt Potter was probably Wesley S. Potter from Brodhead, Wisconsin, Co. D, Thirty-Sixth Wisconsin Infantry. However, Taylor must have been mistaken about the

discharge because official records reveal that Capt Potter resigned May 25, 1865 (Aubery, *Thirty-Sixth Wisconsin Volunteer Infantry*, 302, 394).

3. Taylor often referred to Sarah as "Sis." We were unable to determine whether that was Sarah's general nickname or simply meant to be an affectionate greeting by Taylor to his wife.

4. Confederate money was printed in every denomination found in the states of the Union. Individual Southern states and even corporations were allowed to print scrip, a practice resulting in additional denominations.

～

Mount Pleasant Hospatol
Washington D.C.
May 28, 64

My dear wife,

I take my pen in hand to let you know that I am yet among the living. I am bout the same as I have bin, some days I feal quite smart and think I shell be able to go to the frunt in a few days but maby the next day I do not feal so well, but I have made up my mind that I shell not be fit to go to the frunt for some time yet. I have bin mooved from the tent that I was in, so to give room for the wounded. We have vary good tent wheir we now are. It is most likely that we shell stay wheir we are now untill we are able to go to the frunt. The docker was gust in hear. He is a old man but he noes his buisness. He told me that it wood be some time before I got well, but he wood fetch me around allrite again. I feal vary well but I do not gain any streanth as I can see, one thing the dockers that have seen me before has not gave me anything to give me streanth. All that I have had is a little cough medison and I should not got that if I did not go to the dock for it, but this old fellow is a going to give me somthing he say that will give me streanth but what it is I do not know. I suppose you are a wouring about me thinking that I am sick but you nead not worery for I am not sick atall that is to feal sick and I am gust as well off hear as I cood be if I was at home. I can go around all I want to, we cannot go outside of the gards but we have got plenty room to go in. It is not like camp randell wheir a purson has not got room to turn around in. In the tent wheir we are now are we can look rite into the sity. We have got a fair vew of the capital. It is a splended bilding it is all made of granic stone. I have not hurd anything from our Reg. since it left Bells Plains but I expect it has gorn down wheir Buttler[1] is. If they have they have got a good genral. Old Ben, is not beate

by meny men, but I do not expect to get down their untill Old Grant & Buttler is both in Richmon for I think by the time you get this theyr will be
inside of the fortifications of Richmon but then they may not, but Grant is
given Lee all he wants allthough Lee is dissputing evry foot of the ground
but Grant still goes on. It is a horable Battle our men are cut down like
grass but as they fall their is more to step rite in their plaices, and on they
go. It seams that Grants army was like grass in the hot sun, it withers in the
day but the coole nites dew revives it up again and in the morning it is as
fresh as evry, but it is not so with Lee when his men falls, he cannot get others to take their plaices. I wrote to you in my last that you nead not write to
me in this place but you may for I do not know how long I may be hear and
if I leave before I get it their wont be no harm don. Write as soon as you
can. I must close for this time. I will write again in 2 or 3 days so good by.

Derrect to Guy C. Taylor

   Mount Pleasant Hospatol, Washington, D.C.

NOTE
   1. Union Gen Benjamin Butler was commander of the Army of the James.

∽

Mount Pleasant Hospatol
Washington D.C.
May 30, 1864

My dear wife,

   I am yet hear and I am gust about the same as I have bin except I am a
little stronger, but not anough to brag of, but I still think that I shell be able
to go to the Reg. again in a short time but I may not. I am fealing first rate
and we have a vary good time hear. We can go around as long as we want
to, and when we get tiard we go and lay down on our bed. We can get what
papers we want to read and that is all we can get unless we by Novals and
they do more hurt then good. I wish that I had some good Book to read but
we cannot get them unless we go to town for them and money is to scurse
to by books but then we can spend our time to good advantage by going
among the wounded. It is a good school for a man to be in the army that is
if he is a mind to make it so. He can lurn human nature rite along, he can
see the diffance between men in bairn pain. Som men I have seen with

their arm or leg all shot to peases and they would not make a mite of fuss, and some with a fingar shot off would swair about the pain and such swairing I nevry hurd before I was in the army, and it is a fact that the roughis men are the men to find falt with evrything. They cannot be suted anyway. I suppose that Edd is fast for going to the war yet, but if he had bin wheir I have bin he would have seen anough so he would think it was no fun and I have not sean the battlefield yet. I would say to anybody that was old anough it is your duty to and help put down this rebelion but it want men and not boys, and men must be orful tough to stand this spring campain. Men are march day and night and som men that you would think would stand anything are coming back all used up. Their was 10 of our Reg. come back to this hospartol yesterday. Their was 6 of them wounded and one was killed on the spot. They was in Co. H & K. They was out on picket duty and they had a schurmish and the other fore was sent back sick. Their was one from our Co. he says that he is on the gain he stop to Port Roral[1] to days he was not able to come but he is so he can get around pretly well now. He was sunstrut[2] twise once he was pick up by our gards and he got a little better and he went to the reg again and he was sunstrut the day he got to the reg again and then the Dock sent him hear. We are a going to get a pass to go down to town tomorrow to get our pay. The paymaster is in the sity and we can get our pay if we can get down their, and some of the boys says that see the clurk, that the Paymaster has not got the alotmant roal yet and if that is so he will pay the bounty to me, and I shell send it home by mail and then you can have it to help yourself with, but he may have got it before this time. I am getting rather short for money. My being sick I have spent money prety frealy but I am so now I do not have to by stuff to eat for I can get a plenty to eate and that is good anough for anybody, so I have got anough money to stand me awhile yet, so if I do not get any pay now I shell not complain, that is if they make out their returns to the Reg so they can send you the allotment, which will be Fifty Dollars, for if I get out of money I shant be a spending it. The boys says that they have bin on the frunt six month to a time without a sent of money and they did not want any as long as they was their. One thing is that their is no chance for spending money and I think that I have got anough while I stay hear. When I first wrote to you from this place I ment to have you send me 50 cts worth of postage stamps but I did not think of it so I wrote to George the same day and told him to send them to me and you would pay him. I can get them hear but I am a little carful what I bye for evry sent counts when a purson has not got but a few dollars. You must not get down hearted but must injoy yourself, for if you do not you will get so you wont cair wheather you live or die. I am injoying myself first rate all that I worry about is home, and I shood not worry about home if I cood hear from their but it seams as so it had bin a long time since I hurd from home but then I can wait with patiants. You mite write to me in case I leave it will do no harm but you will loose your stamp you put on it. I must close for this time I will write again in a few days so good by.

Derrect to Guy Taylor

Mount Pleasant Hosparital
Washington D.C.
Write all the newse

NOTES
1. Port Royal on the Rappahannock River replaced Belle Plain as Grant's supply base.
2. Sunstrokes happened frequently on the march, especially when soldiers were oppressed by tight-fitting clothes and heavy accoutrements and when obliged to march in close order.

ᨃ

Washington D.C.
June 2, 64
Mount Pleasant Hospotal

My dear wife

I received the mail yesterday that has bin sent to the reg. and you must know that I was glad to hear from home. Their was six letters and two papers for me. I have bin down to the sity today and I am prety tiard, it is about two miles but we did not walk more than ½ amile and then we got into a streat car and went rite wheir we wanted to go. We went down to get our pay. Their was not only 7 days pay due me but it was anough to get the bounty which was forty dollars. The way it comes that I get the bounty is that the paymaster has not got the alotment role yet, and if I did not go and get it he would have gorn to the frunt and paid them and then we would not have got any untill the next pay day, so I thot it best to go and get it so he cood report to the reg wheir we are and then the reg cood report to the state. Their is good meny men hear that has not taken any pangs to let their reg know wheir they was so they have bin reported to they state as deserters and their folks cood not draw any money from the state untill they sent to the reg. a sertificat from the docker stateng wheir they was, and then the reg. had to report to the state. I thought that would not pay. I shell send the mony home but a little and I shell send it in letters at diffance times. I will put in ten dollars to a time and I will send it as fast as I think it is proper. I do not want to send it all so it will be on the rode to a time, but by the time you get part the rest will be on the way. I am getting along prety well now but my legs are bout the same. I am so I can eate like a hog now I feal first rate in body and mind with the exception of my runers.[1] I must close for this time I will write again tomorrow or nextday and file a little acount of what I see at the sity so good by for this time.

From you husborn

Guy C. Taylor

NOTE
  1. We assume Taylor is referring to his legs.

Washington D.C.
June 4, 1864
Mount Pleasant Hospertol

My dear wife,

I take my pen in hand to let you know that I am still among the living. I am on the gain, if I was not laim I should apply for a discharge from the hospertol and go to the reg but their is no use in my trying to walk yet to think of marching for I cood not cary the heft I should be ablige to and walk ½ of day without makeng me so laim I cood not stur. I told you in my last that I would tell you what I see in the sity. Well we started from hear at ten oc and went ½ mile and then we got into a streatcarr and went to the office of the Paymasters, and then we went to the Smithsonain Institution.[1] It is a splended bilding it is granet stone. As we went up the steps we went into a small room wheir was all kinds of refreshments for sail. We pass threw that room into the museam hall. The hall is about 100 feat long and fifty wide and their is glass cases on each side which is about 12 feet by 8 reaching from flore to flore, and shelf as they wanted them. Well the first I see was birds of all kinds from the humingbird to the conder. As I look

Smithsonian Institution, between 1867 and 1869 (courtesy Library of Congress Prints and Photographs Division)

from case to case it brot fresh to memry what I have read and aspeshly the condor the largest bird in the world, as it is the pleasure for you to sore so high and rest your vary wings on some high Andees peak wheir the foot of man nevry tread. As you look at the bird, and realize that when you get up so high the air is vary lite, we do not see how it can fly but the truath is their bones are vary large and they are hollow so they are vary lite. Well we must go on saying I shood think their was 2000 birds. The next was the crockadile from the smallest to the largest kind & then come the shark & the jaw of a whale & all kinds of sea fish & then the seals of all kinds. As I looked at the great Newfoundland seal it made me think of the picturs in geography of the native with their spears a seal fishing, and the next was the snakes all kinds from the little green snake to the anaconder. The next was stones that had formed with teath in it and all kinds collars and shape and we pass along and the next was wild mamels from the mouse up to the roan lion. The next we see Dr. Cane[2] as he was drest in the Artic regons. The next was the old atiant wepons of war. Hear was a study, as we look back to formor days and think how they led large armeys to battle we cant see how they cood take a strong place, but when we can see the wepons they had, we somewhat chainge our minds. To look at the lance and bow it looks like wepons of war, as much so as the old rev. musket dos compaired with the guns that we now use. Well I will have to stop, I did think that I would send home all of the money but their has bin one of the boys in our tent that has come down with the Small Pox, and I think I had better keepe a little money so in case I have taken it, I can get some things that I cant get any other way except to by, but I shell send you some more in the next letter I write to you, and I shell write in two or three days again. I must close for this time, so good by.

From your husborn,

Guy C. Taylor

Derrect to Mount Pleasant Hospatol Washington D.C.

NOTES

1. The Smithsonian Institution was established on August 10, 1846, from money willed by James Smithson, a British scientist. His intent was to increase and diffuse knowledge among people.
2. Elisha Kent Cane was born February 28, 1820, and died February 16, 1857. He was a medical officer in the U.S. Navy and a member of two Arctic expeditions that attempted to rescue explorer Sir John Franklin.

Mount Pleasant Hospital
Washington D.C. June 6, 64

My dear wife,

I received your letter on the 4 and I was glad to hear from home and to know that you war all well. I am on the gain, I am in hopes that I shell be able to go to the frunt in a few days but I shant apply for a discharge untill I am as well as I was before I had the measles. I am some laim yet but not half so bad as I was one weak ago. I shell send you ten dollars in this letter and by the time you get this I will send som more. You said you solt the old B plow for six dollars you don well. I got a letter from Amanda yesterday so I hurd from leads[1] and was glad to hear that they was all well. I wish I cood hear from John. When you hear from him you must let me know how he is a getting along and when I get to my reg. I shell write to him and see if I can hear from him and to Swanton. I have not got a letter from George yet but I look for one evryday. You spoke about farthers folks, it is no more than I expected, but I am in hopes that it has not got so the old cannot turn yet. You wrote somthing about a pair of boots, what their is their is in your hands to do as you pleas with. If you want to keep anything that is all right and if you want to sell anything sell it. You said you paid to George Chipman 7 dollars on Georges account, when he was owing you, (well that is allrite) you are now going to the school of experance and I have no dout that the 7 dollars has bin well paid out. You must try and improve what you have lurned and turn on him and receive the benifit of going to school. Well anough of that. You must not set rite down and say that you wont stur from home because I am gorn. You must go what you can and pas away the time the best you can. You said that your side bothard you again you must be vary carful and not do anything to make it any worse if you can help it. I suppose you have hurd that out reg. has bin badly cut to peases[2] and our Cournal[3] has bin shot. Their is not much morning with the men over his death, and a good meny thinks that the ball that hit him came from his own men, but I do not know nor do I cair he has killed a good meny of our boys, he made them march day and night, and good meny fell rite in the rode and died, and their was no call for such marching, but the tyrant wont kill any more men. Their is nine of our boys hear that is wounded. We do not know yet how meny men our reg. have lost but anough. I wish that I cood go home from hear as quict as I cood from Madison but I cannot, so I have to hope that you are all well and let it go at that and pass away the time the best I can, and day coms and day goes vary fast with me. It dos not seam as so I had bin from the state more then 2 weaks and it has bin 4 of them tomorrow. I must close for this time I will write again two or three days. When you receive any money do not let it be known around for maybe their may be som merstake in the muster roal and I may want to send som more.

From your husborn

Guy C. Taylor

Derrect as before

NOTES
    1. The town of Leeds is located in Columbia County, Wisconsin.
    2. The Thirty-Sixth Wisconsin suffered large numbers of casualties on June 1 at Bethesda Church, Virginia, and on June 3 at Cold Harbor, Virginia.
    3. Col Haskell was killed June 3, 1864, at the Battle of Cold Harbor.

Mount Pleasant Hospital
Washington D.C. June 7, 64

My dear wife,

I take up my pen again to let you know how I am agetting along. I cannot write any diffrance from what I have before. I do not think that I am any better than when I wrote before. I feal prety well one day and the next day I do not feal so well. It is a good deal owing to the weather I think. It is vary warm hear one day and the next day you want a heavy coat on to keep warm. I think it is the rhumatic pains for one thing that ails me. In case I do not get any better in a weak or so, I shell try for a furlow. I do not know wheather I can get one or not, but I can try and see, but if I cannot get one I can stay hear (that what is that matters) as long as they want me to, but I am in hopes that I am a going to get so I can go to my reg. in a weak or so but I do not know, but you must not worrey about me for in case I get vary sick I shell get sent to our own state, they are a sending the men off vary fast. I have sent 20 dollars to you in two letters. You must rite wheather you got it or not. I think I will not send anymore now. I will wait untill I find out how I get along for in case I should try for a furlow and get one I shell want som money. I suppose you expect to hear som news when you get a letter, but you cannot get much news from a hospital. The most news that I can tell you is I see a row betwean a man and a woman. The man was as large as F. W. Duston[1] he pict up a stone that would way 4 lbs, and went to strike hur with it, and she run rite for the camp. She came up to the gards beat and the gard stopt hur, and it was not no time hardely before their was 40 or 50 men up to the beat and they told him if he raised his hand to strike hur that they would hang him and they told him if he did not go away from their they wood thrash him untill he wood wish he never see a stone or a woman eather. I have not got the smallpox yet but it wont do for me to feal to well yet for I may have them yet, but I do not think I have taken it. I received .25 worth off stamps of George. You may pay him if you have a mind to sometime when you can. Have you payd James Ostrander[2] yet for that days work he don for me last winter? I must close for this time I will write again in a day or to. You must write ofton and tell all the news and the first paper you get with the list of the kill and wounded I wish you would send it to me.

Guy C. Taylor

NOTES
    1. A neighbor from the town of Bristol (http://www.danecountyhistory.org/1873plat/bristol.html; accessed June 23, 2011).
    2. Ibid.

∾

Mount Pleasant Hospital
Washington D.C. June 10, 1864

My dear wife,

I just received a letter from you, and I was vary sorrey to hear that you was not well. You must be vary carful, and take care of yourself. I think it is the best thing you can do is to wean Charley. I am on the gain we have got a new Doc and he gave me som medison for my laimness and it has help me rite away. I feal prety well I am a gaining in streanth prety well now. I think that we will start for our reg. in a few days that is if we keep on gaining, but after we start we may not get to the frunt for a weak or two, and we may get their in 4 days. You said that bad news come to Sun Prairie about our reg. It is bad if it is true but their is som dout about it. The Cournal is ded and thank God for it. The old tryant ort to have bin kill long ago. He was worse then a highway rober. You wrote about them boots. If you want to keep them do so by all means, and what Edd says or anybody elcs says pay no regard to it. Gust tell them that you can tend to your own afairs. As to the money I sent to George for, I wrote to you as soon as I got hear and got rested, and I did not think to tell you to send me som stamps, and I did not think that I shood be hear long anough to get more then one letter from you, so as I was a writeing to George the same day, I thought that I would tell him to send me som stamps. I did not want money, for I had anough of it. It was the stamps that I wanted and he sent me 25 cts worth. I have sent 20 dollars in two letters and I will send ten more before long. Write when you receive any money that you have received ten letter or the mount that is in it. Do not put in that you have received any mony, for in case the boys know that anyone is sending mony they have a good chance in case they have mind to, for sometimes you have to send a letter to the office by how you can and if you write that you have got the ten letter or six or whatevey the sume is, they can not tell in case they do see the letter. I have not got anything new to write but one thing I will tell you, that is that you must not give up but you must try and take good cair of your health and

Petersburg, Virginia, "The Dictator," September 1864 (courtesy Library of Congress Prints and Photographs Division; David Knox, photographer)

try to injoy yourself the best you can, and if you are sick trey and get help rite away. I wish it was so I cood see you and be with you, but it cannot be so yet, but I am in hopes that I shell be so to go home in one year from now and I shood not be surprised if I did have a chance before that time. Our men are at work in urnest now and the reb get whiped evry time. I think that I shell be in Richmon on the fourth. The men that got hear last night say that they are a planten the large siag guns[1] in fore miles of the sity. The Rebs will have a vary warm time of it. I must close for this time, I am in hopes that you will get well rite away, but you must write how you are. If sick write so and not wait and see if you dont get better and then wont let me know anything about it. I will write again in a day or to so good by from your husborn.

Guy C. Taylor

Be carful of your health

NOTE

1. Siege guns were heavy and cumbersome cannons, mortars, and rifles, which were effective but difficult to maneuver. They were used extensively in the ten-month siege of Petersburg. One of the most famous mortars was the flatcar-mounted, 13-inch 200 pounder known as "The Dictator."

Mount Pleasant Hospital
Washington D.C. June 16, 1864

My dear wife,

I take my pen in hand to let you know that I am well and hope you are injoying the same blessing. I am getting as well as evry again. I am sorry to hear that you are not vary well. I am in hopes that by the next time I hear from you, you will be well again but I am afraid you will be worse instid of better. You must try and take cair of yourself and keepe up good currage for that is half of the battle. I got a letter from Amanda last night and they are all well in Leeds. She wrote that it was so dry their that evrything was drying up. I am in hopes that Wis. will raise a good crop this year, for if they do not it will be hard times for a good meney, but they will see good times their for what they do around hear. In case it looks like having a poor crop you had better try and sell that note againts Mossey and get it in shape so you will be shure of it, for he will not be able to pay unless he can from wheat and you must look out for number one and in case that George Chipman dos not pay you for the plowing you had better make him give you a note and be carfull about stamping the note, and when you take a note let the one that gives the note stamp it. I have sent 20 dollars to you I growed 40 dollars and my being sick I had to by stuff to use, and to eate, and it cost a good deal. You can guess what it cost to get a pint of brandy it cost $2.00 dollars and evrything elce is gust so, but I have not spent more then I have bin abliged to and get along. Out of the 40 dollars I have got 10 left and I let one of our boys have 5 dollars he cood not draw any and he lent what he took with him to the boys in the Co. and when he fell out he was left without any mony. He was that little cook in Madison. I do not know but what I shell be sent to the reg. in a day or so, but I do not think that I shell stay their meny days for I think that as soon as I go to walking it will bring me down again as laim as evry, and if I do get down again I shell try to get to my own state, and I think I can get their if I shood try. I mite gust as well bin in Madison now as hear if I had onley nown it in time. I think that they will send me to my reg. in a day or two and it may not be so that I can write again for some time. We hurd that the mail has bin stopt goin to the frunt, but I do not know but I am in hopes it is not so but if we cannot hear from one another for some time we must look on the brite side, and hope it is all well with one another. I do not think that we shell have much more fite-ing around Richmon except by canons. They are now fixing for a seag.[1] You had not better answer this letter untill you get another unless you derrect to the reg. in case I am not sent away I will write again day after tomorrow. Well I must close. I wish that I cood see you and little Charley. When I get losome I go out under a tree and set and read in the testerment, and once and a while look at yours & Charleys picture, and it seams as so you was rite with me but when I look over the road it looks a good ways. You must try and be a good girl and when I com back I will get you a stick of candy.

From your husborn

Guy C. Taylor

High Private in the rear rank.

NOTE

1. Actually, attacks on Confederate fortifications occurred June 16–18 prior to the beginning of the siege of Petersburg (Trudeau, *The Last Citadel*, chapter 3).

Mount Pleasant Hospital
Washington D.C. June 17, 1864

My dear wife

I take my pen in hand to let you know that I am well and hope that you are injoying the same blesing. I have bin pretty well now for some time and the dock said the other day that I cood go to the frunt in a day or so, and the order come in to our tent this morning to go to the headqurtars to be exa-mend and I was one of the number to go to the frunt, and I will start now in a few minits but I expect to stop at Alaxander for a few days. I do not know when I can write again but you may rest ashuard. I shell write as soon as I can. You had not better write anymore to Mount Pleasant Hospital. You must not get downharted if you do not hear from me for som weaks for the report is that the mail has bin stopt going to the frunt for a while. You must hope for the best and I will do the same. Tell all of our folks that I will write as soon as I can. You must be a good girl and keepe your Cloths Clean. I must close so good by.

From your husborn

Guy C. Taylor

◌◠◡

Washington D.C. June 18, 64

My dear wife

As I am laying at the Soldiers Rest[1] waiteing for orders to moove, I thought that I would write a few lines today and then I would write the remainder tomorrow. I got a letter from you last night and I was glad to hear that you are not any worse. I am well and in good spearits. Their is at the rest about 250 men. We will go to Alaxander from hear and I do not know how long we shell stay their. O Sis, I can see what good the good Tempilers are a doing. Since I have come into the army I have found a good meny men that say that they youst to drink before they took the pledge and now they wont tutch it. Their is a grate deal of drinking don in the army. Their was one man had the deleierm tremons in the rest hear this morning. He was hear about 2 hours and then they took him away. At ten o clock we started for Alaxander and we got hear at noon. We come on the cars. We may stay hear for a weak and we may leave in a day or to. When I got hear I found 3 of our men hear awaiting for anough to com to make a squad. They wont send less than 600 to a time and their is not hardely any hear. We have a vary good place to stay and I am in hopes that we will stop hear for a while. I think that if we do that it may save the lives of som of our boys. Their is 2 of the 3 that is pretty bad off and if they cood stay hear for a few days it mite do them a grate deal of good. I am fealing pretty well now but I do not know how I shell feal when I get down to the frunt and hear the balls whize by, but I shell soon know, that is if Grant does not take Richmon before long but at the rate he is a going on, the rebs will begin to get their eyes open before long and in case they do not they will get som more eye holes in their heads. You wrote to me that you hurd that our Capt.[2] was wounded it is trew, and more then that we expect that he is taken a prisiner. Mr. Marr is sick I do not know how bad off he is but I guess not vary and wheir he is I do not know but one of the men of our company that was wounded said that he got off the boat at Washington and most likely that he is in the sity somewheir. You wanted to know if I sent a pair of gloves home when I was in Madison. I did, Mr. Marr took his with him so you need not send them to Mrs. Marr (for if you want to give hur a present give hur somthing worth more than the old gloves). Well I must close for this time, but one thing more I want you to pay no regard to what is said about my going to the war, if any one ask you what was the reason tell them that they must write to me if they want to know and I can tell them in a vary few words. Good by for this time.

From your husborn

Guy C. Taylor

NOTES

1. Lodges were established near railroads by the U.S. Sanitary Commission in order to give soldiers temporary shelter.

2. Prescott B. Burwell, from Sun Prairie, Wisconsin, was captain of Co. F, Thirty-Sixth Wisconsin Infantry. He was wounded and taken prisoner June 1, 1864, at Turner's Farm (also known as Bethesda Church), Virginia, and died from his wounds June 28, 1864, in Libby Prison, Richmond, Virginia (*Roster, 36th Wisconsin Infantry Regiment of Volunteers and Draftees*, 124).

❧

Alaxander, VA
June 21, 1864

My dear wife

I thought as we was not agoin to start for the frunt today that I would write a few lines to you, and let you know that I am injoying good health and I hope you and yours are doing the same. I am getting vary fleshy for me and I never felt any better then I have for a few days back. We are having vary hot weather down hear and it is vary dry to but it dos not make much diffrance hear wheather it is dry or not for their is nothing raised hear any-way. Va. is a ruined state the old Solgers say that we are in as good section of the state as there is, and a sivalize white man cannot live hear. It is vary hilly, and the soil is sand and it is as stoney as it can be, and not be all stones. It has bin covard with scrub pines but all the bigast of them has bin cut off. I have gust got back from a ramble[1] and I went upon the top of a high hill and look around and I cood see the lay of the country for sevral mials around me, it was a good plaice to go to pas a way time but hard work to get to it. I had a vary fair vew of six Hospitals Camps, and of the river[2]

I cood see some ten or twelve sail botes and sevral steamers, but no farm houses war to be seen except wheir they war close to the camps, and they are youzed by our men. Their is som vary nice orchards left undissturbed yet but they would not be if they did not bair fruit. It will be so the boys that are not able to go to the frunt can have small fruit now for the land is covard with blackbarrys and they are getting ripe, and it will be a good thing for the boys if they do not make to big a hog of themself and eat to meny of them. Their is a sturing times now in Camp that is in talking, it is on the next election.[3] It beats all about the old army of G. B. McClenon, the most of them are strong slavery men. It is no wender that they have had hard times in this army hear before for it is slave men against slavemen, it is like a man trying to fite himself. I do not know when we shell start for the frunt but I think we will tomorrow and it will take about 8 days to get to our reg. You must take good care of Charley, if he has the measels and not let him get cowl. You must write often and derrect to Co. F 36 Reg. Wis. Vol. via Washington. I must close for this time and I will write as soon as I can again so good by from your husborn.

Guy C. Taylor

NOTES

1. Fortunately, Guy Taylor liked to go on exploratory walks and write about what he saw along the way.
2. The Potomac River.
3. On July 27, 1861, George McClellan was appointed by Abraham Lincoln as commander of the Army of the Potomac. He was relieved of command by Lincoln in 1862. He challenged Lincoln for the presidency in 1864.

∽

June 22, 1864
On boad of a steamer

My dear wife

We started from Alaxander at about 3 oclock pm. I am well and feal well. Their is nearly or quite 2000 men on board. It is a large bet we will go rite to Petersburg. We shell get their in to days, but when we get to the landing it may take ous 3 or 4 days to get to our reg. I hurd today that our reg. was 40 miles from the landing that was 4 days ago but it is hard telling. Oh Sis, if you cood gust see ous hear on this boat you would think that we war some

heathen tribes of men. We look so kinder rough and then we are so durty
that we do not look like white men. You see we was camped 4 miles from
the sity, and this morning we started and march down to take the boat and
we had to march rite in the road and the dust was so bad that we cood not
hardely see and when we got their we had to stay in the yard by the dock,
and it was about 1½ deap with coal dust and the boys must run around any
way. Their is a good meny Negroes on board, and it wood be hard to tell
them if it want for their curly head. As we go down the river we can see som
vary prety farms but the most of the land is vary rough indeed and the soil
is all gravaly sand. The crop is all corn and it has bin so dry it looks bad,
they wont have half of a crop this year. As I am siting hear and writeing we
are apasing George Washingtons home. It is a one story house[1] it has 16
windows in frunt and only one dore. It is situated rite on the bank of the
river, and rite under a hill that is covard with timber. When we look at the
home of the father of our Country, and think how our fore fathers fort for
our freedom it seams as so it put new life into ous, so we are redy to stand
whair our fathers stood, and sware before high heven to maintain the freedom that they have won for ous, and by so doing if we have to lay down our
lives, we know that we have left a Country for our children wheir freedom
rains, and wheir those are left can injoy the blesing that a free Country
afards. Sis, you said in your last letter that you did not know as you ever
would see me again, that may be the case, but I hope not. At any rate you
must not think that untill you are ablidge to, and if it shood be the case I
am in hopes that we may meat hearafter wheir their is no war, but let ous
both hope for the best. It will be time anough to get downhearted when
the worst has com. Tell Lydia and all the rest of the folk how I am. It will
not be so that I can write hardely any and what I do will be to you and the
rest will have to hear from you but tell them to write often and I will when
I can. Well Sis you must be a good girl til I get back and take good care of
Charley, but then I am not atoll afraid of that. I wish that I cood gust see you
and the rest of the folk before I go to the frunt but I cant so I must wait with
pasiants untill I can. I will write again as soon as I can so good by. Derrect
to the Reg. Co. F 36 reg. Wis. Vol. via Washington D.C.

From your husborn Guy C. Taylor

NOTE
   1. Apparently Taylor had a distant or an obstructed view of Mt. Vernon because the
mansion has three floors.

June 23, 1864

My dear wife

   This morning fines me well, and injoying the cool breaze of the salt watter. I am now out of site of land. It is the furst time in my lief, but we will
soon be wheir we can have a chance to try our legs again. The wind is a
blowing prety hard and the waves run vary high but the old boat runs as
stidy has can bee. We have got about 8 or 9 hundred of men on board that
has deserted and last nite their was som 18 or 20 that gump overboard and
one of them was struct by the corner of the wheal house and went to the
bottom and the rest jump clear of the boat but it is doutful if they did not
most of them go to the bottom before they reach shore. Their was som
susspision among the officers that their wood be a row on the boat last
night, but they got redy to receive the deserters in case they tryed to com up
on deck that the volontears was on. The gards had their guns well loaded
for them and a good meny that warnt gards, but their was no stur and I am
vary glad their wasnt. We have just past Foartest Monrow[1] and it looks so it
was a place that it wood be vary hard to take. The shore is lined with larg
seag guns and the river is fild with gun bots. The wind has gorn down and
it is vary plesant rideing now. We have a fair vew of the shore on the west
side. We can see some vary prety resadances, but the most of the land that
we can see is covard with timber. Sis I lent 5 dollars to James Parker[2] and
in case that I do not get it from one of the boys in the reg. he will send it to
you, so you may know what it is for if you get it. You had better wait til tord
fall before you let out any money. In case you get any before that time
which I am in hopes you will. Unless you can get it in the fall when you
want it, so if you do want to build you will be shure to have the money to
work with but I am in hopes that by fall their will be som turms for pease,
but be perpaird for the worse as well as you can and then you will be allrite
anyway. I do not know as I have anything more to write this time so I will
bid you good by for this time.
   From your husborn

Guy C. Taylor

NOTES

1. Fortress Monroe, a vast installation at the tip of the Virginia Peninsula, was one of the most imposing fortresses in the United States. It remained in Union hands throughout the war. After the war, Confederate President Jefferson Davis was imprisoned at Fortress Monroe.

2. Pvt James L. Parker, age 35, carpenter, Princeton, Wisconsin, Co. F, Thirty-Sixth Wisconsin Infantry (*Roster, 36th Wisconsin Infantry Regiment of Volunteers and Draftees*, 138).

CHAPTER 3

In the Ranks

June 26 to July 25, 1864

From June 26 to July 25, 1864, Guy Taylor served in the regular army ranks in or near the front lines of Petersburg. His first impression upon reaching the front was how decimated his regiment and company had become during his hospitalization. As he experienced life at the front, he filled his letters with more observations and descriptions of a Civil War soldier's activities.

His letters revealed his torment of not knowing what to expect from day to day, such as when a move was about to be made, where he would be sent, or whether he would survive the war and be able to return home.

During this time, Taylor continued to support his wife, Sarah, from afar, and sought to stay informed about conditions on the home front. He and Sarah began to number their letters to deal with the problem of irregular mail delivery. His health continued to be problematic, and as a result he formed a very important bond with Dr. Elijah Woodward, assistant surgeon of the Thirty-Sixth Wisconsin.

According to James M. Aubery, "From the 24th of June until the 25th of July we were camped in various places, working in the trenches, picket duty, etc. The whole army, or as much of it as is not on picket, seems to not have turned their swords into pruning hooks, but stacked their muskets and taken a shovel."[1]

NOTE

    1. Aubery, *Thirty-Sixth Wisconsin Volunteer Infantry*, 101.

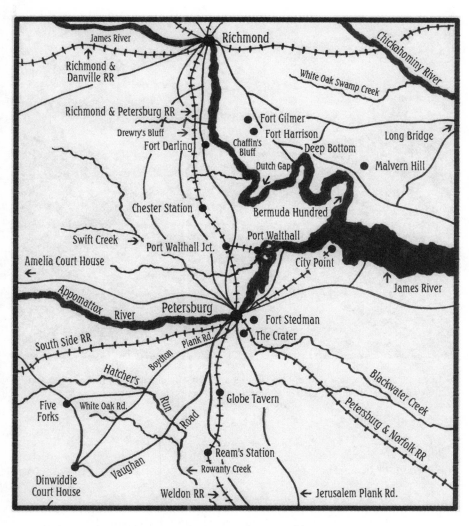

Petersburg area, June 1864 to April 1865 (map by Patsy Alderson)

City Point, Virginia, rear view of Gen Ulysses S. Grant's headquarters, between 1860 and 1865 (courtesy Library of Congress Prints and Photographs Division)

June 26, 1864
Camp in the field

My dear wife,

It is with pleasure that I take my pensel to write to you to let you know that I am well and I am in hopes that thees few lins will find you and the rest of the folks are injoying good health. I got to the reg. last night at sundown. We took the boat at Alaxander and we landed at sity point[1] and we march 3 mils that day and then we laid over untill the next day at 4 oc AM and we had a durty time of it now I tell you. Oh Sis you said that you had hurd bad noos from the reg. I can tell you they have seen hard times. Our company was 89 strong now it is 14 strong. You wrote that John Slingland[2] was among the mising that is not so for he is well and to work at the meat buisness so I hav not seen him yet. Their is only 300 men in our reg. now but they feal first rate, but they do not want to go into a fite gust yet. They would like to rest awhile now. They have had about anough fiteing for awhile. Mr. Marr has bin detail at Washington in the hospital I am in hopes that I can now stay with the boys but I am afraid that I cannot stand it, it is so hot when we was a coming their was twenty of the men that was son-struct and 5 of them died rite away. I stood it first rate but I work so hard in the sun when the men fell to keepe life in them that I com vary near going down but I got in the shade and I got over it in a little while, but the rest was worse and the men work over them and they did not any die then but their was 3 that died that nite. We are under marching orders now but we do not know wheir we shell go but I think it will be to the frunt. I must close for the mail is going out now. So good by.

Guy C. Taylor

Write ofton to the reg.

NOTES

1. During the final ten months of the Civil War, City Point, Virginia, was the nerve center of Union operations. Located on a bluff above the confluence of the James and Appomattox rivers, City Point was where Lt Gen Ulysses S. Grant directed the operations of all Union armies. Today City Point is located in Hopewell, Virginia, and is part of the Petersburg National Battlefield.

2. Pvt John Slingerland, age 33, butcher, Sun Prairie, Wisconsin, Co. F, Thirty-Sixth Wisconsin Infantry (*Roster, 36th Wisconsin Infantry Regiment of Volunteers and Draftees*, 141).

June 28, 1864
Camp in the field

My dear wife

It is with pleasure that I take my pensel to let you know that I am well and I hope you are injoying the same blessing. We are about 12 mils from sity point and 6 from Petersburg. We went to work yesterday and fix up our tents in good shape for the officers said that they thought we would stay their for 2 or 3 days and their was 4 of ous went to work and get ous a nice tent up and gust laid down to rest and the order com strike tents and be redy to march in a minits warning so we had to rout out and pack up, and we gust got pack when we had to fall in, and we march about 2 miles and we camp and we are hear yet but we do not know what minit we may start again and we do not know wheir we are a going to. We are like a dog go wheirever our master goes. I like camp life vary well. We cannot march but a vary little now anyway. It is so hot and dusty when we was marching yesterday it was so we cood not see the man that stood before ous for good sheir of the way. Their was one man in our company sun struct and he is prety bad to. Our hole company now numbers 14 men 8 men are fit for duty this morning. The Reg. numbers 250 men when we started it numbered 964 men so you can see wheather they have don anything or not and their is a good meny that are not able to cary a gun but they keepe along. Their is 230 guys in the reg. but they have got threw doing much work for awhile

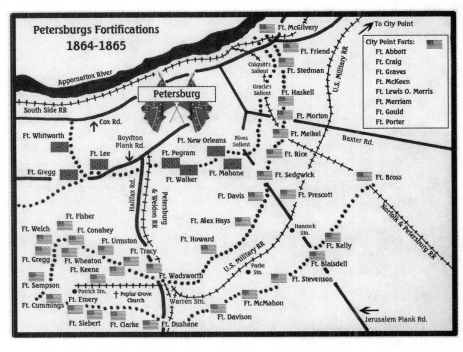

Petersburg fortifications, 1864–1865 (map by Patsy Alderson)

the officers cannot make them go in to another charge for a good bit of awhile. The talk is now that we are a going to sity point and do gard duty their untill we get rested and recruited up som but we do not know we may and we may not but time will tell. It is clouding up and the wind is a riseing and looks so we mite have som rain and I am in hopes that we shell have som. Oh Sis I wood like to have you gust com in camp and see ous, see how neat and clean we are. We lay down in the dust and swet and the wind will blow dust on ous so when we get up we look like a dust stack. You wood not know any of ous, we have to go ½ mile for water and we can not get it to wash with neather. We have to wash when we can som of the boys has bin 3 days without washing, but you may bet they wash in urnest when they get a chance to. I must close for this time you must write ofton as you can and I will write when I can but you must not expect them vary often derrect to the reg. so good by.

Guy C. Taylor

June 30, 1864
Camp in the field

My dear wife,

It is with pleasure that I write to you to let you know that I am well and I hope that all the folks to home are the same. Since I wrote to you last we have mooved twise. Yesterday we was out on picket duty but I happen to be luckey and did not go but was sent with 6 more back wheir our provisions was to gard it, but not against rebles but against theifs for their is no reb anywheir near ous. At one oclock the provision wagon started to go wheir our reg. was camp and got most their when we met the Colonel ordely and then the wagon had to stop and go back and the gard had to go and report to the reg. and we gust got their when the order was to fall in forward march and we marched about 3 miles and hear we are now but how long we shell stay hear I do not know, and wheir we shell go to in case we start I dont know. We are now behind som brestworks. We have hurd that the rebs are trying to flank ous on the left but if they try that gaim they will find that they will run themself into truble for we are all ready for them. The 6 army Corps has mooved to the left of ous and have got in posision before this time, so let the rebs com as soon as they will and we will lay in wait for them but their is no dout but they will draw back and give up their flanking for this time when they find that they have got to fite ous in the brestworks for as we are hear we can shoot them down as fast as they com up in shooting distance but we shant have a chance to shoot for the rebs are not the men to charge on brestworks they dont like that kind of work . . . we gust got orders that we are to be mustard for pay at 10 oclock today. I am vary glad of it to, and sis I want you to get your papers made out and draw your money from the state as soon as you can, and dont put it off, for I have som reasons for haven you do so that I will let you know before long, and get your pay as often as you can. Now dont delay for if you get it, you will be shure of it. Most of the boys are well and they are in good sperats and som of them get most to much spearits in them. Their is a good deal of licker drank in our reg. and it dos them any good but it dos them a good deal of hurt. Folks may talk about licker being a good thing, in the army it is no such a thing they have to drink it rite up, and it makes them half drunk, and their is som that wont draw it and then som that wants to drink will get it and they will get so drunk that they cannot hardly stand, but I must not try to write evrything that is don in the army but if I live to get home again I can tell you better then I can write, but their is one thing I am bound to try and keepe myself strait and pay no regard about others, for it is all that one man wants to do to keepe himself strait. But I must close so good by.

Guy C. Taylor

Write often Der. To the Reg.

❧

July 2th, 1864

My dear wife

We are camped in the field 12 mils from Sity Point and about 3 mils from Petersburg. We are on the frunt line of works but their is two lines of pickets ahead of ous. We are in a good plaice and we have got a gay old line of brestworks. The works are so strong that one man is as good as 4 at least, and we have got men anough hear to form to lines so when one line gets short for amunition the other can take their plaice. We are the rear line. Our camp is on the brink of a small hill and it is a good plaice to camp. Last night the act Colonel which is Capt. Warner[1] had ous pull up our tents and build them in good order and they are now laid out in regler streats. It looks

Fortifications in front of Petersburg, Virginia, 1865 (courtesy Library of Congress Prints and Photographs Division)

as so we was a going to stay hear for awhile and I am in hopes that we will. The boys are agetting so they feal first rate, and are getting in good flesh again. I am agetting as fleshey as can be and I never felt and beter in my life then I do now. I suppose that you think that we are a seeing hard times for we are in frunt but it is not so. We have beter living now then we had in Madison and we do not do anything but to cook and eat except one or two haves to go out on picket evryday but it is no duty to speak of for they are not on but twise a day and two hours to a time, and their is no danger wheir they are for their is two lines of Cavaly in frunt of them, but they are to cary nouse to the regiment in case their is any stur but not to shoot unless they are ablige to, but to run inside of the line as soon as they can for the Cavaly cannot get in except in rodes and men can run in all along the line and give the alarm, but their is no danger of the rebs atacking our works unlesst they are abildge to, to get somthing to eat for the rode that runs into the sity is all in our hands and they cannot get any surplises now. We was mustard for pay on the last day of June so I suppose that you will get your alotment before long and you had beter look well for your cloathing and living for acorden to what acounts we get hear you are not agoing to rase anything this year, but then I hope it aint so bad as it has bin stated to be. I have not got any letter from you since I left Washington. You must write often and tell all the rest to write, I wood write to them but we cannot get no paper nor stamps hear so what I have got I am agoing to keepe to write to you and the rest must go to you if they want to hear from me. I wood like to write to them all if I cood but they can write to me and hear from me by you. Good by for this time.

Guy C. Taylor

NOTE
    1. Lt Col Clement E. Warner, age 28, Windsor, Wisconsin, Thirty-Sixth Wisconsin Infantry (Aubery, *Thirty-Sixth Wisconsin Volunteer Infantry*, 293, 335–37).

∽

July 4, 1864
Camp within 3 mils of Petersburg

My dear wife,

    I have gust got in from picket duty, so I thought I would write to you and let you know that I am well and I hope that you are injoying the same blessing. We are camped in the woods and they are to work a cleaning up the ground and burning the rubish. We think now that we will stay hear awhile but we do not know but I am in hopes we will for it is a nice plaice to camp and their is no danger of the rebs a trying our works for they are so strong that they cannot get over them no how. We have cut the timber in frunt of the works and fell it crossways so a man cannot hardely get threw it and then rite in frunt of the works their is logs laid along and large limbs stuck in the ground and the tops are cut off so the prongs sticks out in evry derrections and they are sharpen to a point. Taket in the nite when they cood not see vary well any armey wood half get killed in getting threw if their was not a gun firad, and then we have got first rate brestwork they are made of large pine logs and the logs are covard with durt and their is a large ditch on the outside of the works, but I must stop writeing about the works, I sed

Petersburg, Virginia, view from breastworks of Fort Sedgwick, April 3, 1865 (courtesy Library of Congress Prints and Photographs Division)

that I was on picket we was about two mils in frunt of the works we was in the thick woods we had pits and logs works to stand behind their was 4 men and one corpal on one stand and the stands are about 4 rods apart and then their is a resurve laying about 30 rods in the rear, so in case their is any attack they can com to surport and if they cannot drive the rebs they are ordered to retreat to the works and let them, but the rebs know beter then to try it. Well Sis I am injoying the forth a good deal better then I expected to. I wood like to know how you was injoying yourself I hope well. I am as healthy as I evry was and I am getting as fat as a hog and as lazy as one. We have not had any raine down hear yet evrything is all drying up. The woods are full of huckelbarys but they are all burnt up so they are not good for much. I got a pint yesterday and made me som sauce and it went nice now I tell you. We have vary good living hear and a plenty of it, it is foal as good as we had in Madison and we are having first rate times now and the boys are all getting fat and lasey now I tell you. Well sis have you got your state money yet, and have you got anymore money from me except the first letter if you have not their is som lost we expect to get our pay now in a few days but then we may not in a long time yet but would not care if it wornt for your having the bounty and allotment for I do not want any hear now for it wood only be a bother to me. The sutlers sell evrything so high I will not by off them for I can live on what the Govermont finds me and it is a good deal healthery then this stuff that you can by. Mr. Marr I hurd was in Washington he has bin detailed their so he will not be back for a good while yet. Mr. Daily[1] is sick to and is back somwheir. I must close for now.

Guy C. Taylor

NOTE

1. Sgt Joseph Dailey, age 34, farmer, town of Leeds, Columbia County, Wisconsin, Co. F, Thirty-Sixth Wisconsin Infantry (*Roster, 36th Wisconsin Infantry Regiment of Volunteers and Draftees*, 128).

∽

July 5, 1864
Camp in the woods on the frunt lines

My dear wife,

I gust got a letter from you and I was glad to hear from you but with good noose their came som bad noose I thought that mother Taylor had talk so much before I com away that she would have nothing to say after I was away, but I see that she must talk anyway, but she may tell all the lies she has a mind to. I don't think she will make meny believe them. As for hur talking with me she did, but we was not sitting on a stone nor I wornt a crying. We was a walking in the rode I was going from Georges up home, it was when I was at home on a sick pas she went awayes with me and their was a not one word said about your trying to keep me to home. She was a talking all the time most about what had bin sed when I was at Madison. She was vary much afraid that I would think that she had sed somthing she hedent orte to, and if I know myself she mite as well bin afraid, but let hur talk as much as she has a mind to you gust pay no regard to it and the folks wont believe their is any truath in what she says. I know it is hard to stand such talk and not resent it but, the truath will com to lite in the corse of time. You know that or at least I believe you know that I did not inlist on any acount of yours, except that I believe it was for the best for you and myself for me to go. If I known that you would had bin talk about as much as you have I would not had inlisted when I did, but I thought that talk would stop when I was gorn, but never mind I shell return in case the Lorde is wiling in the corse of time, and when I get back I think that thoes that has talk so much had as live see the vary eavle one as to see me for they will be glad to try to take back som of their talk you must try and get along the best you can and keepe up good chear untill I get back, and then we can look back and see what we have past threw and we will both know better how to appreciate a quite home. You can gust tell the folks that if they want to know what made me inlist they can find out by writeing to me. You must try and drive the thought of danger (that surounds me), from your mind as much as posapol—for we are not in as much danger from the Rebs balls, as we be from the balls of King Alcohall. Whiskey is as free as water most, but I think I can stand against all such enemys. I have seen so much roudyism that I have got intialy sick of it. I cannot write you any noose in this for I have writen one letter to you and it is now in my pocket and, you most likely will get them both togeather you have not writen how much money you have got from me. You must write often as you can and I will do the same.

I must close for this time

So Good By

My Dear Wife

Derrect to Co. F. 36 Reg. Wis. Vol.

Via Washington DC

Be of good chear and wait for better times for they will com.

If you can get the Wis. cheife[1] I wish you would send me one or any temprance paper.

NOTE

1. The *Wisconsin Chief* was a temperance and antislavery newspaper published in Fort Atkinson, Wisconsin, by Thurlow Weed Brown.

☙

In the field 2½ mils from Petersburg
July 9, 1864

My dear wife,

It is with pleasure that I take my pen in hand to let you know that I am well and I am in hopes that this will find you injoying the same blessing. We are in camp wheir we was wheir I wrote to you last. The boys are all well we are in a vary healthy plase. I was out on picket last night. I was apointead as corpral on gard so I did not have to stand on gard. We had a nice time in the woods. We are in 1 mile of the rebs pickets. They com over to our line

Petersburg, Virginia, Federal picket line in front of Fort Mahone, April 1865 (courtesy Library of Congress Prints and Photographs Division)

and traied papers with ous, and they go back again they dont want to fire on our line nor we dont want to fire on them we are on good turms now and we dont want to get out with one another for fear it may create a row, and somebody mite get hurt and the rebs thinks we are most to strong for them, so I think we will remain on good turms for somtime. We have hurd that we would go back to Marysland. The rebs are going in their but we do not know as we will. We are in hearing of the guns at Petersburg. It luls ous to sleap at night and it is moosic in the morning for ous. Last night their was a dewal to our rite betwean two battears and it was prety sharp work. It was two miles from ous in gust good distance to stand and hear. I got a letter from you the other day and I was glad to hear that you was well. I have written two letters evry weak, but I got no answer yet, but I expect that I shell get them by the dozens byme by, at least I am in hopes so. I wish you would send me evry good temperance paper that you can. We cannot get any such thing hear and I think that if the ministers that are preaching so much hear, would spend one half of their time in giving temperance lecturs they would do twise as much good as they now do, but you dont hear a word in faver of temperance hear. It is all whiskey and it is a killing more men then the balls are. Oh Sis, I hope you will not leve the Lodge[1] for I want you to let me know what is going on their. I hope that Mr. Rood[2] and his co workers will find that the majoyety of the people of that neighborhood is in faver of temperance. I think he had better get converted to or three times more, and then see if he cannot form sum man principals for he cannot have any now nor no other man that will oppose a temperance sosiety. (That is in my vew of the mater) if the men that oppose the Lodge was hear they would say that a temperance sosiety is a good thing and ort to be surported. Well Sis you must keep up good courradge and make up your mind that you do not care what folks say as long you know that you are doing what is wright for if folks want to tell things that is not so they have the worst of it and the truath will com out in the coarse of time. You must write often and tell all the noose, and write all about the crops. I have hurd that you had not had any rain their since we left. It is vary dry hear evrthing is burning up for the want of rain. I must close so good by.

G. C Taylor

NOTES

1. The lodge that Taylor was referring to was a temperance lodge.
2. Mr. Rood was an early citizen of the town of Bristol, Wisconsin (http://www.dane countyhistory.org/1873plat/bristol.html; accessed June 23, 3011).

In Camp
July 10, 1864

My Dear wife,

We was orded to strike tents and be ready to march in a minuit warning. It was at two oc in the morning and we got ready to march, and most of ous made up our minds that we was agoing in to a fite but we got grately fooled for we march onley ¾ of a mile to the left and camped. Well Sis I suppose that you are vary losome but you must try and pas away the time the best you can. It is harde to be seprated so long for all of ous, but I am in hopes that when we get togeather again we shant have to be seprated again on acount of war. I am in vary good health. I was never any beter and I shood injoy myself first rate if I onley new that you was injoying yourself but I know that you worry about me and then you feal bad about what has bin sed about my inlisting, but you must try and let such things pass and pay no regard to what is sed, for what has bin sed is false. Oh Sis would I not like to hear that this war was over so we cood all return to their homes again, but that has not come yet but it is on the way, for pease must come in the coarse of time, and I think that time is before another year roals around but we cannot tell, and we cannot tell what may happen in the coarse of this year but I am in hopes that evrything will com out allrite. I do not think that I shell be with the reg. grate deal longer for awhile at any rate, but I do not know how it will be yet. I want to stay awhile yet at any rate if I can. Oh Sis we have bin mustard for pay, and I suppose that you have got the bounty and ten dollars a month before this time, and if you have not you must write as soon as you get this and let me know and if you have you can do as you have a mind to do with it but if you let it and take a note be shure and see that the note is Stamp acorden to low, for you dont want to loose any money, and you must see that you dont let it go so you will be short. You must keepe anough for you and Charley for you cannot get anything without money, and I want you to keepe yourselfs well cloathed. Well I must close for this time you must try and hold up good courradge and I will try and do so to and wait paisantly for the time when we can be togeather again. Well good by from your husborn.

Guy C Taylor

Derrect to Co F 36 Reg Wis Vol via Washington
1 Bregrade
2 Divition
2 Army Corps

~

3½ miles from Petersburg
July 11, 1864 in camp

My Dear Wife,

I gust got the letter that you wrote on the foarth, and I was glad to hear from you, but I am sorrous that you are so unwell, but I am in hopes that you will get better before long. I am well and getting vary fleshey for me. We do not have much to do I have bin on picket twise since I got to the reg. onley, and we have traveled about 10 miles, and I have bin hear 17 days, so you can see how hard we have worked since I have bin hear. I am sorrous to hear that the crops are so poor for it is hard time anough their now and if the crops faile it will be a vary hard thing for Wis. Well Sis, I cannot tell you any nouse for we are in the same plase we have bin in for sevral days and I have written sevral letters since we came hear. They have bin clean-ing the ground in frunt of the works. That is all the change of looks their have bin. They are to work of building a large foart[1] 2 miles to the rite of ous it is on the plank road that runs from the river to Petersburg and it is about 2 miles from the sity. I think that they are a carcalating to shell the sity from the foart. Well Sis, you must try and take good care of yourself and do not work to hard you had better keepe still for a while and try and see if you wont get better. I am sorrous to hear that Mother is sick and I would like to go and see hur if it was so I cood, but I cannot. I hope that she will think back a few months and see if she has lived as she ourt. You had better try and Bye evrything that you will want for another year this fall for evry-thing will be as cheap then as it will be most likely and then if you get a years ahead you wont run short, and you can bye cheaper by bying a large amount to a time, and you will want to look out and bye as cheap as you can for you may want evry cent you can get. We cannot tell yet how the thing will com out, but I hope allrite. Well Sis, I dont know as I can write any-thing that will interest you, but I have kept a memarandom since I first got to the reg. and I will write it down and the charges that the boys made before I got to them. June 1 they charge on the works of the rebs at Danes

Bluffs[2] and was repulsed our Co. lost 26, 1 killed Mr. Hackmaster[3] and the rest was wounded, and taken prisners I do not know how meny their was wounded. That is wheir we lost our Captain, and it was a great lost to our Co. June 3, they made another charge at Cold Harber[4] and was repulsed. I do not know how meny we did loose their was 1 killed, Frank Casady.[5] On the 18 day of June they made another charge on strong works of the enemey at Petersburg.[6] Their they hill the ground that they took and the rebs left their good brestworks. I dont know how meny was lost their but their was none killed. We had 83 men when we left Madison, and 63 of them are sick, wounded or killed. We have 20 men now in all and 4 of them have bin detaile so they are not with ous it leaves Co. F 16 men strong. I wish Sis you would take down the names of the killed and the plaise wheir so you can get them put in the Chart of the company for if I do not get back the chart may be worth a good deal to you and Charley when he is old anough to know what such things are, and you can take it to Madison somtime and get them marked acorden to the chart. Well I must close for this time so good by.

From your husborn.

Guy C. Taylor

Write often so will I.

NOTES

1. The fort that Taylor was referring to was Fort Davis, located on Jerusalem Plank Road (Mark R. Terry, "The Federal Forts at Petersburg," http://www.petersburgsiege.org/fedforts.htm; accessed July 21, 2011).

2. The battle of Danes Bluff, also called Bethesda Church, was fought on June 1, 1864.

3. Pvt Heinrich Hackmeister, age 42, stonecutter, Arlington, Columbia County, Wisconsin, Co. F, Thirty-Sixth Wisconsin Infantry (*Roster, 36th Wisconsin Infantry Regiment of Volunteers and Draftees*, 131).

4. The Battle of Cold Harbor was fought on June 3, 1864.

5. Pvt Frank Cassidy, age 18, farmer, Princeton, Wisconsin, Co. F, Thirty-Sixth Wisconsin Infantry (*Roster, 36th Wisconsin Infantry Regiment of Volunteers and Draftees*, 127).

6. Taylor was writing about the June 18 Union assault on the Confederate lines at Petersburg. The Thirty-Sixth Wisconsin Regiment referred to this assault as the charge over the melon patch (Aubery, *Thirty-Sixth Wisconsin Volunteer Infantry*, 87).

Petersburg, Virginia, summer quarters, August 1864 (courtesy Library of Congress Prints and Photographs Division)

In camp 5 mils of Sity Point
July 14, 1864

My Dear Wife,

I am sitting in my tent injoying myself as well as a soldier can. My health is vary good. We march yesterday about 5 miles and camp in the woods about 5 miles from Sity Point. When we left wheir we was we tore the brestwork all down flat. It looks as it was labor don for nothing, but we do not know what it is allrite, we cannot tell anything about what our work amounts to. We do not know eaven what our a Corps are a doing. We can see what our davision is adoing for it is so small we can look all over it and see evry man their is not more then 3000 men in it and I do not think their is as meny as that. The men are in good health as a genral thing, grate deal better then they woir in Camp Randell, and the men are all getting as fat and as lazy as a hog. It is allmost inposibal to get them to do anything, and they would not do anything if they was not afraid of getting punished and they do not like the stile they punish. Well Sis I do not know wheather you get my letters or not. I have not got but one from you since I left Washington but I suppose it is owen to the mail not being reglar. I got a letter from Martha the other day and she wrote that she had not got a letter from me attall, you can tell hur that I have written to hur prety often, surtain wonce a weak when I was in Washington. Now I cannot write so much so when they want to hear from me they must go to you, for I cannot get the things to write on. I cannot write you any noose for I dont know any. It is dry hear yet, it has not rained since I got to the reg. and they said that they had not seen any rain for 3 weaks, and you can guess how dry it must be in this hot plaice to be without rain for 7 weaks. It is so hot that we cannot do anything hardly in the heat of the day. What we do we do mornings and nights, and lay in our tents in the day time and finley we are in our tents most of the time anyway. If you hear from Mr. Marr I wish you would let me know wheir he is, so I can write to him. There is onley one boy left that I new fore I inlisted and that is Chapins[1] all the boys that was from Leeds have gorn back to the rear except Chapins. Well I will close for this time you must write often. I do not know as you can read this for I am holding my paper in one hand and write with the other. Well good by.

From your husborn

Guy C. Taylor

NOTE

1. Pvt Marvin J. Chapin, age 26, farmer, Leeds, Wisconsin, Co. F, Thirty-Sixth Wisconsin Infantry (*Roster, 36th Wisconsin Infantry Regiment of Volunteers and Draftees*, 127).

∽

In camp 2 miles of Petersburg
July 18, 1864

My dear wife,

I sit down once again in my little house with my pen in hand to let you know that I am injoying good health, and I hope that you are injoying the same blessing. We are camp in the pines, and it is a vary nice plaise for a camp. We do not have much to do as a genral thing, but for the two last days we have bin on detale. Part of the reg. have bin to work on a foart, and the remainder have bin cutting down the woods around the foart, so to give good chance for the big Guns. Their is som prospect of noisey times in afew days, but I do not think that it will last vary long for I think that our army have got the rebs in a tite plaise. I think that the sity of Petersburg will be no more unless they surrender before long. Our big guns are in such persision that they can throw shells anywheir they want to in the sity and the brestworks that run from one foart to another is so strong that it is inposable to drive our men out of them for they are covard by the foarts and then their is large guns all along the works. Our men as a genral thing are eager for the fite for they think that they will have the pleasure of goine into the sity and then to Richmon, for when Petersburg is in our hands we are all around Richmon so they cannot get anything to live on. Folks may talk but it looks to me as so this war is about over, but I do not know. Well Sis I cannot write any noose this time as we are laying in camp and we do not see anything nor hear anything. John Slinglan is back to Sity Point sick. He has bin prety bad off but he is getting better now. The health of the reg. is vary good som of the boys are getting sick on acount of their eating so meny green apples. They will eat them rite down by the dozen. Wel I do not know wheather you will get this or not if you do I wish would send me som paper and invelops. Get a large invelop and send them in. I have writen twise a weak but I do not expect that you get one half of them. I have got onley one letter from you since I got to the reg. and that was writen on the foarth. You must write often and tell all the rest to write, and I will write as much as I can on acount of paper and Stamps. Well I must close for this time By Biding you good By.

From you Husborn

G. C. Taylor

Tell all the folks to write

～

Camp near Petersburg
July 25, 1864

My dear wife,

I received a letter from you this morning and I was glad to hear from you and to know that you are as well as usual. I am in good health. I am as

strong as I ever was in my life. I never was any healther in my life, and
I should injoy myself first rate if I onley new that the folks at home was
doing the same, but I know that you are not injoying yourself attall. You not
being vary well and then I know that you are a wouring about me, and all
togeather you give to your fealings. You must not woury any about me for
I am in a plaise wheir I have nothing to do but to take care of myself, and
when you get a thinking about me you must go to work about somthing to
draw your mind away. Why if I should sit down and let my mind run on
things at home I should bin ded long ago. Their is nothing that will make
a purson sick as soon as to be homesick. Their have bin good meny sent to
the hospital and the Dockes say that it is on the count of their being homesick, and their is a man in Co. G. that has soured so much about home he
has becom foolish and sick to and they are trying to get his discharge. You
must gust make up your mind that you are agoine to injoy yourself let what
will com, and let folks say what they will. It is a long time yet before I shell
get back, for if I can get the plaice that I think I can I shell stay as long as I
can for I shell be making good wages and be in a plaice wheir I shell get
better if their is any such thing as getting any better.[1] At least it will not be
like farm work, but I have no idea but the hole army will go home in 8 or
10 months, and go about their own business for the rebs are getting in a
tite plaise. Well I guess you will think that I am givine you a real lecture on
being homesick, so I will stop. Wel Sis we have mooved twise since I wrote
to you before and we went 1½ miles in the two mooves. We are in the
pretest plaise I ever see for a camp it is on a high pease of land that is covard
with young pines they are from six inches to 1½ feete threw and the land
have bin planted to corn somtime. You can see the rows gust as plaine as
so it had not bin more then 3 or 4 years since the crop had bin taken off,
but thoes that pretend to know how to tell the adge of treas says that it has
bin about 15 years. Down hear they plow their corn vary deep and hill it up
vary high so it will show for great meny years. The prospects is that we will
stay hear for quite a while, and I hope we will. I am so I can go anywheir I
please so I go around and see the works.[2] I did want to go to the frunt and
see the big guns but the boys sed so much I give up goine. The shells fly in
their evry little while. I think that I will go to the rear tomorrow and get som
apples their is a orchard that is loaded with fruit. Som of our boys went into
it and brot a mest of them to me and we are agoine to cook them for our
super. I am tenten with Nat Crampten.[3] He is a real nice young man he is
vary tidey and temperant and that is a rare thing in the army. The reg. is on

dress praied now while I am sitting in my tent a writeing to you. You wanted me to write and say what paper that I would like and you would send it to me. You nead not take any on my acount but if you do not take any you do as you like if you was agoine to send it to me after you have read it. I should choose som religes or som temperance paper I am not perticular what paper it is. I wish that you would send me a pactedge of paper and a cuple bunches of invelops we cant get them hear and if I cant get som from home I cannot write for I have not got onley six sheets of paper left and that will not last long. If I onley had paper I should write so you would hear from me as often as twise a weak surtain, so if you do not get letters you may know that I am out of paper to write on. When you write again let me know whether you have got your State money or not and if you have not got it you had better for in case I do not get the plaise I think I shell I shell go in for a discharge and then your state money mite com out this small end of the horne if it com out at all. Well Sis I guess that their will be no truble now about my getting your letters the mail is reglar now and I get your letters reglar. After this let ous number our letters. We will commence on this one for number one then we can tell what letter is lost in case their is any lost. If you do not want to take a paper you can take the money that the paper cost and get the white paper with and send it to me and I will scrible on it and then send it back again. If you send a hole packedge I can sell the bigest sheir left then. I must close for this time good by.

Guy C. Taylor

NOTES

1. Apparently Taylor was still suffering from medical issues and seeking a special assignment.

2. This indicated that Taylor was in a situation in which he had more freedom of movement than someone confined to the regular army ranks.

3. Pvt Nathaniel A. Crampton, age 17, blacksmith, Sun Prairie, Wisconsin, Co. F, Thirty-Sixth Wisconsin Infantry (*Roster, 36th Wisconsin Infantry Regiment of Volunteers and Draftees*, 128).

CHAPTER 4

In Transition

July 28 to October 6, 1864

The combination of measles, heatstroke, and "a breach in a vary purticaly plaice" caused Taylor to be partially incapacitated. On August 8, 1864, he also developed intermittent fever (a symptom of malaria) and two days later was sent to the division hospital and then on to City Point.

As a result of his illnesses, Taylor found himself in an interesting situation: he was unable to meet the rigorous demands of being in the ranks but was too useful to be discharged because he could cook, wash clothes, care for horses, and perform other duties.

Eventually he was taken in by the regimental surgeons. He helped them with various tasks and was excused from carrying a gun. It appeared as though his role as an aide to the doctors became secure. At that point, however, the doctors who had been sent to treat the wounded after the August 25, 1864, Battle of Ream's Station were taken as prisoners. Prior to their capture, Taylor had been instructed to care for Dr. Woodward's horses, and he continued to do so during the doctor's absence. After Dr. Woodward's release and subsequent return to the regiment, Taylor's position as the doctor's aide continued.

His relationship with the doctor allowed Taylor an unusual amount of mobility, and he was frequently able to witness much more of the war than the typical soldier. He also had the advantage of being in less danger than the other men in the ranks.

In the section of letters covering July 28 to October 10, 1864, Taylor continued to describe a soldier's routine and life at the front. He became much more philosophical and reflective, especially in regard to God, duty, politics, and matters of life and death. During this period, he also described feeling the "blues" because of company casualties and what appeared to be a serious illness suffered by his wife, Sarah.

Gaps in his letters occurred between August 7 and August 14 because Taylor was ill and between August 22 and August 31 during and immediately after the Battle of Ream's Station. As was customary for Taylor, he filled in the gaps with a summary letter (the letter dated September 22), which covered the time period of June 18 to September 22. I believe that letter is one of Taylor's most informative and interesting letters of the war.

∽

On the banks of the James
July 28, 1864

My dear wife,

When I wrote to you the other day I thought that we would lay their for somtime but it was not more then a hour after I mailed the letter when the . . . 5 days rations.[1] When we started we made up our minds that we had got a long march to make. We traveled all nite and in the morning the boys said that they wished we wood run on to som of the rebs and then they wood have to stop, and it was not long before we cross the James river[2] and gust got up the bank and we see a line of works about twenty rods ahead of ous and we went and layed by them and the first we new the canons began to fire and then we new we was to our gourneys end for a while. Nat Crampton & myself went to work to get ous som breakfast and as we sat a eating a canonball from the Rebs com a bounding rite over ous but we cood not leave untill we got threw eating let what wood com for we had som tea and we cood not afoard to loose that. After we got threw we stood and wasched the skurmish line awhile and see them take the guns that was so sausey at ous and then we went back to the rear. This Nat is sick so he dos not go with the company. He is my tent mate and a nice young man he is to.[3] As I am a sitting in my tent a writing to you their is a gun boat rite close by ous that keeps up a perfect rore from their big guns. They are a throwing shells about 2½ miles into the rebs works.

July 29

We went 1½ miles to the frunt and stop untill night and then went back. We went threw the woods that the rebs was in wheir our big guns drove

U.S. gunboat *Mendota* on James River, near Dutch Gap Canal, Petersburg campaign,
between 1864 and 1865 (courtesy Library of Congress Prints and Photographs Division)

them out it was a site to see the treas war all shaterd to peases by our shells
wheir a 90 lbs shell struct it swep evrything. Large pines that are two foot
threw are cut rite in to half way up them and som of them are cut off twise.
The rebs got up and run like white heads and I dont wonder at it for it was
anough to make anybody run if their was any run in him. We are now on
the bank of the river wheir we cross the other day. It is call Jones landing.[4]
The reg. is about ½ mile rite in frunt of ous. We lay rite under a steep bank
so the rebs cant drop a shell into ous. Their is not onley a vary feue that is
sick and their is not any of our bregade that has got wounded except slite

wounds, so they cood go rite to the hospital. Our reg. has not had a chance to fire off their guns yet but they may be in before long and get more then they bargen for, but I do not know the rebs act rather strong. They get evrytime we make a advance, but I think they will have to make a stand somwheir before long for our men are getting on all sides of them. The calvary captured 500 yesterday and the infantry took good meny to. We lost 200 by their not obaying orderds. They was out on picket and they was orderd back and 200 would not hurry any so they got taken. I think that they did not care much.[5] Well Sis I have gust got back from goine out after som corn for the Dock[6] horse and as I am tired I thought that the best way to get rested was to finish this letter. I got a letter from Mother today and I wrote one to hur, but I do not know when I can send them out. You must not worey in case you do not hear from me vary often for awhile. The mail coms to ous pretty reglar so you must write if you do not get any from me, but I shell write as often as I can but I must close for this time for I want to go in swiming tonite yet. We can keepe prety clean hear for we can go into the river as often as we want to. I will close By Biding you good By from your husborn.

Guy C. Taylor

Write often and long letters.

NOTES

1. A line of Taylor's letter is illegible, but the original line probably referred to preparing for the long march to Deep Bottom, Virginia.

2. The James River begins in the western part of Virginia and flows 340 miles to Hampton Roads and into the Chesapeake Bay. The river played a major role in military operations at Petersburg and Richmond.

3. If Nat was sick and not with the company, and he was Taylor's tentmate, then it is probable that Taylor was not directly with the company either.

4. Jones Landing on the James River was the site of one of the famous Union pontoon bridges.

5. The engagement Taylor described was known as Deep Bottom (fought July 27–28, 1864). Gen Grant was attempting either to break through to Richmond or, at least, create a diversion to mask an assault on the lines at Petersburg, scheduled for July 30.

6. Dr. Elijah A. Woodward was born March 3, 1817, in Litchfield, Connecticut. He married Mary Newton, October 6, 1839, in Plymouth, Connecticut. They had a daughter, Belle; a son, G. B.; and an adopted daughter, Emma. In 1842 Woodward graduated from the Berkshire Medical College of Massachusetts. He came to Madison, Wisconsin, in 1855 and practiced medicine there for four years. In 1859 he became Sun Prairie's first doctor. In the fall of 1861 he entered the service as an assistant surgeon to the Twelfth Wisconsin Volunteer Regiment and resigned in 1862 because of rheumatism. Dr. Woodward reentered the service in 1864 as assistant surgeon of the Thirty-Sixth Wisconsin Volunteer Regiment (Klein, *Sun Prairie's People*, 45).

Jones' Landing, Virginia, pontoon bridge over the James, from the north bank, between 1860 and 1865 (courtesy Library of Congress Prints and Photographs Division)

In same camp 3½ miles of Petersburg
July 29, 1864

My dear wife,

I received a letter from you yesterday and you may think that I was glad to hear from home. My health keepes yet and I feal first rate genral. We march 1½ miles this morning and then camp. We are now on the rear lines of works the brestworks are vary good and then their is a foart with 12 guns in it so in all it is a strong line, and vary little prospects of the rebs trying the streanth of them, for they dont want to try to get around to the rear and then have to charge on a line of works, they still keep up a roar of artilary on our right and the Negroes pickets keepe up a roar of Musketrey, while the whites are rite in site of one another and they do not fire any at all they dont want to bring on a fite untill they are ablidge to, but the negro dont care how much they are a fiteing. Folks may say what they have amine to about the negro rase. They are grate deal more inteligant class of people then I had any fear, and if they had their freedom for a few years they wood be more able to take care of themself then their masters are. I got a letter from William the other day they are all well as usual. I wrote to you awhile ago that I mite get home. I do not know what to do wheather to try to get home this fall ore to waite till another summer. Docker Woodard told me that he thought that he cood get me a chance in the dockters tent so to be with them all the time. When we was ready to march this morning the Dock made me sine over my gun so I do not have that to cary, and it was that what cause my being so breached, and I do not think that I shell cary a gun again while I am in the armey. I would like to stay hear for if I go home I cannot do anything this winter to mount to anything and when I am hear I am a getting prety good wages and laying still all the time you mite say and if I go with the Docters I shell not be in any danger of the enemeys balls. The doc says that I can go to the hospital any time I want to, but he wants me to stay with them, so you must not worey about my being shot for in a few days I shell be in the hospital or with the dockers. As it is to late to send this out today I will stop and get my supper. I wish you cood com and take supper with me. You mite sit on my napsack and I would sit on the ground. I again take up my pen after taken supper of beaf soup and hardtack and coffe. It is great deal better living then you think it is, it is not like home but it dos vary well. Oh Sis I wish that you would send me som papers. We cannot get anything to read except now and then a paper. When I get my Madison paper¹ the hole company and good meny others are run- ing after it so I cannot hardely read untill it goes the rounds. I get once and awhile som papers from Amanda. She puts to papers in one invelop so it dont cost onley a peny a paper. If you can send me som temperance or religes papers I would be vary much pleased with them. I think that we will get our pay in a few days now so you may look for some at Sun Prairie for the alotment role has bin all fixed, and you had better get your pay from the state as soon as you can and write to me when you get it so I may know if it is allwrite or not. I have hurd that some of the woman have tryed to get theirs and cood not but the reg. have sent in another repoart so if you cannot get yours I can go to the colonel[2] and have him look after it and see what is the matter for it is allrite if the officers are rite, but I must close for this time. Please send me som writeing paper or I cannot write to you much more and som invelopes. As for stamps I can send them without and you may pay for them or send som stamps good by.

From your husborn

Guy C. Taylor

Write often and tell all the noose and try and be a good girl.

NOTES

1. The Madison paper Taylor was referring to was founded in 1839 as the *Madison Express*. It became the *Wisconsin Daily Journal* in 1852 and the *Wisconsin State Journal* in 1860. The *Wisconsin State Journal* is currently the second largest daily newspaper in Wisconsin.

2. The acting colonel at the time was Clement E. Warner, Windsor, Wisconsin, Co. F, Thirty-Sixth Wisconsin Infantry, (Aubery, *Thirty-Sixth Wisconsin Volunteer Infantry*, 293, 335–37).

Camp near Petersburg
July 31, 1864

My dear wife,

It is with pleasure that I take up my pen to let you know that I am well and hope you are the same. We are on the old camp we was when I wrote to you before. Since you got the last letter we have had a great time. We was orded to fall in that vary nite that I wrote to you and we marched all nite and stopt at Jones landing and took 4 peases of artiley from the rebs and som prisiners and then we advance 1½ miles and threw up som works and at nite we fell back again and threw up another line of works and the next day layed still untill dark and then we left and went to Petersburg marched all nite and got to Petersburg gust as our men blew up the foart and then begun the battle.[1] Their was a purfect rore of artiley and we staid their untill nite and then we marched about 8 miles in around about way and stopt on our old camp ground. I wrote a letter at Jones landing our lost at Jones landing was 1 killed 92 wounded and 4 or 5 taken prisiners. They was out on picket. At Petersburg we did not go to the frunt atall, but once an awhile the rebs would throw a shell at ous. One shot struct one of the tents and nock it down but the boys got up and laff at them it did not hurt anybody. As I do not cary a gun I was not up in range of them but was rite in fair vew not more then twenty rods. I went out and got upon a old foart to see the charge on the line and as I was standing their with a mest of others the rebs thought they would try ous they threw one shell and it struct about 40 rods in frunt of ous in the corn field and tore up som of the corn, and the next time they fiared it went rite over ous and struct the ground about 40 rods to our left. You would laffed to see the men got down from the old foart the first that I new I was standing their alone, and I new that I was as safe their as anywheir I cood get to see the charge so I thought I would stay and see it out, but it was onley a few minits when their was another com and bursted in the air onley a few rods from me, and I thought it best to get from (dat dare plise mity sudden) and I got down and started to go back when a shell bursted to my rite and kill 2 muls, but the greatist shooting I have seen yet was by our gunboat at Jones landing. Their is no use of my telling anything about it for you cood not beleive it unles you see it let who would tell it, but it is a fack that the balls cut down treas that was a foot and ahalf threw, the balls waied 90 lbs. of iron and six lbs. of powder and when one of them burst it makes evrything jar. Well Sis I wrote to you that I thought I shood be with the dockers but their is som dout of it yet and as for getting a discharge that is all plaid out at preasent anyway but I shell try and get home by the last of December or the vary first of January if their is any chance for it anyway. I do not know how long we may stop hear but I hope for somtime for it is a pleasant plaise to stay and a vary healthy plaise to. Well Sis I have got the Chief and I am vary thankful to get somthing that speaks in faver of temperance, and in case we go into winter qurters you will hear of a regamental Lodge that is if I cannot get home. I have had som talk with the boys and I can find 35 or 40 that are good templers that has not drank anything onley when they was all drill down and it was given to them by the Docks, and they say they will go in for surpoiting a Lodge. I would have writen to the lodge before now onley I have bin carful how I have let my paper go for I thought that I had rather write to you then to the lodge but as soon as I can see wheir I can get paper then I shell write all around to the folks. Well Sis you must try and take good care of yourself and try and make yourself as confible as you can and get a warm plaise for

this winter let it cost what it will. I am in hopes that we shell get our pay
before long, so you can get your money if the compiney ever gets the payrole
made out rite. It has bin sent to Washington and it has bin sent back to the
reg. for to be rectified and they are to work again on them. The Paymaster
is redy to pay ous as soon as the payrole is made out rite but I must close
so good By.

Guy C. Taylor

NOTE

1. The Battle of the Crater was fought July 30, 1864. Union forces attempted to breach
Confederate lines in front of Petersburg by tunneling under and blowing up a section of
the Confederate fortifications. The Union's spectacular explosion created an excellent
opportunity for a breakthrough, but because of Union bungling, the attack failed. Grant
later described the assault as a stupendous failure. Casualties for the Union were 504
killed, 1,881 wounded, and 1,413 captured or missing (Aubery, *Thirty-Sixth Wisconsin
Volunteer Infantry*, 274). Total losses for the Confederates were estimated to be nearly
1,500 (Trudeau, *The Last Citadel*, 127).

Aug. 2, 1864
In camp near Petersburg

My Dear Wife,

   I am sitting on my bed with John Slingland he got back to the reg. yesterday he is prety smart now but he is not vary strong yet, but they had to
send all of the sick ones that was able to walk to the reg. on acount of their
being so meny wounded ones to go to the hospital. That was a blody battle
at Petersburg[1] and I guess that we did not gane anything neather, but I do
not know, I do know that their was a slew of men killed. I was wheir I cood
have a fair vew of the lines and I stood and look at the chargen untill the
rebs began to throw them roten balls at ous and after two or three com prety
close to ous we thought it wood be gust as well for ous if we got from their,
so we went down from the foart and I went back to the rear about 40 rods
and layed down and went to sleap and when I woke up the Dock told me
that their had bin a orful charge made since I went to sleap, but guns dont
wake me now, as soon as a buzz of Muskets did when I was at home. The
boys dont think nothing agoine to sleap rite on the battlefield when they get
relieved. Well I do not know as you care anything about the field of battle
but they are vary interresting to anyone that is in vew of them. It did seem
to me as so I would like to have a hand in with the boys, but I new that I

cood do no good if I was with them, but did it not seem strang the next day to lay in camp wheir it was as still as cood be. Most of the boys layed in their tents and sleap well. Sis I am agoine to stay with the Company for awhile at any rate the dockers says that they cannot get me a discharge and if they send me to the hospital they will send me back on acount of the wounded. Leut. Russell[2] says that he will try and get me detail in som hospital in Washington so I may get somwheir yet so I can be in one plaise and not exposed to camping life alltho camping has agread with me first rate so far. Well Sis you are to home in Wis. wheir you have the comfoits of life around you and it seems hard to you I know and it is hard to. I was thinking the other day when we went on the James River what would our wimon think it they see such hard times as the wimens do in old Va. As I was walking along the road I pass 3 young ladyes one of them had a child in hur arms she was I shood say twenty and the rest was not so old, and I think that they was 3 sisters and they was left without anybody to look out for them and our men built the line of works rite up to the house on each side and the men tore down evry out building to make the works with but their was a gard put over the house so the boys cood not go in. Well Sis I suppose you are vary losom and I know it is vary hard for you but you must try and make the best of it. I think that I can get home this fall but I do not know. I can go to the rear again if I wanted to but I don't want to not yet for we are in a good plaice hear and we dont have to march any to speak of, but as soon as we have to march I shell go back for I cannot travel and cary the guns equipadge. I mite as tell you what is the mater with me. It is a breach in a vary purticaly plaice it is not bad but it is so I cant stand it to walk[3] so I think you had beter wait a while before you do anything about building for in case I do get home you wont want a house their. Sis I nevry felt any better in my life then I do now with the exception of this breach. I am getting as fat and as lazy as a hog. Oh but I wish I cood see you and Charley but I can wait with paciant untill I get home again. Sis as I was out on picket we was in the rear of the picket line hilled as a surpoit in case of atack and we was laying on the ground having a good time of it and I was talking as I awlwais are and I was scratching in the leaves and I found a nice 3 blaided nife. We was laying on a old battlefield. I have got the nife and I shell take it home with me if I dont loose it. Well Sis you must write gust how you are and how you are getting along and dont make it any better then it is. You must write how the crops are, and how Moses folks are ageting along and if his is going to raise anything or not. You must look out for your alotment role and you had better get your state money as soon as you can. Good by my dear wife and child.

From your husborn

Guy C. Taylor

NOTES

1. Battle of the Crater, July 30, 1864.

2. Lt Oliver N. Russell, age 22, merchant, Princeton, Wisconsin, Co. F, Thirty-Sixth Wisconsin Infantry (*Roster, 36th Wisconsin Infantry Regiment of Volunteers and Draftees*, 124).

3. Taylor never revealed the specifics of the breach.

In our old camp near Petersburg
Aug 5, 1864

My dear wife,

I gust got a letter from you and glad I was to hear from home and to know that you are well. I am injoying first rate health yet. We are now laying on our oars we do not have any duty to do at all, not as much as to gard our own camp, and we are now getting the vary best of living such as bread potatoes onions cod fish mackerel & coffe & sugar, so you can guess what hard times we see. To be shure any reg. will see som times that is hard we have seen it onley a few days ago, and we may see it again in a few days but wheir they see one hard day they see three easey ones, and we have seen onley 5 hard days since I got to the reg. but their is men that complain, and they would if they was in their own state and doing nothing but to stay at home and draw their reglar pay at that, but they have to stay hear if they dont want to. Well Sis I suppose you want to know what I am about day after day well the first thing in the morning is to get breakfast and eat it that you know is vary hard for me for I eat so much, and the next thing is to take a good wash, and if we want to wash any clothing then we go in for washing if none to do we lay in camp read somthing sum the bible som novel som nouspapers, when they can get them. Their is now a noose boy that comes with papers evryday for 5 cents we can get a paper so the boys get more reading now then they did. Well Sis their has bin one grand order given Genral Grant gave orders that no more whiskey is to be delt to the armey so all the whiskey their is now is what the officers bye off the sails wagons but you wont know what I mean by sails wagons. The officers bye their vuitals and their is wagons a purpos to bring it to the field and they bring whiskey with them and a privat cannot by anything unless they get a order from their commanding officer and they cant get a order evryday, but their is a great deal of licker drank for all that for the officers dont make anything of drinking a canteen full evryday. Their was one lieutenet got so drunk last nite that he cood not get to his tent and layed out all nite and sombody was good anough to go and cut off his sholder straps, and it is a great pity they did not cut his head off, then he would not be a torment to himself nor to anybody eles. Well I begun to tell you what we do hear in camp, but I see that I rune rite into whiskey, so I will go back again. After we get tiard of laying in our tent reading or writeing, we go out and get som of the darkeys a rashing and then it goes to boxing caps and gumping and then to diner, and the same rite over again and then to super, and then to dress prarade and then they get together in small companeys and talk about things in genral untill nine oclock then roal calls and then they all turn in for bed. It is evryday a like anybody dont know when Sunday comes unless they keep the rune of the days of the week and their is not one half of them but what hast to ask the day if they want to know. The boys say that they want to moove so they will fix up around and then they are shure to have to go and leave it so they have gorn to work and sat post and made a shed over evry streat so they are in the shade all the time when they are in the line of camps and it looks nice now I tell you to see shed covard thick with pine bows they are so grean and clean to, and they have all got their beds about 1½ feet from the ground they are fixed with polls and they are covard with pine bows so they are vary easy to sleap on and they are vary healthy to for what the ground is and then they can keep so much cleaner to but they will get the gra back lise[1] on them anyway. We have to fite them evryday or we cood not live. It seams as so the ground was all alive with them and you cannot get them all out of your cloths onley by boiling them and it may be two days and you get them again. Well Sis I have bin to work since I wrote the first sheat, and I have gust got it don, and I wish that you cood gust stept into our camp gust for one minuit and see it. I do not think that you would say that we look like soldiers that was doing much work for the hole camp looks so it had gust com out of a banbox for what it did a few days ago. John Slingerland is camping with ous he has bin throne out of his plaise and it is a shame, because a man is sick to have another planner around to get in his plaise but John wont cary a gun he will get into som lite buisness so he is in a good anough plaise now. Well Sis you said that you would send me som things I guess that you had not better send anything except paper and Stamps or som such things for as for stockens and such we throw away when we march I thros away a new pair of homemade socks a few days ago and the army socks are great deal the best. If you want to send anything send a good coten hankief of som darkish coller,[2] but the most that I want is paper and such things for writing. Well Sis you tell Father Thompson that if he wants som reglar gray back Shirts that I think that I can send him som they are first rate shirts for winter. I can get them for 1.53 cents a pair and it will not cost much to send them by mail. Send two to a time and they will go rite threw I think. Well Sis I wrote about the alotment but you wont get your money from the alotment untill we get our pay hear and I do not know when that will be but I think in a week or two, but in case we do not get it their will be more when it comes. You had better get what is dew you this fall & if you stay at home if he wants money you had better let him have what you dont want I think that you had not better build for we dont know what may turn up by next winter. It may be that we may want a house somwheir eles by next spring but I cannot tell yet but I have som hopes. Well Sis you must try and be a good gall untill I get home and tell Faney[3] to write and Heney[4] to and all the rest, and perticular yourself. Write often and long and I will do the best I can but I cant write vary well and I cannot think what to write so you cannot expect much for a few days again.

From your husborn

Guy C. Taylor

NOTES

1. *Grayback lice* was a nickname given to lice by Union soldiers.

2. I suspect Taylor requested a dark hankerchief to reduce the chance of being targeted by sharpshooters.

3. Frances was a sister-in-law.

4. Henrietta was a sister-in-law.

∼

NO. 1 LETTER

Aug. 7, 1864 in camp near Petersburg

My dear wife,

I received a letter from you last nite and was glad to hear from you and to know that you are well. I am injoying good health and injoying myself vary well. I never was as fleshey as I am now and keepe groine fat evryday. We are in camp on the old ground yet and things looks as so we would stop hear for somtime, but we do not know. We have got the ground all cleard off as nice as it is their at Madison and we sweep it evry morning so it keepes clean. The boys say that if they do not moove pretty soon that they will be so fat they cant walk at all. I got a paper from you to with the letter and I was glad to get somthing to read. I do not get the State Journel vary reglar and it cuts me short for reading, but I get along vary well for I go to the Dock tent and get somthing to read. Oh Sis it dos not seam posible that John can be ded he was such a stout healthey boy, but after all, them are the vary ones to be taken sick, at least it is so in our reg. Well Sis if such is the case their is one thing that will comfert his mother that is he has died in a noble cause. It is far better to know that he died like a good Soldier then to know he was shot for not doine his duty. When I wrote to John I wrote about the Lodge urgeing him to live up to his pledge so when we both got back we cood say that we had lived up to our pledge, and I thought that I shood see John again in the Lodgeroom but oh alast, little do we know when we may be call from this world to eturnity, but let ous hope that he is in a better plais then he was hear on earth, wheir he will not have to go in the field to fite a wickerd enemy, but he can rest in ease wheir war is not hurd of. Well Sis you say that you want me to com home as soon as I can. Well Sis as soon as I can get a discharge I will do so, but I cannot get one now for their is a order not to discharge anyone in this campain so their is no prospect of my geting home untill late in the fall, but the dockers says that they will try and get one for me as soon as their is any prospect of get-ing one, so I think that I can get one somtime this fall, but it wont do to be to shure, for I may not get one then but their is one thing surtain that I never can cary a gun any more so you may rest ashured that I shell not be in any battles for they wont let me go to the frunt anyway, but as long as things are as they are I shell try and get home but if it was not so, I would stay untill spring anyway for then I cood earn somthing this winter. Well Sis you said that you had not hurd anything about the alotment yet nor will you untill we get our pay, and I am in hopes that will be before a great while but it may not be for two months yet. I wrote to you awhile ago and spoke a numbering the letters and the vary next one I wrote I did not think to number it so I will try again and call this number 1, and then you do the same and then we can tell if we get all of the letters or not. Well Sis I do not know anything new to tell you so I will close by bidding you good By.

From you husborn

Guy C. Taylor

Write often and tell all the childin to write I have not hurd a word from Faney since I left tell hur to write or elces I will give hur a regler blesing one of theas days.

NO. 2

Aug. 14, 1864, Sity Point Hospital

My dear wife,

I take my pen in hand to let you know how I am, I am not vary well but I am beter then what I have bin for a few days past. The next day after I wrote to you I was taken sick with the intermittent Feaver[1] I was in the company to days and then sent to Div. Hos. and from their to Sity Point[2] I am now pretty well except being weak I do not hav any appatite to eat anything

City Point, Virginia, tents of the general hospital, October 1864 (courtesy Library of Congress Prints and Photographs Division)

and we have evrything most a purson cood ask for, but as I am on the gain
I will rest but what my eating nosion will com back again, it is a vary prety
plaise it is situated on James and Adamadic River[3] the point is long and
narrow so it takes the cool breeze from both sides. I wrote a letter to you 4
days ago but cood not send it so I thout that I wood write another and keepe
the other to look at. Well Sis I have lost my reg. or elces they have run astray
and finely the hole core. I think that I shell send to the Madison State Journel and adativement to see if I can find out wheir they are. You know that
I take that paper and get one once in fore weaks, but the reg. I do not know
wheir it is the hole core came to the point and got onto boats and started
down the river good meny thinks that they are to go to Washington and
then into my Maryland I hope that it is so for they wood not com back into
Va. not untill next spring I dont believe.[4] Sis I want you to write to me gust
how it is with you about money maters for I do not know for surtain but I
think that I shell not get any this pay Day for they are a paying the men off
now so I have hurd in my not being their gust fools me but if you need the
money rite away I will write to the reg. and get my disscrptive list and then
I can get it hear or at any plais I shood be so you be shure to write about it
the next time for if I have to send to Madison to find out wheir the core is
it will take quite awhile to get my list. Well I will close for this time and try
and write again in two or 3 days if I comboozled all over the army of the
Potomac. So good by from your husborn.

Guy C. Taylor

Sity Point 2 Div. 2 Armey Corps Hospital Secion C Co. F 36 Wis.

NOTES

1. *Intermittent fever* was usually one of the symptoms of malaria.

2. Taylor was sent to City Point Hospital, located at the Army of the Potomac's base
at City Point, Virginia.

3. The Appomattox River, which flows into the James River at City Point.

4. On August 12 the Second Corps marched to City Point, boarded transports, and
started down the James River. After dark, the ships changed direction and headed back
to Deep Bottom for another assault on the Rebel lines in front of Richmond. In the fighting, the Thirty-Sixth sustained the following casualties: 3 men were killed and 28 were
wounded (Aubery, *Thirty-Sixth Wisconsin Volunteer Infantry*, 118–20). One of the wounded
was Lt Col Clement Warner who lost his left arm (ibid., 335). Union losses were 328
killed, 1,852 wounded, and 721 missing. Confederate losses were estimated at approximately 1,000 (Trudeau, *The Last Citadel*, 170). The Union forces were unable to break
the Rebel lines and marched back to Petersburg, arriving exhausted on the twenty-first
of August.

❧

Sity Point Hospital
Aug. 18, 1864

My dear wife,

I take my pen up to write a few lines to you to let you know how I am.
Well I am not vary well but I am on the gain. The Doc says that, the most
that I want now is to keepe still and eat lite foode. I get tea and good tosted
bread with plenty of butter and Apple Sauce and then their is a mess of stuff
brot in evryday from the Christain commisioners[1] so we have evrything that

City Point, Virginia, soldiers' graves near general hospital, between 1861 and 1869
(courtesy Library of Congress Prints and Photographs Division)

we nead and then they find ous shirts and drawes cotton so we can be as clean as so we was at home, and that is one half, their is a good meny sick that would be better off now if they had kept half clean in the reg. It is no plaise in the armey for a man that is afraid of watter for a man must wash evry 2 hours to keepe clean and he must wash in good earnist to. Well Sis I expect that you are expecting a long letter but it will not be this time for I have no noose to tell you except that of war, and war noose is sometime bad noose. We have hurd that our Colonel[2] has lost his arm and Nickels[3] of Leeds and Fuller[4] of Madison is wounded in the foot. Nickels & Fuller are in our Company and nobody knows how meny may get hit before they get back but such is war and men know it and have made up their minds to stand the storm let what will come and when the mind is made up to stand anything that is one half of the battle. We can see it evryday see men that would way from 165 to 200 that now they are nothing but skin and bones and they seam to be well except weak but they will not talk atall unless you talk about their folks at home and not onley that but they write to their folks a reglar homesick letter and that of coars keeps them in a fret and they are gust big fools anough to write a piting loving Sicking letters back. It is no plaise for coating in the army espsaly for a man that has bin married and got a girl 12 years old. Anough of this but when I write to you a homesick letter I want you to gust send it back and say you don't want me to write any more unless I can write drifrant from that for I know in case I shood let my mind run gust as it will I shood be in the ground in a short time for I have not got streanth to stand it to worrey, and nobody elces, not for a great while. I like to see folks onest and write as they are and how things are, but deliver me from fretting. I suppose you would like to know who I was a hiting on, well it is anough to say he is a man in our company that wares stripes on his arms. It wont do for me to say anything against my supearhohe. Well I must close for this time I think that I shell not try to get stamps I can send them gust as well by putting on the letter Soldiers letter well good by.

From your husborn

Guy C. Taylor

Der. To Sity Point Va.
2 Div to armey Corps Hos. Sec. C.
Co F 36 reg. Wis. vol.
The plaise is laid out in sections and the sec. runs by letter

NOTES

1. The Christian Commission was an aid society for Union soldiers. It was founded in New York City, November 14, 1861, by the Young Men's Christian Association. It worked together with the U.S. Sanitary Commission. The Christian Commission provided services such as free box lunches, coffee wagons, volunteer nurses, reading rooms, writing materials, and postage (Faust, *Historical Times Illustrated Encyclopedia of the Civil War*, 140).

2. Lt Col Clement Edson Warner, Windsor, Wisconsin, Co. F.,Thirty-Sixth Wisconsin Regiment. He was wounded August 14, 1864, in Deep Bottom, Virginia. His left arm was amputated, and he was mustered out July 12, 1865 (Aubery, *Thirty-Sixth Wisconsin Volunteer Infantry*, 293, 335–37).

3. Pvt Myron C. Nichols, age 27, farmer, Madison, Wisconsin, Co. F, Thirty-Sixth Wisconsin Infantry. He was wounded in action August 16, 1864, in Deep Bottom, Virginia. His left arm was amputated, and he was discharged January 24, 1865 (*Roster, 36th Wisconsin Infantry Regiment of Volunteers and Draftees*, 137–38).

4. Cpl John G. Fuller, age 36, saddler, Madison, Wisconsin, Co. F, Thirty-Sixth Wisconsin Infantry. He was wounded in action August 14, 1864, in Deep Bottom, Virginia, and discharged for his wounds May 20, 1865 (ibid, 130).

U.S Christian Commision sends this as the Soldier's messenger to his home.
Let it hasten to those who wait for tidings.
"Behold! Now is the accepted time; behold, now is the day of salvation."

NO. 3

August 19, 1864 Sity Point Hospital

My dear wife,

It is with pleasure that I write to you to let you know that I am again getting so I can eat my reglar grub. I am getting quite smart again. I suppose that you have bin a worring about me evry since you hurd I was sick and gorn to the hospital, but Sis you must not fret any about me, for when I am well I am allrite and when I am sick I have first rate care. The senetary Commision and Christian Com. brings ous all kinds a fruit and chicken & Mutton soop, so you can see that the hospital is not a man killing plaise after all. All I wish is I was shure as good living at home allways as I get hear. Well my dear wife I know that time must seam vary long to you but you must hold up good curradge and pass away time the best that you can I am in hopes that I can get home this winter on a furlow or som other way but I do not know. I have applide for a discharge but I do not think that it will do any good whatever, but it has don no hurt and it may com round allrite yet, but I have little faith. In case that I do not get home this winter you must be vary carful and take good care of yourself, and dress warm let it cost what it will. I want you to write to me gust how you are off for money and whether you will want som before fall or not in case you do nead any I think I will not draw it from the govament untill fall and then their will be anough so it will be of som acount, and you can youse it to som advantage I think that I shell cook for Lieu. Russel[1] as soon as I get back to the reg. again, and that will be in a few days. The Lieutenant wanted I shood cook for him and he came to my tent to tell me and he found me sick, but he said as soon as I got well again he wanted me to cook for him. It will be no work hardely and when we moove I shell not [corner of letter missing] for I will have a [missing] can put evrything on his [missing] makes marching so hard it is the load they have to cary. If they did not have no load the march-ing wood be nothing to speak of. They do not travel fast nor do they pay any regard to how they stept, they walk the best way they can gust keep in order so not to get mix up, but vary oftan Co. get mix up togeather and sumtimes reg, but when reg. get mix it makes a bother. If you cood see the men a marching hear you wood think they never drill in Madison in room of tuch-ing elbows we walk about 4 or 6 feat apart when we can so to let the wind have a chance to pas throw and then it is not so bad about the dust. Well Sis I suppose that you have hurd before now that our corps cross James River and fot on Melvern Hill[2] we lost good meny men but they dun a good pease of work our Co. had 3 wounded Fuller was wounded [missing corner] the knee it is a flesh [missing] Leeds had his arm taken [missing] wounded in the finger[3] flesh [missing] and most likely stay hear untill he go to the reg. the other two may go home and may not get any further then Wash-ington. Well Sis I do not know of anything more to write that will interrest you so I will close by bidding good by.

From your husborn

Guy C. Taylor

Write often and dirct. To the reg. for I think I shell be their in a few days.

I must tell you again not to worey about me for I am well anough off, and you must try and injoy life. Life is given to be injoyed and it is our duty to injoy it if we can. We must not let our mind run at its own will but when we get a thinking about thoes that is far away and get gloomy we must start up and go to work about somthing or put our mind on somthing to change the thoughts.

Kiss Charley for me and tell him to be a good boy as I cant get stamps you will have to pay the postage their.

NOTES
   1. Lt Oliver N. Russell, age 22, merchant, Princeton, Wisconsin, Co. F, Thirty-Sixth Wisconsin Infantry (*Roster, 36th Wisconsin Infantry Regiment of Volunteers and Draftees,* 124).
   2. Malvern Hill was near Deep Bottom, Virginia.
   3. Taylor was referring to Cpl Mike Eichner, age 19, blacksmith, Madison, Wisconsin, Co. F, Thirty-Sixth Wisconsin Infantry. He was wounded in action August 16, 1864, in Deep Bottom, Virginia. He later returned from the hospital to his regiment and was mustered out July 12, 1865 (*Roster, 36th Wisconsin Infantry Regiment of Volunteers and Draftees,* 129–30).

NO. 4

Sity Point Hospital
August 21, 1864

My dear wife,

As I have got tirad of reading I thot that it wood rest me to write to you and let you know how I am a getting along. I am a getting along first rate I have got well again and are redy to go to the reg. anytime the Dock says go but I shant ask to go yet at any rate, for I had gust as live stay hear untill the reg. gets settled again as not for I dont care about traverling vary much when I can get red of it. Well Sis I do not know what to writ, today it is pleasant and warm. We have had rain for the three last days. It has bin fine weather for the wounded Soldiers and their is alot of them they have bin fiteing now for 7 days and nobody knows how much longer it will last but our boys feal allrite for they have whipe the rebs evry time. The rebs made 3 charges on the 5 corps and was mode down each time like grass before the syth. Their was a sharp fite last nite, but I have not hurd the result but their was a squad of prisiners com in about 60 in number, I am ancious to hear how the fite com out but I hope allrite.[1] The rebs are getting in a warm plais and they know it and they mean to braik our line somway, but if they do they have got to work for it and they will have to walk over their own ded and a pile of them to. Well Sis I would like to hear from you but I must wait untill I get back from the reg. I know that their is som kind of nouse their for me eather good or bad. One of the boys that is hear says that their is three letters for me in the company and I am in hopes that their will be som more by the time I get their. I know that you write often but it would not hurt my fealings atall to hear from home three times a weak, but I suppose you do not get time to write so often and I know how it is you cannot think of much to write but anything gust so I will know how you are a getting along I suppose that you are or have got your plais for this winter pick out and you must write and let me know wheir you and how you are agoine to be this winter and tell me gust how you are a getting along. I want to know all about it if I am not with you I want to know wheather you are injoying yourself or wheather you are living in misery all the while. Life is not given to moarn away and if their is any caus for you to moarn I want to know it. I am in hopes that you do not moarn and I hope you have no caus to moarn. I know that you will be losom my being gorn but you must get over that and say well he is gorn and I am not goine to fret any about it if he comes back it will be a hapy meating and in case he dos not it is time anough to moarn when I know it to be a fact, but untill then I mean to injoy myself as well as I can but I do not expect that you will feal vary well for a good while yet but try and pas away the time as fass as you can. It is a hard plase to leave a woman wheir you are, but if I had nown how it was I shood of not left Madison quite so chearful but I thought that if you had nothing onley you and Charley to look out for you cood get along pretty well but you must try and make the vary best of it you can and you may be healthear afterwords but it is a hard way for dockering. I am in hopes it will all be for the best now. Well Sis you may be shure that it was a day of rejoising when we hurd that Capt. Burell was still a living the letter that I got from you that spoke about it the others boys got letters the same day but it did hurt to of the boys vary bad one wanted to be first lieutenant and the other seckon lieu. But as long as the capt lives their cannot be any such promotion the first lieu was vary glad to hear from the capt[2] he is not one of theas kind of a fellow that wants other men to dye so they can gane a little by it. Well Sis I will close for this time I will write to the lodge in a few days. You must write often and I will do so to, but you must not worey if you do not get letters reglar for it may be for weaks we cannot send out a letter nor get any. Good by my dear wife for a few days.

From your husborn

Guy C. Taylor

NOTES

1. Taylor was referring to the fighting in Deep Bottom, near Richmond, and the Weldon Railroad at Globe Tavern, south of Petersburg. Union losses at Deep Bottom were set at 328 killed, 1,852 wounded, and 721 missing; Confederate losses were believed to be around 1,000 (Trudeau, *The Last Citadel,* 170). Union losses at Weldon Railroad were 251 killed, 1,149 wounded, and 2,879 missing or captured (ibid, 174).

2. Taylor was referring to Lt Oliver N. Russell, who would later become captain of the Thirty-Sixth Wisconsin (*Roster, 36th Wisconsin Infantry Regiment of Volunteers and Draftees,* 124).

NO. 5

In camp near Petersburg
Aug 22, 1864

My dear wife,

I got to camp today and I found a letter hear from you and I was glad to hear from you and to hear that you are well as usual.[1] Well Sis I am well and feal first rate. I am som tirad as I have gust got hear from the hospital and we march prety fast but I shell soon be rested again then I will be allrite again that is as near rite as I can be. I am sorry to hear that so meny of the boys are dien off that went to the war from our plaise I was in hopes that we mite all get back again, but life is not ours to controal their is a power that is able to take life and it is not for ous to say why do you do so, but it is the duty for each and evry man to look well and see wheir he stands for life is like the grass, today it is grean and tomorrow it is dry. Well Sis we had a fine time coming from the hospital we started yesterday at about 11 oclock and we march and stopt all the afternoon at nite we got six miles and then we stop for a hour and then we had a cavalrey gard to go with ous and we started again at sundown and we march about twenty minutis and we see that we was goine to have a hard rain and we begun to onfold our rubers and gust got mine on when the rain began and it rain in good earnist I tell you, but on we went and it got so dark we cood not see wheir to stept and we cross a ditch and the watter was about 2 feat deap and som of the men would try to get to near the watter before they wood stept down into the watter and they wood slip off from the bank and they was shure to mesure their leanth in the watter and they would get up as wet as watter would make them, and you may know what kind of talk would follow. After we went and march a mile after we cross the ditch we stop for the nite. I was lucky I was dry except from my kneas down and we stop wheir their had bin a old camp and I hunted around untill I found a bunk made of poals and large staves and I turn the staves over and they was dry and I layed down and put my ruber over me and slep untill morning when the gard com around and waik me up and said they was all redy for a start. I got up and got me a bite to eat and I felt all rite but their was good meny of the boys that sat up all nite and kep up a fire and they had no ruber and they was wet anough in the morning for it rain evry little while all nite but I was well covard with my ruber and I thinks let it rain I am allrite and the rest mite be if they wornt to lazy to cary a blanket, but I am now to the reg. and am allrite. It has com up fair and not vary warm but warm anough for benifeit. Well Sis you must take good care of your self & Charley I wish that I cood see you all but I cannot at preasent so I will wait with pasiant untill time coms when I can see you. We cannot have evrything gust as we want it but we can learn to take things as they com without fretting, and when we learn that we can get along well anough if we do not have evrything gust as we want it. Well I do not think of much more to write so will close by biding you good By.

From your husborn

Guy C. Taylor

Write often and long and be a good girl

I cant stamp this letter for I have not got the stamp nor can I get any hear.

NOTE
1. Taylor arrived back at camp the same day his regiment returned from Deep Bottom.

∾

NO. 6

Aug 31, 1864
In camp near Petersburg

My dear wife,

It is with pleasure that I take pen in hand to let you know that I am well and I hope that you are the same. Well I suppose that you want to know what I am about now days. I am taking care of Dock Woodard[1] horse. He and Dock Miller[2] was sent back by Genral Hancock[3] with a flag of truse after the battle on the 25th[4] to take care of the wounded and we expect that they and the men that went with them are in the hands of the rebs and we do not know when they will get back. When they went away Woodard sed that he wanted me to take care of his horse untill he got back and I am redy to do it. All I have to do is to go to the wagon and get it oats and hay and watter it and if I take a notion to go anywheirs I take the horse and go and then we live gust as well as we have amind to we get all kinds of can fruit and vary best of crackers and lemons, and most anything you can ask for, so we draw our hardtack at the reg. and fead it to the horses. Docker Winch[5] has bin discharge from our reg. and has gorn in the 42 Wis. as head docker so we are left without any Dockers but if any of the boys are sick they go to som other reg. docker that is in our brigade so they get along vary well, but I am in hopes that our own dockers will get back before long but it is hard to tell what the rebs will do. I think it will be doutful wheather the men that went with them will get back or not but then they may. I suppose that you got the letter that I wrote to Mrs. Slingland in and in case that you hear from John by the way of hur I want you to write and let me know for I have alot of mail that belongs to him and if he cannot get away he will write home most likely and then I wood send the mail rite back or elces write to hur and find out if their is anything of any importants in the letters if not I would burn them. Well Sis you wrote that you sent me som paper and invelops but I have not got them but you nead not send any more for I can get all I want to the Senatorys. I have got now quite a lot on hand but you may send me som postage stamps if you have a mind to for I cannot get them hear at no prise, and I got two letters from VT. One from Cousin Louisa M. Taylor from Salisbury, VT & the other from Cousin Mary A. Damon of Ripton, and I want to answer them and I will not send a letter their not being stampd and stamps are all out of the qustion in our reg. so I cannot borrow and if I cood I cood not pay them back so if you will send me som they will com vary exceptable but do not put more then 5 or 6 in a letter and then if a letter gets lost their will not be much lost and put som in to or three times and then I shell get som if not all of them. You wanted to know if I was agoine to try and get home this fall, I may and I may not get home but you had not better make any cackalations on my geting home. Their was one while the Dockter thought he was shure of geting me my Discharge & he try yet in case he gets back but we do not know when he will get back if at all, and in case he dos not get back I haven no hopes of geting home so do not expect me but do the same as you would in case you new I was not agoine to get home. You said that you had not hurd from the alotment yet I am well awair of that but it is allrite I guess you cannot get the allotment not untill we are paid in the field and then it will be sent to you. We was mustard for pay yesterday & we expect our pay on the 15 day of this month and if we get it you will get yours in a short time after gust as soon as the paymaster can get word to Madison. Well I do not know of much more to write that will intertain you so I will close and draw a plat of the battle of the 25 August for the boys for I do not expect you want to know anything about the mode of fiteing. Well I will close by biding you good by.

From your husborn

You must be a good girl and Behave yourself and write often and tell the rest to write to. Mother wrote to me once and I guess she got scared out of writing for she has not wrote since.

Guy C. Taylor

Ream's Station Battle

Aug. 25, 1864

Rite in frunt of our works wheir the cavaly skurmishers are, the fite[6] began. The rebs advanced on our cavaly and then fell back and then they began to fire on our cavaly in the shugar cane field for the purpose of drawing our men that way but our cavaly was to much for them and then they com in line of battle on our frunt again and drove in our skurmishers they com in on that road that cross the brestworks and a good meny of our men fell their. As the cavaly com in our men got down behind the works and when the rebs got in good range they raised up and poard a voley into them and down and loaded as soon as posable and the rebs com on with a yell but they met cold lead and that did not stop them they closed rite up and kept rite on and they was within 8 rods of our works and our men let them have another volley and they cood not stand that and broke and run and our canons played in to them nisely, but they was not agoine to give it up so and they got in line again and com on ous as before and met the same fate and they tryed it 4 times and was repulsed but they got reinforsement and they com on and when they was about 10 rods from our lines our frunt line got panic striten and broke and run and they run rite over the rear line and the rear line was orderd to take the brestwork but the rebs got them

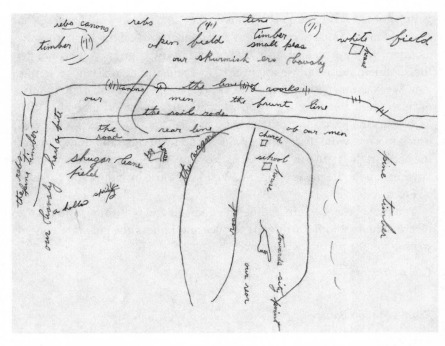

The Battle of Ream's Station, drawing by Guy C. Taylor (re-created by Patsy Alderson)

first and all that our men cood do was to run or give up so they took to runing but they found that the rebs got in the shugar cane field and was a heading them off and their was good meny killed and good meny give themself up but their was a ratling down the road now I can tell you. Our reg. lost 140 men kill wounded & mising I do not know the hole lost on our side but it must be 5 or 6 thousand but the rebs must lost a good deal more for when they made the 3 charge the ground was covard with their ded and som laid one a top of another and the 4 charge was the hardest on the rebs of any. It was a orfull battle for both sides but if we had half as meny men as they had they cood not sturd ous but we had onley 2 divisions beside the cavaly and if the frunt line had not got panic striten we would held them untill we got reinforsement for we got reinforsement in about ½ hour after we lost the works and the gards stop our men and formed in line a battle again and made a charge on the rebs and drove them back to the works again so it give ous a chance to retreat without their helping ous along with their led balls.

NOTES

1. Dr. Woodward entered the Rebel lines by order of Gen Hancock to take care of the wounded and to see to the burying of the dead after the Battle of Ream's Station. Along with two Rebel assistants, Woodward performed forty major operations from sunrise to sunset on August 27. He was then taken to Libby Prison in Richmond, Virginia. After a week, he was sent back north in the first truce boat that was sent out. Of the twelve men who volunteered to go with him behind enemy lines, only four survived the war. His hospital steward, Dr. Hand, a graduate of Beloit College, was one of the twelve who did not survive. He died of starvation in Georgia's Andersonville Prison (Obituary, "Dr. Elijah Woodward," the week of April 8, 1907, Sun Prairie Historical Society Obituary Collection, Sun Prairie, Wisconsin).

2. Clarkson Miller, Geneva, Wisconsin, was a surgeon in the Thirty-Sixth Wisconsin Regiment. He died December 20, 1864, in Geneva of disease (Aubery, *Thirty-Sixth Wisconsin Volunteer Infantry*, 293).

3. Gen Winfield Scott Hancock was commander of the Second Corps of the Army of the Potomac (ibid., 325).

4. The Battle of Ream's Station was fought August 25, 1864; Taylor included a diagram and description of the battle with this letter.

5. George D. Winch, Otsego, Wisconsin, was assistant surgeon of the Thirty-Sixth Wisconsin Regiment. He was promoted to head surgeon of the Forty-Second Wisconsin Regiment on July 29, 1864 (Aubery, *Thirty-Sixth Wisconsin Volunteer Infantry*, 293).

6. Ream's Station was located south of Petersburg on the strategic Weldon Railroad, which was a major supply route for the Confederate troops at Petersburg. In the battle, the Thirty-Sixth Wisconsin sustained the following casualties: 5 killed, 10 wounded, and 128 taken prisoner with 74 eventually dying in Rebel prisons, most of them in Salisbury, North Carolina (Aubery, *Thirty-Sixth Wisconsin Volunteer Infantry*, 131). Total Union losses at Ream's Station were 140 killed, 529 wounded, and 2,073 captured or missing for an aggregate of 2,742 (ibid., 274).

NO. 7

In camp near Petersburg
Sept. 3, 1864

My dear wife,

As I had nothing elce to do I thought that I would write a few lines to you to let you no that I am well and I hope that theas few lines will find you injoying the same blesing. I am yet takeing care of the Docks horses. I have two in rume of one now. We have not hurd a word from the dockers yet nor from any of the men that went with them. I shood not wonder if they wood have to stay their for somtime, but I am in hopes that they will get back before long for their is som falt finding about the grain and fead for the horses and I think that I shell stay with the Dock as long as he stays in the armey and I do, for when he went away he told me that he wanted me to stay with him and the other man that had charge of the pack horse thought that I was trying to rut him out and he began first to make a fuss about that hay and he found that I had bin to the man that deals out the hay and got gust what belongs to me and then he began about the oats and I don the same again. I told the man that I wood help him anough about dealing out the rations to make it allrite if he wood give me my grain separate and he did so, and when the other man found out that I was redy for him at any state he com to his rite mind a little and said as long as the other docker had gorn home he wood not have anything to do with Woodards horse, so I told him if he said that he wood have nothing more to do with it before the others boys that I wood take the horse and he gave it up to me, and that was gust what I wanted for he is out now anyway from having anything to do with the Dockters things at all so their is a fair show for me but I do not know how long I may stay. The Dockers are both mad about my coming back from the hospital, they ment to got me discharge if it was in their power to do so but the Dock at the hospital sent me so I had to go. The Dock ask me what made me com back and I told him I was sent back by orders and he swore anough about the Dock at the hospital to turn evrything blew (this was Miller) the head Surgent and he said that he should send me rite back the first chance he got and he wood send a line to the Docker that wood not be so pleasant neather but the next day the battle com on and he had to go back and I do not know what he will do if he gets back. They are trying to break up our reg. becaus we lost the stars & stripes in the last fite.[1] The man that bore them was shot ded and the rebs was rite on him as you mite say and no man in the world cood get them but som of the officers say that we mite save our flag but they say that the 36 is a set of cowards and evry other flag was on the run before our state flag turned and when he turned the rebs was holling to him to surrender and he started to run and the other man was shot rite by his side and he had sevral holes put threw his flag and one shell tore it vary bad but he got off with it and to have it took from ous now it goes rather hard but I think that they will fetch it back again. The Boys all say if they do not give up the collors again that they will not do any more then they are ablidge to and if the boys set out to shurk they wont be good for nothing for it is the greatist plais in the armey to shurk that ever was. Well Sis I have not got a letter from you for 2 weaks but I know that it is not your falt but the mail is vary eareglar now but write and if I get them it will be allrite and in case I do not get them I shell have to go without hearing from home untill they can com reglar. When you write I wish you wood put in to or 3 postage stamps each time for awhile. I do not know as you get my letters but I write two a weak you said in your last letter that you had not hurd from your alotment yet, you will not untill we get our pay and we expect that on the 15th day of this month but we may not get it but I am in hopes that we will. In case you have more money then you want to use when you get your alotment you had better keep it or let sombody have it so you can get it in case you should want it for you do not know how much money you may want to youse but I must close by biding you good By.

From your husborn

Guy C. Taylor

Dont try to send any thing by mail except stamps.

NOTE

1. Maj Gen John Gibbon, commander of the Second Division of the Second Corps, issued General Order No. 63, dated August 30, 1864. The order deprived the 164th New York, the Eighth New York, and the Thirty-Sixth Wisconsin Infantries the privilege of carrying the national colors because they had lost their national colors at the Battle of Ream's Station. Why these three regiments were singled out when several other regiments lost their colors as well is puzzling. 2nd Lt George E. Albee of Co. F, Thirty-Sixth Wisconsin, who was taken prisoner at Ream's Station, was soon paroled and on hearing of the order denying the Thirty-Sixth Wisconsin the right to carry the colors expressed his displeasure to those in command—all the way to President Lincoln. After a full investigation of the matter, Maj Gen Gibbon was subsequently ordered to present, in person, a new regimental set of colors to the Thirty-Sixth Wisconsin, which he did in November 1864 (Aubery, *Thirty-Sixth Wisconsin Volunteer Infantry*, chapter 6).

In camp near Petersburg
Sept. 5, 1864

My dear wife,

As it is washing day with me and I have got my close on a borling and have got time to write a little while I thought that I wood write a few lines to you, and let you know what I am up to now days. To tell the truath I am doing nothing to speak of so I do not know what to tell you I am up to. I have charge of two horses yet. We have not hurd a word yet from the Docters and I do not think we will for somtime for if the rebs was agoine to let them off they wood have bin hear before now, but we have had a docter Detailed to our reg. so the men are cared for. Their is a good meny of our men that has bin sick are now coming back to the reg. so we shell soon have quite a mess of men again. When I wrote the last to you I said that they had taken our collors from ous but they com back that vary nite I wrote. They found out the truath of the matter and they sent for our staff bearer and when he com back he bore the flag of the 36 Wis. Vol. The flag looks vary hard it has bin ridle with balls and one shell went threw it but then we mean to keep it as long as their is one partacle left of it, and when it is all gorn we will send to the governer for another.[1] It has bin a long time since I have hurd from home but their is no one to blaim as I know of. I got a letter from Amanda this morning and she said that George & Moses had both inlisted I do not know but they have don the best thing but I do not beleave that they will do one weeks duty for they cannot stand it. The hardest of the marching is on the longest. They have got to cary a knapsack or they will suffer with the cold, and they must cary their haversack & cankeen, and they all draw rite across the longues. Their is a good meny strong looking men have to do without what they nead on that acount. If you know what reg. they are agoine in I wish that you wood write and let me know, but I am inclined to think that they will both be throad out, for any Docter will know that they cannot stand it, but they may get in som good plaise wheir they will not have to do duty if they look out for it. Well Sis I will say once more, (for I do not know as you get my letters) that the allotment you will not hear from untill we get our pay, and as for you makeing any caculation on my coming home this winter you may not for it is doutfull, and I want you to do gust as so you new I warnt coming and then you will have a plaise to stay. Do gust as you wood if you new that I had got to stay 3 years. I want you to write gust how it is with you about money matters if you are out of money or not and whether Chipman has paid you or not, and what is father agoine to do in case that George goes to the war. I have wrote sevral letters to Wis. and I have not got onley two for about two weeks, but I keep a writeing and I think that I shell get a pile of them byimby at least I hope so. I wrote to you that I had hurd from two of my Cousins in Vt., and I have got the picture of my cousin Marys husborn and I will send it home. It is taken from another. He is in the 7 Vt. Reg. and reinlisted. He is in a band so he is not in much danger of the rebbles balls, well I must close By Biding you good By.

From your husborn

G.C.T.

NOTE

1. The tattered Thirty-Sixth Wisconsin flag of which Taylor was speaking is now in possession of the Wisconsin Veterans Museum, which is located in Madison, Wisconsin. The captured national colors of the Thirty-Sixth was recovered in Richmond after the war and then kept in Washington until it was returned to the state of Wisconsin in 1905. It is also now housed in the Wisconsin Veterans Museum.

∽

NO. 8

Sept. 7, 1864

My dear wife,

I got a letter from Mother last nite, that was written to me when I was at Sity Point, sick and another that you wrote, that was written on the last days of Aug. When I got Mothers letter and found out that you was sick I wish myself to home for the first time since I have bin in the armey. I was afraid that your sickness wood prove to be fatle, but earley in the morning our orderley sent me your letter which stated that you was in the gain which has gave me som hopes, as for me I have not felt so well (that is so free from any pains) since I have bin south, but their are reasons for it, for I cannot march and keepe in the ranks, but what my legs will pain me so I cannot sleap. It is the load that we have to cary, but I am not in the ranks now nor I dont think that I shell be anymore, as long as I stay in the armey. Wheir I am now the horses cary the load and me to, and I find that it is gust as well for me to get som such a plais, as to gust lay around the camp and lug all my stuff, and let sombody elces get the chance to go with horses that is able to do duty evryday rite alonge. Well Sis you said that you expected that I new all about how you was. I think I do but I do not know by hearing from anybody except from Mother and all she said was that you was vary sick, but the docter said that good care wood fetch you up again. I have not got any letter from Lydia for a long time and I cood not think what the reason was but now I think that she wrote to Sity Point and the letters are their. The way that I got this of Mothers was by one of our boys being their and he brot it up to me. Well Sis you must be vary carfull and keep vary queit untill you get your streanth again, and do not worey about me, for I am in a plais now wheir I can take pains and take care of my health I am gust wheir I want to be as long as I stay in the armey. I suppose that you want to know what I am up to well I am cooking beans I take my paper in one hand and my pen in my mouth when I want to do anything and then sit down or stand up gust as it hapens and write. We are expecting to moove back to our old camp ground and I am bound to write so to get it out at this mail if posibol. I have got one letter hear that I wrote to you 3 days ago and gave it to one of the boys to put into the mail bag and he has carred it in his pocket untill this morning he gave it back to me, so I will send to this time. One of our boys has gust com from the reg. and he says that they have gorn rite in their old plais and they are behind som orfull strong works now and in a nice plais to camp. We will go up to wheir they are this afternoon. You say that you expect your pay off Moses and you are agoine to let it out. I wood not let it for no longer then spring if I cood help it, and do for heven sake keepe anough to be shure that you will have anough, and som to spair for no one noes what we may want money for by spring (at least I dont know) as for that of Chipmans I will write to him myself and I guess it will com. Well I must close I will write again in a day or two so good by.

From your husborn

Guy C. Taylor

Write often

[NOTE: NOT NUMBERED.]

In camp near Petersburg
Sept. 9, 1864

My Dear Wife,

I wonce more take my pen to write to you to let you know that I am well and I am in hopes that you are on gaining ground. I wish it was so I cood be to home with you while you are sick, but I cannot, so I mite as well try to content myself and hope for the best. You said that if I cood see you I wood not know you, if that is the case you are vary low and you must be vary carfull and not try to stur around to soon and let your mind be at rest to for if the mind is not at rest, their is no rest for the body. I am with the docters horses yet, we do not hear a word yet from the Docters nor from any of the men that went with them. We have made up our minds that they have all gorn to Ritchmond to stay awhile, and it may be that they will try to get Jeff[1] to com to a settlement with the govarment. Well I suppose that the folks are all awaik about the draft.[2] I think that the best way they can disspose of the draft is to inliss and then they wont get drafted. Folks may talk about pease, their is no pease untill the north whips the south rite to it and they will do it to. Great meny of the men in this armey are crying pease but they are the men that never had pease to home for a drinking man dos not know what pease is (this is my vew), and it looks so strange that you cannot find a irish man nor a drunkard scurisely but what is a McClynon man,[3] but old Abe is at the helm yet and I am in hopes he will be for 4 years more. When I wrote to you before I said that we had our flag taken from ous but we have got it again, but the Stars and Strips are in the hands of the rebs, that was a hard fite on the 25 of Aug. but the repoart that we get from the fite we come off a great deal better then I had any ide we had. I expected that our lost was nearly 5000 in all but it seams as so the most that was lost was rite wheir we was, and the first repoart was that the rebs broke our line on the exsteam left and I expected that the resurve that layed in the cane field was all swep or nearly all, but it seams that they got off with vary little lost. Their was one Mass. Reg. that onley 3 men com out of the fite, they had good meny killed. We got a letter from Lieutenant Russell[4] and he says that his wound is not one half as bad as he thought it was. The ball struck his sholder (in frunt) and the bone clanse the ball so it com out of his arme gust below the sholder, and it did not shatter the bone but vary little. He says that he will be back to the reg. again this fall. I tell you the boys wood be glad to see him, but poor Capt.[5] he has gorn wheir their is no rebels to fite. He was a man to home and a man & a officer in the armey, and he has died like a trew Soldier, at his post. Well I must close or I cannot send it out today and I will bid you good by by caushing you to be vary carfull of yourself.

From your husborn

Guy C. Taylor

Write often and tell all the rest to do the same

NOTES

1. "Jeff" refers to Jefferson Davis, president of the Confederacy. He was previously a senator from Mississippi.

2. The first National Conscription Act was passed on March 3, 1863. Prior to that time, the North had obtained its troops from volunteers and state militia called into Federal service. Opposition to the act was widespread. The act declared that all able-bodied males between 20 and 45 were liable for service. It itemized exemptions, permitted substitutes, and provided elaborate methods of enforcement. By the end of the war, the draft had provided 46,000 conscripts and 118,000 substitutes, a number making up only about

6 percent of the Union force (Faust, *Historical Times Illustrated Encyclopedia of the Civil War*, 225).

3. Union Gen George B. McClellan.

4. Lt Oliver N. Russell, age 22, merchant, Princeton, Green Lake County, Wisconsin, Co. F, Thirty-Sixth Wisconsin Infantry. He was wounded in the right shoulder on August 25, 1864, at Ream's Station near Petersburg. He was hospitalized until December 1864, but his wound rendered his arm nearly useless. He returned to his unit, was promoted to captain, and was mustered out in Jeffersonville, Indiana, with his company July 12, 1865 (*Roster, 36th Wisconsin Infantry Regiment of Volunteers and Draftees*, 124).

5. Taylor was referring to Capt Prescott B. Burwell, Thirty-Sixth Wisconsin Infantry, who was wounded June 1, 1864, at Turner's Farm (aka Bethesda Church). He was taken prisoner and died of his wounds in Libby Prison, Richmond, Virginia, on June 28, 1864. He was buried in Richmond, Virginia, as P. F. Barwill (ibid., 124).

NO. 10

In Camp Near Petersburg
Sept. 11, 1864

My dear wife,

I take my pen up once more to let you know that I am well and I am in hopes that by the time you get this that you will be so that you can write more incouging nuse, but I do not want you to write that you are a getting along well unless it is so, for I want to know the worst of it. I am in the same plais as I have bin. We hurd from the docters they are reliesed, and are both in Anapalas sick. Miller is vary low it is doutfull whether he comes back again or not but Woodard we shell expect back in a cupple of weeks. He sent me word to stay with the horses and I shell stay as long as I can, but I want to see the Dock back now for this campain will soon be over and I want to know what I am agoine to do this winter and I think I can tell prety soon after he gets hear. We are having a vary easy time now. The reg. dos not have any duty to do hardley they are call out once and awhile to work on a foart, but they do not work vary hard, not as men do on a farm in Wis. Well Sis you must try and take care of yourself and not try to get smart two quick, for if you do you may get down again worse then evrey, you said that Lydia had writen to me I have not got a letter from hur for 3 weeks and I have written to hur asking what was the reason she did not write. I got a letter from you 4 days ago and I look for one last nite but no letter com. I wish that you wood write often when you are sick, incase you cannot write get som of the rest if they do not write more then 3 lines. This letter I have numberd 10, I think that I did not number the other ones, but I do not know but I did, I am sorroy that George and Moses has inlisted for they can nevry stand it. A man wants to be made of steal to stand what the armey has to hear, but one thing the hardist work is over. They will not have such hard marchis anymore. This reg. has march 20 miles in the nite and work the next day & nite and the next nite march all nite again and then lay rite in the hard sand expecting evry minit to have to go into a fite, but it is all over with now and the boys are a fealing first rate. They are geting incourage to for we can see that the south is groine weak vary fast. Well if Fan has got home I shell expect a letter from hur in a day or two. I will Close By Biding you Good By.

Guy C. Taylor

NO. 11

In Camp Near Petersburg, VA
Sept. 14th 1864

My dear wife,

I pick up my pen to let you know that I am injoying vary good health and I am in hopes that theas few lines will find you injoying the same. I have not hurd from you since the 31 of Aug., and you may be shure that it seams like a long time. I am to the Companey evry nite looking for a letter but I have to go back Dispointed. I do not know hardly what to think about it, somtimes I think that the letters do not com and again I think that you are vary Sick and dont want to let me know it, but if that is so (that you are vary sick) I want Some of you to write and let me know it, and in case that your letters are lost their is no one to blaim but you must be shure to write. I am in the same plais that I have bin in evry since the battle, we have hurd from the docters. They are at Annapalas MD. we rather expect Woodard back before long but it is doutfull about Miller for he is vary sick. Miller the Steuard[1] has got back (he is the docks brother) and he will have charge of the Sick now. He has studard medisons considerbly and then the men all like him and they all hait the Docter that has bin detailed to this reg. and a man had better be ded then to get the ill will of the men he has controal over. I cannot write you any neus this time. It is curringly at the frunt vary noisey. The roads are lined with teams and the canons in frunt are belching out their tremendes roar. While som of our men are geting blown to atoms, others are laying (rite in hearing) as though their was nothing goine on at all. The men can lay rite by the side of a foart and sleap gust as well as so they was at home while the guns are makeing a deafing roar. Their is more stur hear today then coming I do not know what it means but I think they are changen their baises of surpleys. They have got a railroad now from Sity Point to the Welden railroad[2] and it strites me that as soon as they can get it so we can get supplyes up by the cars their will be another moove to cut the rebs road west of the Welden road. It is reported that Lee has fortified himself on that road but he will have to get from that in the coarse of time and I think that time is not vary long neather. Well I will close and send this out today. Write often and let me know gust how you are and how you are a geting along, and do not vary from the truath, so Good By.

From your husborn

Guy C. Taylor

of Co F 36 Reg. Wis Vol. via Washington D.C.

NOTES
   1. Pvt Alanson Miller, Geneva, Wisconsin, Co. A, Thirty-Sixth Wisconsin Infantry, was promoted to hospital steward April 1, 1864. He was mustered out July 12, 1865 (Aubery, *Thirty-Sixth Wisconsin Volunteer Infantry*, 294).
   2. The Weldon Railroad connected Petersburg, Virginia, to North Carolina. The railroad was an important supply route for Lee's army and for Richmond until it was permanently severed by the Union forces at the Battle of Weldon Railroad, or Globe Tavern, August 18–20, 1864.

∾

NO. 12

In Camp near Petersburg
Sept. 17, 1864

My dear wife,

   I have gust got a letter from you and glad was I to hear once more from home, and to hear that you was geting better, I am injoying vary good health onley I must say that I have had the blues or somthing elces. Time has seam so long since the battle on the 25 of Aug. for at that time our men was more then one half gorn and we did not know but what they was kill & wounded and a few days after I got a letter from you that stated that you was vary sick, and then the first that I hurd from you was this morning, so you can guess somwheir near how I felt, it has bin 18 days that I have look for a letter and it has com at last. I know that you write often but the truble is in the mail. The letter that I got this time was No. 6, the last letter was No. 3 so it shoes that the mail is not reglar and then I know it is not by my papers I do not get one once in 3 weeks. You said in your letter that you had not got any letter from me to Mrs. Slingland[1] I wrote to you and to hur and sent it to you and I forgot to number the letter untill I had got it seald, so I thought I wood let it go, as for the paper and invelops I never got them, nor neather have I got onley 4 papers from you. I vary well know that I do not get much more then one half of the mail that is sent to me. I have not got a letter from Lydia for more then 5 weeks and I know that she has writen (I say I know, at least I believe she has) and I have wrote to hur and ask the reason she did not write and no letter com yet. Well I have no nuse to tell you, for we are in camp and we do not hear anything onley by mail eather by letter or by the Press. We have gust hurd threw the State Journel that the boys of our reg. that was missing are all in Lybia Prison[2] except one and they do not know what has become of him but I prosume that he is in the Speartual World, but I am glad to know that our men was not killed nor wounded, the rebs drove ous from our works but it was a dear thing to them they layed one a topt of another all along our works, our men barred 2000 of the rebs, their lost must have reach 5000 kill & wounded while we had onley a bout 6000 in the fite, one of the rebs papers say that they lost five thousand while another says that they lost in kill & wounded 700 onley and we barred two thousand of their men. Well Sis you must be as carfull as you can of your health and gust make up your mind that you are agoine to take the world easey let what will com, and pas away time to the best advantadge you can. Well I will close By Biding you good By.

From your husborn in the armey

Guy C. Taylor

I will write again in two or 3 days you must write often to if I do not get all of them and tell them all to write and I want to know whether Lydia dos write or not.

NOTES

1. Wife of John G. Slingerland, Co. F, Thirty-Sixth Wisconsin Infantry.
2. Libby Prison was a Confederate prison located in Richmond, Virginia. For the most part, Union officers and high-ranking civilians were held there. Long after the war, the

building was dismantled and reassembled as a museum at Chicago's 1893 World's Columbian Exposition. Most of the prisoners from the Thirty-Sixth Wisconsin Regiment captured at Ream's Station were not sent to Libby Prison but to a Confederate prison in Salisbury, North Carolina.

∾

NO. 13 RECEIVED NO. 6

In camp near Petersburg, Virginia
Sept. 20th 1864

My dear wife,

I have gust got a letter from you and was glad to learn that you are on the gain, but I am afraid that you are getting smart to fast, for your own good. You had better keep prety still, untill you are strong again and then do as you have a mind to do, but I suppose that you will do that anyway strong or not, my health is vary good the best it has bin since I left the state. I began to feal like myself once more, and I am in the vary plais to have good health what little work that I do is like doing work at home on a farm, it is not like caring a gun and being up nites on gard, when nite comes I can go to bed and lay their untill morning, and then we can have better tents and can fix up our beds in som shape, and another thing we can keep clean, my tent mate now is a young man by the name of Hart[1] he is a smart boy to, he is clurking now for the docters that has bin detailed to our reg. He is a vary pias man for a young man in the armey, he has hill out so far and no dout but he will as long as he is in the armey, but that is not the genral case with boys in the armey. It dos seam as so men lost all manhood in the armey. Their is som of coars do not give way to the inflance that is around them. I have warctht it once prety close, and I can see that the men that are the most corrupt in their ways are the men that are the most homesick, they get discurage and homesick and then they dont seam to care for anything and go into gambling, swaring yes evrything that man can to make him worse, well I am in hopes that this war is most over with and men can go back to their homes and settle down once more and try to be men again and most of them will be men, and men that are men to for they will see what influance & hardship will do to men. Well Sis you say that you think somtimes that if it warnt for Charley that you would like to be with me in som Hospital, well I am not in a hospital now nor I shell not be as long as I can help it. I am in a good plais wheir I am and I shell stay hear gust as long as

I can. It is the plais that I wanted as soon as I got to the frunt and lurnt how the thing was a runing and I am hear now and it is better then I had a ide it was at first. What is the reason that I do not get any letters from any-one from home but from you their is a dozen of you in one house, and onley one that writes, is it that you do not want to write ore that you dont care about my hearing from home or what is the reason, or is it becaus I do not write to you each in person I cannot write anything more then what I do write and when I write it is for all & then Lydia I have not got a letter from hur for 5 weaks. I shell write to each one bi & bi and give you all a reglar dutch blesing. Well I must close for I got a letter from G. Taylor this morning and I must answer that to. Write often this letter is the answer to No. 6 you wood all do me a favor by writing. I will close By Biding you all good By.

From your husborn

Guy C. Taylor

NOTE

1. Walter Osgood Hart, Bloomfield, Wisconsin, Co. A, Thirty-Sixth Wisconsin Infan-try (Aubery, *Thirty-Sixth Wisconsin Volunteer Infantry*, 295). Hart had enlisted as a sur-geon's assistant along with surgeon Clarkson Miller and hospital steward Alanson Miller. In 1917–18, Hart wrote *Plodding and Thinking*, which gave the details of his Civil War experience. Guy Taylor is mentioned several times in Hart's manuscript. *Plodding and Thinking* can now be found in the Wisconsin Historical Society collections. Hart also wrote *Maps of the Battlefields Where the 36th Regiment Wisconsin Volunteers Was Engaged*, which is located in the special collections department at the University of Virginia Library in Charlottesville.

NO. 14

In camp near Petersburg, VA on the Petersburg & Norfork Railroad
Sept. 22th 1864

My dear wife,

As I have not got anything to do to pass away the time, so I thought that I wood spend a little time in writing to you & let you know that I am still numbered with the living, and am injoying one of Gods great blesings, that is good health. We are in camp in a open field by the edge of the timber. Our crew is in the timber so we can get the horses in the shade and then we had rather be back a ways from the reg. for it is so much stiller. I thought that you mite want to know wheir we have bin, so I will send my minuits that I have kept, so you can tell vary near by looking on a map. I started from Mount Plesant Hos. on the 18 day of June and we stoped in Washington Sity that nite the next morning June 19 we took the cars and went to Alaxander we went into camp their June 20 we drew our guns and amunition June 21 we started again and marched to the sity and took the boat for Sity Point and landed at the Point lait in the afternoon on the 22 & camp, morning of the 23 we started for the frunt and it was vary warm & we had not marched onley 2½ miles when their was 15 of the men Sun Struck, we got 5 miles and camped. At 4 oc on the morning of the 24 we again set out and I got to our reg. that nite. The reg. laid som 4 miles from Petersburg near the Petersburg & Norfork R.R.[1] We was in camp or making short mooves untill the 28 we then march about 3 miles and cross the R.R. on the 30 we was mustard for pay, and on the 2 of July we mooved to the rite about ¾ of a mile and camp behind a strong line of works, we was about 1 mile south of the R.R. and about 3 miles of Petersburg, we was laying in camp doing picket duty untill the 11th, we then struct tents and had the pleasure of puting them up again at the same plais but the next morning we had the pleasure of strikeing tents and of tairing down the brestworks and then we marched about 2 miles and camp near the R.R. in about 2½ miles of Petersburg. We layed in camp the 13, 14, 15, 16 we was sent out on fategue choping wood and returned to camp on the eavening of the 17 on the 18 Docter Woodard returned to the reg. on the 21 their was 10 of our company went out on fategue 22 we march about 1 mile and went to work on the line and we broke camp again on the 26 we started gust at nite and marched all nite and in the morning we laid ourself down to rest on the bank of the James River after a march of 15 miles, in the morning of 27 we cross the James River on a pontoon Bridge and met the enemy, and after a little fiteing we took 4 peases of artilary, and a number of men,[2] after sheling the woods our men went to the left about 1 mile and threw up som brestworks, and the next nite fell back to the lines that they took from the rebs in the morning of the 27 work all nite in makeing another line and the next day the 28 they layed by the works untill nite and then we recross the river and marched all nite and in the morning of the 30 we was in frunt of Petersburg. Gust as we got their the rebs foart was blown up and then began the battle.[3] Our reg. marched down into a hollow and was hill in reddiness in case that they mite be neaded, but they did not moove untill nite then we

march back to our old camp on the Petersburg & Norfork R.R. and we laid
in camp untill the 12 of Aug. on the 10 I was taken sick and sent to the Div.
Hospitol & the 12 I went to Sity Point and the hole corps mooved they went
to sity point and took boats and went up the James River about 12 miles and
then landed and was marched to the frunt and charged on the rebs. at
Melvin Hills[4] and drove the enemy from their works and hilled their line
and on the 16 they started back again and cross the Petersburg and Norfork
R.R. camp about 3 miles south of the R.R. On the 22 I started from the
Hospital to join the reg. and joined them on the 23, 3 miles south of the
R.R. on the 24 we broak camp and marched 7 miles and com to Reams
Station on the Welding R.R. and on the 25 you well know what took plais[5]
that nite after the docters had got threw examining the wounded we set out
and march nearley all nite and went into camp the next day near the Petersburg & Norfork R.R. again and we have layed in camp and don fatague duty
evry since but wheir we shell go to next the good Lord onley knows, but I
do not think that we shell have much more marching to do. We may have
to moove good meny time before we get into winters quarters, but it will be
short mooves, but we cannot tell what *old grant* may have for ous to do yet
before winter, their is time anough to whip old Lee yet, in case that they get
men anough, but that is what is the matter I expect that the men that are
left at home are to work a plowing and takeing care of their corn. While
they are turning the soil we are trying to turn the rebs, and I think that they
are geting turned pretty well now, since the fall of Atlanty[6] & Early's defeat[7]
our boys have seam to have woken up from their slumber. It did look as
though the men did not cair what did become of the Country in case they
cood onley get out of the armey, but now they are awaik & wide awaik and
they begin to think that they are a doing somthing after all, and they do not
think so much of that pease party[8] as they did, they began to think that old
Abe is agoine to whip the rebs and not let George B. McClenon[9] make any
kind of a compramice that old Jeff[10] may ask for, they began to get their eyes
open and see wheir they stand, now for a few days we have got noose from
Shurmen[11] & from Shurden[12] and you can hear chears after chears all along
the lines, and then you go to a reg. and in rumes of seeing the men laying
on their bunks they are all alive and sturing around and talking over the
prospects of the coming election[13] & war matters in genral. It is amusing
for anyone to go and stand and hear the talk, & it is interresting to for their
is som smart men to talk and their is som that *think* that they *are* smart,
som boys that cant tell one letter from another, will talk as though they new

evrything that is agoine on in the war department, when in reality they do not know what is don in their own company. Mr. Miller[14] is hear with ous he is Brother to Docter Miller, and he is the hospital stuard he is a doing most of the doctoring now for the boys are all down on the docter that is in charge of our reg. and they will not go to him untill they are abelidge to, but you see that Miller cannot excuse any one from duty that is the buisiness of the docters, he (Miller) is a vary fine man and he is around with the men all of his time to see if their is any one sick and if their is any he cannot do to much for them. I am in hopes that he will get to be asistant surgent, but then I do not know as they can get him in, for I have hurd that their was a man in Wisconsin that was trying to get in, you see that Woodard will become first assistant now that Winch[15] has gorn we are having a vary nice time in our little camp most evry nite we sit around our camp fire and lysing to Millers singing he is a vary good singer and he can sing from morning untill nite and sing good morrel songs to, and their is not much church music that he dos not know it dos seam somtimes to hear him & Williams[16] & Hart sing that we was back in old Wis, in som meating but (if not their in body we are in minds) and I am in hopes that it will not be meny months before we shell be their body & mind to, but not untill the rebs are whipt so they are wiling to lay down their arms and cry for turms, and then let ous return home and know that we have not work in vane but our work of strive & blod is dun, and we can see the benifit of our laber, not onley can we see, but to hear the cryes of joy from nearly fore millans of bondsman that has bin set free. Well I must close for this time, and I will write again in a day or to, and you must write and tell the rest to write So good By

   From your husborn

Guy. C Taylor

NOTES
   1. The Norfolk and Petersburg Railroad connected Norfolk, Virginia, to the city of Petersburg, Virginia.
   2. Demonstration north of the James River at Deep Bottom, Virginia.
   3. The Battle of the Crater.
   4. Part of a second Union army demonstration north of the James River near Deep Bottom, Virginia.
   5. The Battle of Ream's Station.
   6. The city of Atlanta, Georgia, fell September 2, 1864, to Union forces commanded by William Tecumseh Sherman.

7. Taylor was referring to Confederate Gen Jubal Early's raid on Washington, June 23 to July 12, 1864.

8. Taylor was referring to the Democratic Party during the presidential election of 1864.

9. George B. McClellan.

10. Confederate President Jefferson Davis.

11. Gen William Tecumseh Sherman, commander of all western Union troops.

12. Philip Henry Sheridan, cavalry commander of the Army of the Potomac.

13. Presidential election of 1864 between Abraham Lincoln and George McClellan.

14. Alanson Miller, Geneva, Wisconsin, hospital steward of the Thirty-Sixth Wisconsin Infantry (Aubery, *Thirty-Sixth Wisconsin Volunteer Infantry*, 294).

15. George D. Winch, Otsego, Columbia Country, Wisconsin, first assistant surgeon of the Thirty-Sixth Wisconsin Infantry (ibid., 293).

16. Probably Cpl Stephen Williams, Trempealeau, Wisconsin, Co. I, Thirty-Sixth Wisconsin Infantry, or Cpl Thomas Williams, Randolph, Wisconsin, Co. H, Thirty-Sixth Wisconsin Infantry (ibid., 316, 314).

~

NO. 15

In Camp Near Petersburg, Va.
Sept. the 24th, 1864

My dear wife,

I write to you once more to let you know that I am well, and hope that you are still on the gain we are in camp on the Petersburg & Norfork R.R. yet, and are having a vary nice time of it. We have not mooved for most two weaks and it has got so it seams more like home but no knowing how soon we may have to moove, the allotment roal is good for nothing the papers was not made out rite so you will not get any money, (onley what I have got a mind to send you). Well we have got our pay after so long a time altho it has not bin vary long neather since I was paid, I do not get any bounty this time for I did not inlist, not untill March, in case I had inlisted in Febuary I wood have got my bounty it is forty dollars, but it will com the next time so it will not make much diffrance, I got 4 months pay it is 16 dollars a month the hole com to 64 dollars, of which I (suppose you claim 40 dollars your due) but seeing that you did not scold me any for not sending you more of that I drawed at Washington I will try and send you 50 dollars this time. I do not know whether I will send it by mail or get a check som say that they can get a check at Sity Point but I think it is doutfull and their is a good meny that are agoine to send their money to Washington by the paymaster and let him express it, but I cannot have the faise to trust him with so much money it is most to tempting I have no dout but what he will have som 8 or 9 thousend dollars to take back, as the mail runs prety reglar from hear to their I do not know but what it is as good a way as any to send it by mail and in case it is lost it is that's all. This money is a note so in case you do not want to use it do not let it out for it is allredy let to Unkell Sam, unless the folks at home their gets cramp any, you can do as you think best but dont let it to anybody elces. You had not better let this letter be red by anyone that you do not want to know that you are expecting money, for I suppose that it is prety tite times their now and if anybody wanted to be mean they mite try and get your mail from the office, I shell not send the money yet for their is so much of it on the road that I shell wait for awhile untill the rush is over, and their will not be one half of the danger well I do not think of anything more to write so I will close By Biding you good By.

From your Husborn

G C Taylor

Be a good girl and Keep your dress clean and write often.

∽

NO. 16

In Camp rite on the frunt line a bout ¾ of a mile from the Sity
Sept. 26th 1864

My Dear Wife,

I take my pen in hand once more to let you know that I am still injoying good health. We are now in the frunt line of works[1] our reg. dos not lay more then 60 rods from the rebs line they are so close that the Sharpshooters are at work all the while threw the day, so that our men dar not rase their heads above the works, for if they do they will get shot at and they shoote rather carless, at least I think so for I went up to the reg. and I thought that I wood gust take a look at the rebs and as I stept upon the bank to look over the works the rebs see my old hat and they let drive and 4 or 5 balls com whizing by my ears, so close that I made up my mind it was no plais for me and after that I thought that if the rebs hit me they wood have to shoot close for their is no nead of my exposing myself in the leise, for we stay a mile back of the reg. and got in a hollow so their is no danger of the

Petersburg, Virginia, sutler's tent, Second Division, Ninth Corps, November 1864 (courtesy Library of Congress Prints and Photographs Division)

shells, well I cannot tell you any nuse this time but you must not think that their is anything the matter with me in case you do not hear from me again for som time for the mail dos not run to the frunt now vary stidy and it may not be so I can send a letter out for sevral days but it may be so I can send as often as usual, this letter will be maild at Sity Point for one of our boys are agoine down their tomorrow to send som money home by express. He has got som $2000.00 dollars to take down for the Boys they are most sending home their money. Well I must close for it is most nite and I have got to put up my tent yet tonite I will send the money in the next letter I

think you must write and let me know whether you get your pay from Chipman or not I have writen to him about it and I want to know whether he is
agoine to pay it or not and has Moses pay you or not and what is the reason
that Lydia dos not write tell hur to write and you do the same as often as
you can you nead not send me any stamps of any acount for I can by them
hear now as soon as the men began to get their pay the sutlers[2] began to
com in and they sell stamps they will get little money from me for stamps
and that is about all they will get for they are a purfet set of cutthrots but I
must close for this time So good By.

From your husborn

Guy C. Taylor

NOTES

1. The Thirty-Sixth Wisconsin was located between Fort Haskell and Fort Stedman.
2. A *sutler* was a civilian merchant who sold provisions to an army in the field.

NO. 16 [*NOTE:* TAYLOR USED THIS NUMBER ON THE PREVIOUS LETTER.
BELOW HE EXPLAINS THAT HE HAD REPEATED THIS NUMBER
INTENTIONALLY BECAUSE HE FELT HIS LAST LETTER WAS TOO SHORT.]

In camp Near Petersburg
Sept. the 30th 1864

My Dear Wife,

I take my pen in hand to let you know that I am still injoying good health
we are now in the vary frunt but we expect to moove rite away for som plais
but when I do not know. We got orders to be redy at 4 oc yesterday morning
to march and we got redy and have had our horses saddle redy for a start
evry since. Last nite we was ordered to the breg. headquarters and wait for
orders we went up their and stood and hill the horses for about anower and
we got sick of that fun and we did not wait for orders but got on to the
horses and went back to our old plais again and hear we are yet at 10 oc this
morning and do not know how much longer we have got to wait before we
set out. I think that we are agoine to have a long march when we do go and
to Richmon I think but it is all guess work we may not go more then 2 or 3
miles, but they say that Shurden is pushing on to Richmon and their has a
large amount of Artilary goine from hear that way well I do not care wheir

we do go but I do not like this being forever a starting but I think that we will get started somtime today and may be go all nite, if so it will be vary hard for the men that are in the ranks for it is hard marching in the dark and then the rebs kept up such a shelling that they thought that they was agoine to try our works by a charge and our men was standing rite up to the works so in case they did com they wood get mowed down like so much grass, the rebs charge five times nite before last on the 9 Corps, and was drove back each time and then they got satisfide that they cood not get over our works, oh what a horable slotter of men their has bin but then they have not laid down their life in vane. They have died in a noble cause and their naimes will live for ages to com as the presurvers of our Country. Well sis what dos the folks think about home their on the war qustian do they think it is agoine to end this winter or that we have got to fite another summer. We all think that their will not be much fiteing after this winter. I am agoine to send a letter along with this one that will contain $50.00 in money and as soon as you get it write and let me know for I shell feal a little uneasy about it untill I know that it is in your hands and in case you do not want to use it you had not better let anyone have it for it now draws 6 per cent from the grovament and that is shure evry time well I must close for this time So good By.

From your husborn

Guy C. Taylor

༄

NO. 17

in Camp in Frunt of Petersburg
Oct the 2th 1864

My dear Wife,

I take my pen once more to let you know that I am well and hope that you are injoying the same blesing. We are now in frunt of Petersburg, our reg. is in Foart Rise[1] the rebs are getting vary uneasey they have tried their best to brake our lines but they found that it is hard to stand our shells and gust the picket line they cannot eaven drive them in. They com in the other nite when the rebs charge on the 9 Corps, after they fired away all their catagest and then the rebs, began to yell and rush for our lines they thought that they cood com rite over the works but they did not com vary far when our boys sed com on Johners, and then gave them arousing chear with musket balls and the Johners did not like such chearing as that and they turned and run they tried it 5 times and then they thought that it was time to stop. This fite was in the nite it began at 10 oc, it lasted for about two houres. We was in our camp in a little hollow and gust laid down for the nite when we hurd the charge on our left and we thought that we wood gust go on top of the hill and then we cood hear plainer wheir it was and gust as we got up the hill they began to throw the shells and it was a splendid site to see they went whirling threw the air like balls of fire. We thought that we wood see which threw the most and we counted then and our men threw 6 to the rebs one, and it did not take our guns long to dry up the rebs. baterys they soon found out that we had not all gorn yet,[2] it seams that we have got around in the rear of Petersburg and our firering into the rebs. on evry side and they see that they are in a tite plais and they know that they must brake our lines or they must give up and surrender their strong sity and a larg amount of their armey. The war is agoine to close before next Spring I do believe the rebs are getting intialay dishearted their own papers say that they are in a tite plais, and they cannot see wheir the men that are coming into our ranks are a coming from they see that our armey is groing strong while theirs are getting weeker evryday. The rebs are coming over as fast as they can but it is hard work for a man to cross from one line to the other without getting shot, for if a man tryes to go out over the works he will get shot at by his own men if he dos not com back. Well Sis I have trusted to the mail to send you that money and if you get it, it is all right and in case you do not get it, it is a good lesson to me som of the boys told me I had better send it to Sity Point and express it, but then it is not saft their is a battle going on now on our left we can gust hear the musketry but the artiley is playing in good urness we will not know how it com out not before tomorrow or next day, but I think that we will get good nuse when we get any for our men do not try to charge but they are flanking them and making them do the charging and the party that charges get cut up the worse well I must close for this time write often so will I.

   Good By My Dear Wife
   From your husborn

Guy C. Taylor

NOTES
1. Fort Rice was one in a string of forts included in Union fortifications in front of Petersburg. It was 200 feet square.
2. The Battle of Peebles' Farm was fought September 30, 1864. Losses for the Union were 1,193 killed or missing and 905 wounded; Confederate losses were estimated to be 1,300 (Trudeau, *The Last Citadel*, 217).

∾

NO.17 [*NOTE:* TAYLOR ALSO USED THIS NUMBER ON THE PREVIOUS LETTER.]
RECEIVED NO. 9

Oct. the 4th 1864

My dear wife,

I wrote to you and sent the letter out yesterday and when the boy com back he brot me one from you and I was glad to hear that you are a getting along so well, my health is good yet and I think that I am agoine to be healther then what I have bin hear before, but still I can never cary a gun again, but if I have my health I am allrite. I have got your letters vary reglar for two weekes or so, and I am in hopes that I shell get them more reglar then what I have don, for it seams so long a time when I do not get a letter for two weeks but for the 3 last that I got has com rite along reglar and it seams allmost as so I new gust how things are at home. Well sis we are in the frunt line not onley a short distant from Petersburg. Our men was in a foart for a few days, but now they are at the rite of the foart they are in the line of works, and they have got a vary good plais wheir they now are, but I do not think that we will stay hear vary long for I think that the rebs are leaving Petersburgs, our canons are playing all day on the works of the rebs and they cannot get any reply at all the rebs are eather left or they are trying to draw our men into a trap, but they will not make much at that, if that is their game for our men are not agoine to make a charge on their works unless they know that their is not meny rebs their, but then wheather we charge or not, their will be som way to find out wheir the rebs are. Old Ben Butlar has got around to our left (unless he has got in frunt) and is a driving the rebs (pell mell) for election, day before yesterday the rebs com on to our cavaly on the left in 3 lines of battle and the cavaly got into a line and met the charge the first line charge and was sweep down and then up com the 2 line and they met the sam fait so did the third line we lost a good meny men of coarse but nothing for what the Johners did,[1] our cavaly had som

7 shooters[2] and som 16 shooters[3] and a line of such men are as good as 4 lines of muskets I am in hopes that I can write to you before long that we are in the Sity of Petersburg and that Richmon is bown to fall and Lynken is bown to be our next Presadent and war is bown to close in a vary few months, and I must close this letter and watter my horses and then go to the reg. and mail this letter so I will Bid you good By for this time.

From your Husborn

Guy C. Taylor

NOTES

1. Taylor was describing a cavalry battle fought southwest of Petersburg near the Vaughn Road.
2. The "Seven Shooter" was a manually operated, lever-action Spencer repeating rifle. The weapon was adopted by the Union army, especially the cavalry, during the Civil War.
3. The "Sixteen Shooter" was a sixteen-shot, .44-caliber, breech-loading Henry repeating rifle. The Confederates complained that it was a damn rifle that the Yankees could load on Sunday and shoot all week long.

∾

NO. 18

In camp in frunt of Petersburg
Oct. 6th 1864

My dear wife,

I once more pick up my pen to scrible a few lines to you to let you know that I am still injoying good health, and hope you are a doing the same we are in frunt of Petersburg yet, but we have got a vary nice plais to stay in, their is bomsproofes built so the men can go into and be saft from the rebels fire, wheir we are we have not got a bomproof but we have got a vary good plais it is built up with hevy logs and then dug down and the durt throwed over the lodges so their cannot any balls com through but it is not covard overhead onley by brush so if a bom shood hapen to burst over or rite in frunt of ous we mite be in a little danger but not much then for as soon as they begin to shell we go down in the plais wheir the lodges will protect ous the plais that is built up is long anough for 6 horses and it is dug down about 2½ feet and the lodge are layed up som six feat makeing the depth about 8½ feet they are a shelling most evry nite but they have not

Petersburg, Virginia, bomb-proof shelter in Federal lines, 1865 (courtesy Library of Congress Prints and Photographs Division)

throwed any shells in our direction they are eather to the right or left of ous, I expect that their will be prety warm times hear before long I think that our men will try the works of the rebs and see if they cannot take the line of works in case they can they are rite into Petersburg the next thing for they can then see all over the sity and they cannot moove any troops unless we will know it and can tell vary near wheir their main streanth layes. Well Sis I suppose that you do not cair so much about the works of the armey, but in case I did not write about that I cood not write anything for that is all we know hear. I know you wood like to know what I am a doing now days. I can tell you that I work yesterday all day long, I cook for our company their is six of ous we lost our cook he had to go back to his company and then the boys lit on me to cook they by evrything that anybody wants to eat and they say that I shell not bye anything it is not much work and then we live like (big folks) and it pays me vary well I think, for you know that I like good vuitals, well I sayed that I work yesterday and I did I went up to the company earley in the morning and the boys wanted me to do som washing for them and I took som cloths back with me and washed them and at nite I took them back and got my $1.80 for my days work and dun som for our own little company besides, so you can guess how much I washed and gust as I got back in com one of our boys and says I want you to do your best on getting supper tonite so they brot me som potatoes and flower & a can of tomatoes & a can of Peaches, and a pown of butter we had Tea & poark & they brot a pease of cheas & a pown of sugar crackers, and we had som fish & good deal of evry such things so you can guess what kind of a supper we had and that is the way we live most all the while all I have to say I can cook it if they can aford to by it. But I expect it will play out when the Docter gets hear for the boys will go by themself but if I stay along with them they may keep the thing up for awhile but they cannot a vary long time for it costs to much but one of our crew makes his money easy and he says that he is going to live while he is in the armey anyway. Well Sis I have sent you 50 dollars but I do not know wheather you will get it or not, but I am in hopes you will for 50 dollars is to much for ous to loose, their was one poor boy in our reg., got all blowed to peases and he had 150 dollars in his pocket and it was blowed out and they cood not find anything of it and his folks are poor and they nead it he was a waiting to get a chance to express it home. I thought that I wood trust to the mail and then in case anything shood hapen to me the money mite go to you saft but I am in hopes that the money is saft and allso that I may yet go back to old Wisconsin allrite again. Well I must close for this time so good By

   From your Husband

Guy C. Taylor

CHAPTER 5

Detailed to the Doctor

October 10 to November 27, 1864

In his letter to Sarah written October 10, 1864, Taylor stated, "I now know what my work is[,] I am agoine to take care of the docters horses." The doctor of whom Taylor was speaking was Elijah A. Woodward of Sun Prairie, Wisconsin. On April 1, 1864, Dr. Woodward was commissioned assistant surgeon of the Thirty-Sixth. On January 6, 1865, after the death of surgeon Clarkson Miller, Woodward was promoted to fill the position of surgeon of the Thirty-Sixth. Eventually Dr. Woodward used his influence to secure the position of hospital nurse for Taylor. From that point on, Taylor's primary military duties involved service to the doctor and to wounded soldiers.

In addition to doing his assigned tasks, Taylor supplemented his soldier's pay with money made by cooking and washing clothes for fellow soldiers of his company.

Of special interest in this section of Taylor's correspondence were references to the presidential election of 1864; the adjustment of soldiers to duty; and the danger, death, and plight of Rebel soldiers as the tide of war continued to turn against them. Taylor's letter written November 6 was one of his most descriptive and philosophical letters of the war.

The most significant event for Taylor and the Thirty-Sixth during this time period was the October 27 Battle of Hatcher's Run, in which the Thirty-Sixth Wisconsin Volunteers captured two enemy colors and nearly 400 prisoners. The Thirty-Sixth was recognized for its role in the battle, and Dr. Woodward received honorable mention for services rendered.

In camp near Petersburg Va.
Oct. the 10th 1864

My Dear Wife,

I received your kind letter yesterday and was glad to hear that you was a getting along so well. My health is vary good yet and I am as contented as anybody can be in the same plais. I have bin a cooking for our gang but I shell do it no more for I find it is most to much work for me their was 5 in our company and then their was 3 Sutlars that wanted to com into our mes and they staid with ous a few days and then they got a cook for themself you see it made a good deal of work for me for they wood bring in all kinds of can fruit and it is a good deal of work to cook it to have it good over such stoves as we have in the armey, so I told the boys that I cood not do the cooking alone and they must try and help me so they took hold of the cooking and they made kareloues work of it now I can tell you and then they will call on me to com and cook the can fruit they will not tuch it. Well we are a having a vary nice time of it we take evrything easy and have a easey time in genral. Well Sis the docter has got hear but he has not sed anything about having any letters for me but he may have som he got hear nite before last and has bin on the go evry since and I have not had any chance to talk with him but it dos not make much diffrance wheather he has got any letters or not for I have got one from you that was writen about the time he left home. You said that Chipman had not sed a word about paying you for the plowing in case he dos not pay you after you ask him for it you gust get sombody to go and masure the land, and put it into the hands of Lawyer Reaves[1] or somones elce to corlect for I have written to him about it and told him to be shure and pay you for you wood want it rite away and in case he wants to be mean I want you to see if you cannot be as mean and a little meanor so he will know that you are a mach for him evry time. Gust pay him in his own corn and give good intrest in the Bargon, and let me know as soon as you can after you ask him for your pay what he says and I will let him know what I think of him, in case he dos not pay you, he will think that the imps from the depth of misary is let loose and they are all at him. Well I suppose that George is agoine up north to make his Fortune well I am in hopes that he will do well up their for it is tough work to cary on a farm and get onley one half and then not have it yeald anything at all in case he can get into a mill up their and try and get so he can run the thing rite along he will get big wages after a little.[2] I wish that I was out of this armey I cood make my 3 dollars a day gust like a book and not work hard neather if I had my discharge now I wood not go home to stay long, for in a few months I cood make more hear then I cood make in Wis. in 2 years. Their is a little drummer in our regiment that is making his fore dollars a day and he dos not work more then one third of the time, the sutlers pay from 40 to 80 dollars a month for men and they cannot get them at that their is a good chance for making money hear but you better believe that a man must have a mind of his own and take all kind of talk and gust mind his own buiss, and then he is allrite but if he goes in with the boys and Drink he will soon go to disstruction in a short time. I have gust bin a talking along with the docter and he says that he told you that he wood start on a tuesday and he got the chance to com with the 5 reg. so it wood not cost him anything by starting on a sunday. He said that he saw George and told him that he wood start on a sunday and George told him that he wood let you know that he wood com so you cood send by him anything that you wanted to but I suppose that George did not go and see you, but it is gust as well for I have got yours & Charleys Pictuars and it is in a case that I can cary and keape them & a common case you cannot carey no time hear before it is spoilt and then you have got no pictures attall as long as I can get letters from you and know that you are well that is the most I care about. Well Sis I now know what my work is I am agoine to take care of the docters horses[3] so I am allrite and I think that I can make what money I want to spend doing work for the other boyes. This last weak I earned anough to bye me a good hat I got it for 3 dollars and this morning I bot a overcoat for 3 dollars it will do me as well as a new one and they cost 8.40. I mean to try to save anough so when I do go home that I shell have my hole pay left or spent for somthing that has bin neaded it will not do me any hurt to earn all that I nead hear, and then I can send the money to you so you can have what you nead it is a shame to see som of the men hear (that has got famalyes at home) spending evry cent of their pay and their wifes are in nead of it at home. Well I must close so good by

Guy C. Taylor

NOTES
1. Mr. Reaves was one of the first lawyers in Sun Prairie, Wisconsin.
2. George Taylor, his wife, and children were about to move north to the town of Clinton, Vernon County, Wisconsin. It was also apparent that George had been a share-cropper in the town of Bristol.
3. Taylor was officially detailed to Dr. Woodward.

∾

In Camp near Petersburg Va.
Oct, 14th 1864

My dear wife

I wonce more pick up my pen to let you know that I am well, and hope you are the same. We are in the frunt lines yet but we do not know how long we may stay hear. We have hurd that we was agoine to be relieved by the 6 & 19 Corps but I think it is doutful but do not know we are in a vary good plais wheir we are their is som danger hear of coarse but they have got it fixed so nothing but a shell can do them any hurt unless it is a stray ball from the picket line. Their was a shell struct the works that the 7 Mishagan was in and went threw the topt and bursted rite in wheir they was a lay-ing and it kill one & wounded 3 others but not vary bad when the rebs began to shell the Boys will get upon the works and hollor and swing their hats but when they can see the smoak from the rebs canons they jump down and as soon as they hear the shell burst up they get again and yell with all their mite and shuch a nois as they make wood scair anybody to death in Wisconsin but we get so that it is lonesom hear when it is still but that is not vary often. I do not know anything new to write to you except that their is a great change hear in political matters the men are a getting their eyes open and can see wheir they are and they began to think that Linkon has don somthing after all, and they are redy to try him again is the talk of a great meny that 2 months ago was for McClenon body & sole, their is som of coarse that is as strong for him now as they evry was but they think that Linkon will be elected without any dout. Well Sis I have sent you Fifty Dollars in a letter and it is time that you had got it and I had got a answer from it but it has bin som 4 or 5 days since I have got a letter from you so I shell not fret any about the money untill I get a letter anyway and not much then in case it is lost for their is no youse in crying for Spilt milk. The weather is vary pleasant hear we had a little frost a day or to ago and it is quite chilly today and I think their will be a frost tonite but let it com we

have got a good warm plais to sleap and anough to eat and that is all a Soldier cairs for. Well I must close By Biding you good By

  From Your Husborn

Guy C. Taylor

NO. 19 [*NOTE:* TAYLOR USED THIS NUMBER ON A PREVIOUS LETTER.
BELOW TAYLOR MENTIONS HE RECEIVED LETTER NO. 13.]

in camp in frunt of Petersburg
Oct 15th 1864

My dear wife,

I received your kind letter today that was No. 13 and was vary glad to
hear that you are getting so smart again, and I am in hopes that you may
continue so, as for my health, it is vary good for me. I have not bin well
since I com down hear, as I was in Wisconsin allthough I feal first rate,
but I have not got the streanth to stand the work, that I did have but I think
it is coised by laying still so much, for it is a genral complaint among the
Soldiers. I do not have hardly anything to do now, for since the Docter has
got back our little company has bin devided and we have now onley 4 in
our mess and then I do not have now onley one horse to take cair of now.
We have had vary bad luck since the docter got back. We have got both of
our horses stolden, it is a bad go for Woodard, but he dos not seam to care
much, for them, onley he wood want them in case we had to moove, but he
has got one he can ride so it will not be vary bad for him after all. I expected
he wood blaim me for I turn the horses out to fead in the morning, and they
was taken while we was a eating our breakfast. As soon as we got threw
eating I went to get them up, and I cood not find them so I got onto one
horse, and one of the boys, got onto another, and we road for about 1 hour,
and then we com in, and then we started out 3 horses to look, and they did
not com in, not till most nite, and they cood not get any track of them. The
docter said it was no youse to hunt anymore, so we giv them up as lost. The
next day he got this other horse, and brot it to me, and told me to take care
of it, and then he went up to the reg, and he com back and told me he did
not blaim me in the least for I was doing the best I cood with them, but he
wanted me to take care of this other horse, and stay wheir I am now. He

said that he had made it allrite at the headquarters, about my staying wheir I am. You see while the docter was gorn home they tryed to make out that I was taken from the ranks and detailed as horsler,[1] and they was agoine to charge the Docter $52.00 a month for me, and I new that he wood not stand that, so I told him how they was trying to work it, and he gust told them that he shood not pay no 52 dollars for me, for he cood hire for less and get a man that cood work rite along but he told them that he shood not let me do any duty anyway, for I am not fit to go to work, and he wood detail me as hospitol nurse, (so I am detail as such,) but you see we has not got any hospitol yet in the reg, so I take care of the horse, and I guess I shell for somtime, but I am not afraid of goine back to my company anyway. Well Sis as the boys are all goine to bed and it is most to early for me to turn in gust now, so I will write a good long letter but their will not be any nuse in worth hearing if you cood gust look into my tent you wood see my tent mate a laying under to woolen blankets and my overcoat, and you cood see me a laying down on the blankets with a candle by me stuck into a pease of soap for a candle stick, and I have got my paper in frunt of me and am a trying to write a few lines to you but I cannot write as you mite say I can onley make marks, but you may pick it out by having good curage and long patiants. You said that I must not get tiard of reading your letters, no I shood not if I got them 5 times as often and 5 times as long. That Picture of yours looks so you was well a heap, but I suppose that was taken gust after you got so you was able to go to Madison. It is a vary good likeness but you look so poor, but I am in hopes that you are better now then you was then. You say that you are agoine to send Charleys I want to see his picture but I had rather see him but then that cannot be for a while yet, but time goes on and the war must close somtime and then when we get home again we shell think that we have bin well paid for our work, but I expect that their is a class of men that wants to throw away all that has bin don and they think they can do it by electing McClenon, but they will get fooled on him for he will not take the chair for old Abe has gust com rite out and told the people what they mite depen upon and that is gust what men wants to know but little Mac has sneak around the pease party and it is nothing but sneaks that will voat for him if I cood have my way about it I wood have evry pease man put into the ranks no matter how old he was no matter if he was 3 score & 10[2] and one foot in the grave as you mite say he shood fite as long as he had any life left and then be barred and trator written on his toomstone you may think I am agoine all beyond reason but when I get a thinking about it, it

makes me mad, to see men cry pease after so meny of our boys has bin
slain and suffard all the hardship of war it is anough to make one mad if he
has got any spunk in him at all, but never mind old Abe will close this war
and then we will get back home again, and in case they do want to know
what the soldiers think of them, all pease men had better do as J. Ashley
did run to Canady but I do not believe that their is meny their that wants
the stinking sneak. As my candle is most out and my eys are getting so they
do not want to stand the lite vary well I will close for tonite and write som
more tomorrow as it will be sunday and it will keep me out of mischief.

Oct 16th 1864

I have gust bin up to the reg. and I got a letter from you and mother and
was glad to hear that you are well. I also got one from Martha and they are
all well. She said that Chipman wood pay you in a vary short time. I wrote
to him in 3 letters but he did not get onley the last one so he is not to blaim
for not letting me know wheather he had paid you or not. You must write
and let me know in your next wheather he had paid you or not for in case
he has not I will write to him again and see what is the matter. You say in
this letter that I got today that you have received my No. 16 letter it was in
No. 16 that I sent the money in but I wrote two No.16[3] for I did not write
much in the money letter. Well I must close this letter and I will answer the
one I got today tomorrow or nex day so I will close by biding you good By
    From your husborn

Guy C. Taylor

NOTES
    1. A *hostler* was a person detailed to care for horses.
    2. *Score* means "twenty," so "3 score and 10" equals 70.
    3. Originally we thought that Taylor had mistakenly repeated the number 16, but he
had done so purposely.

NO. 19 [*NOTE:* TAYLOR USED THIS NUMBER ON TWO PREVIOUS LETTERS.]

In camp in frunt of Petersburg Va
Oct. 18th 1864

My dear wife,

I take my pen in hand to let you know that I am well, and I am in hopes
that theas few lines will find you injoying the same blessing. We are laying

near Foart Rise yet, but I do not know how long we may stay hear but som
think all winter. I am in hopes we will for it is a vary good plais the watter
is vary good and then their is timber to make vary warm tents. You wrote
to me that I nead not send you so much money, but it is no youse but for
you to say anything about it, for I shell not let you know when I get money
time anough to tell me what to do with it before it is gorn and then I do not
want it and if I keep it I may spend it for Whiskey and get drunk and then
how wood you like *dat dar*. Well Sis I can tell you the reason that I sent 50
dollars. Their is no youse in my spending money hear of any amount as
soon as I sent the money I went and brot me a mess of Stamps & paper &
invelops and I had gust 4 dollars left and since that I have paid 3 dollars for
a hat and have payed a little for stuff at the sutlers and have got 7 dollars
now, so you can see that I am in a plais wheir I can work and earn what
money I shell want to spend and it may as well lay in your hands as mine
and better to for knowone on this earth knows what may hapen, to me yet,
all we can do is to live in hopes that all will be rite and so it will for in case
I am not premited to return home again I shell not be doing more then
what it is my duty to do. I did not com down hear without knowing that I
shood be in danger, and my life is not any better then anybody elces, for life
is dear to anyone, and it is for evryone to take cair of himself, but it is a duty
that falls upon him to go and fite to maintain the country that his fore-
farthers fot and bled for, so we mite injoy the blessing of a free govament,
and we are redy to fite the traitors that has arm themselves against ous, and
their is a great responsibility resting upon the people at home, and that is
to see that the sneaking traitors at home is whip at this coming election and
in case they are whip at this falls election you may be ashure that you will
see ous coming home before another fall meating with the rebs whiped at
the South. You spoke about the money that Chipman owed you in one of
your letters awhile ago and I wrote to him about it and I have gust got a letter from them stating that they wood pay you in a few days and in case he
dos not do it I want you to let me know it and I will write to him again and
see what he mean to do about it for he is able to pay it at anytime and he
must com to time. I wrote to you day before yesterday and sed that I got
your picture but I will say again that I have got yours and mothers and I do
not cair if you will send me all the rest of the folkes but send Charleys anyway and tell Fan to write and send me hurn and all the rest. As it is getting
late and I have got to hury to get this into the mail I will not write to mother

in this letter but try to write to hur tomorrow or nex day. I must close by biding you good By

From your husborn

Guy C. Taylor

Be vary carful in your Derrections and they will be more shure to com.

∼

NO. 20 RECEIVED NO. 15

In camp in frunt of Petersburg Va
Oct. the 21th 1864

My Dear Wife,

I have gust bin up to the reg. and I found that this morning mail brot me good nuse from you and I have gust got threw reading it, and I thought that I wood scrible a few lines to you and let you know that I am well and getting as fat as a hog, and gust about as lazy. Well we are yet having fine weather it is vary warm in the day time but chilley at nite, the roads are vary good and genral Grant is improving the opaturnity and plaising his artilary in plaises wheir they can moove in case of bad roads. It is time now for the rainey season hear so they all say but it is as dry yet as it is in mid summer, and I am in hopes that we will not have much rain this fall for in case that we do the armey cannot stur and I want to see it on the moove now if it is ever agoine to, for the rebs seams to be vary much discuradge, and evry few days they must get nuse that dos not suat them vary well, for they get whiped prety hard, and then they can see that we are getting our ranks fill up full and runing over full they can see our trains of cars runing back and forrad and caring men each way and they do not no what that means Grants railroad fools them orfulley they have tried to shell the cars the best they new how but they soon got sick of that, for our men let som big shells fall rite over in their works and they did not like that kind of ball play they like to play ball when they can do all the throwing but when the other side began to throw they do not want to play vary long for som reason or other, but then it dos not make any odds with our boys they like the throwing part as well as the rebs, and they do as much of it, and I guess a little more. As a genral thing we throw 5 to 6 to their one. I wrote to mother yesterday but

I did not get so to mail it untill this morning, and I wrote in that that the shells was a bursting in the air and so they was and our guns was a fireing at an orfull rate and we did not know what it meant, but this morning reveild the caus it commence by our fireing a salute for the victuary gain by Sheurdein in the valley[1] he took 40 peases of our artilary, and the rebs replyed to our guns at a fearous rate and our boys answard them as sausey, and the rebs dry up in a little while, and it was vary still last nite the pickets was fireing as yousal, but this old Grants express is at work (that is a name the boys gave to one of our big guns) at the rebs and it makes evrything *get* in good earnest. I wish that you cood gust be sat down hear wheir I am for about a houre when the pickets are a fireing *rite smart* and they are at work with the big guns to. You wood think that the nois was anough to tair evry-thing to peasis. Well Sis their has bin a new order com out that all men that are in the rear a taking care of horses shood go to their companeys and repoart for duty but I am detail for hospitol nurse, for I was detail by orders of the bregade Docter but it was threw the influance of Woodard so I am allrite on (the goose qustion) well I must close by biding you good By

From your husborn

Guy C. Taylor

I am vary glad that you have got that money for I was a little afraid of it being lost.

NOTE

1. This reference was to Gen Sheridan's victory at Cedar Creek on October 19, 1864.

NO. 21 RECEIVED NO. 15 [*NOTE:* SARAH REPEATED THE NUMBER.]

In camp near Petersburg Va
Oct. the 23rd 1864

My dear wife.

As it is sunday and I have not nothing to do I thought that I wood write a few lines to you. I went to meating this forenoon and lysen to a good sur-mon delivard by our Chaplain.[1] He got hear 3 days ago, and after meating I took a ramble, and went to our rite for about one half mile and then rite faised and went about one mile and then com to our division headquarters and then I left obleek[2] and went across a field and I found that their was coten their but it was so choked with weeds that it cood not grow to mount to anything but I thought that you wood like to know how cotten look a growing so I pick a few buds of it and then rite about faised and went home, and now I am a sitting in my tent a writeing to you, and as I am a writeing to you, the gun boats are a speaking to the Johney rebs, way on our rite som 8 or 9 miles but they speak in thunder tone for we can hear them vary plaine I will send you one cotten blosem one bud and one in the matuared state the blosem is not a vary good one but it was the best that I cood find it is so late in the year,[3] but you can form som idear by theas how they look and how the darkey must look in the feald picking cotten. You said in your last letter that you shood not youse that note of Moses nor that of Fathers nor this fifty of Unkell Sames, and I am afraid that you are agoine to try to be to saiving for your own good, but you know best and I know that it will be no youse for me to say anything for you can do as you have a mind to, but I will say be carfull of your health. I wrote in my last letter that I was detailed to the hospitol but wheather you get it or not I cannot say, and I may not go to the hospitol this winter but I had gust as leaves for it will be a warm plais to stay, but then it dos not make much diffrance to me wheir I am, I am at home at any plais I am a having a vary nice time of it now and have had most all the while, when I was sick it was not quite so pleasant as it mite be but then it is allrite now, it is all in a persons life time. Our reg got orders to fix for winter and they went to work yesterday and they have got them a vary nice plais. It is rite in under the ground wheir the balls of the rebs cannot get, and then it is vary warm and they have got fire plaises fixed in them so they can cook in their. Well I must close for this time by biding you Good By

From your husborn

Guy C. Taylor

NOTES

1. Peter Van Nest, Geneva, Wisconsin, Thirty-Sixth Wisconsin Regiment, who mustered in July 22, 1864, resigned and was honorably discharged January 6, 1865. He was honorably mentioned in the official report of the Battle of Hatcher's Run, October 27, 1864 (Aubery, *Thirty-Sixth Wisconsin Volunteer Infantry*, 393).

2. *Oblique* is to advance at an angle—in this case, to the left.

3. The cotton samples that Guy Taylor sent to Sarah were still with this letter.

Oct. the 25th 1864

My Dear Wife,

I received a letter from you yesterday, and was glad to hear that you are in such good health. My health is good and I am vary fleashey for me, and I feal so that I cood do reglar duty, but I know that it wont do for me to go to puting on the Straps again so I think that I can get along vary well wheir I am, in case they call me to the hospitol, I shell have a vary good plais their, and I wish that they wood call me their before it gets to be vary cold, for then I wood have a warm plais this winter to stay in. I wrote to you day before yesterday, and then we was at Foart Rise we are now at Foart Bross[1] it is on the rear line we was releived last nite at 11 oc and we march to the rear and stopt at the same plais that we was at before we went to the frunt line we are on the rear line on the norfork & Petersburg railroad. Our camp is not in the same plais. Our reg. is in the rear of the Foart, so to be close to the reg. we have gone into a pease of pine woods on the north side of the field. We was on the south side before. We have gust got settled down so to know wheir we are agoine to stop but we have not put up our tent yet and I do not think that we will tonite for som of the officers seams to think that we will have to make another moove by tomorrow but we may not. They do not know but a vary little more about it then we do and we do not know any more about wheir we are agoine then you do their in Wis, and we have got so we cair gust as little as we know. When we get to a plais and stopt then we know wheir we have bin travaling for and not untill then. You said that you did not want to youse the money that I sent home and had rather that I had kept som of it for my own youse. When I sent it away I did not think that I shood want any of it to youse and I do not know as I shell now but in case that we get evrything stold from ous two or three times more I may want som. The other day we had our camp kittle and our sider poark butter coffee sugar flower and bread all stold from ous and then they was not sat-ifide in robing ous of all we had to eat so they took our plaits nives & forkes spoons & salt from ous to. Sombody got a good hall, but if they had bin cetch at it they wood got a good brall. When we got up in the morning I went to get somthing for ous to eat and I found that we had not got nothing to cook and nothing to cook it in so we was as well suppleyed as we was at nite, but it did not satisfy our appatite quite so well, but we had som money and we bort our vuitals at the sutlars for 2 days and we have bort things again to cook with but we are all prety near strapt for money but then I guess that we can stand it in case they do not make another steal on ous, and in case they do we may take the same play and I think that I can steal as well as som others in case that I take a start to. Well I must close and go and see if I can send this out tonite so good By for this time

From your husborn

Guy C. Taylor

NOTE

1. Fort Bross was located on the secondary rear line in front of Petersburg.

NO. 23

Oct. the 29th 1864

My Dear Wife,

I wonce more take my pen in hand to let you know that I am yet injoying vary good health and I am in hopes that you are injoying the same. Well Sis since I wrote to you last we have seen prety warm times. We have march good meny miles and have seen som orfull fiteing we started from camp on the 27th at 2 oc PM and march rite south we cross the Welden railroad at about ten oc at nite and layed down and slep untill 3 oc that morning and then started again and at about 8 oc we com upon the enemy and we drove them for 3 miles and then we stop to rest our men a little and started on and went about one mile and com upon the enemy again and they give ous battle they drove in our rite a little and the rebs began to chear and they dove onto one of our reg and took them prisiners and they thought that they had made a fine hall but the first that they new they got a voley and then a shout from the 36 that made them turn their tune and we took alot of them and all of our own men back again and then the rebs com on again with a hevy line of battle but they was repulsed with a vary hevy lost but they had one batary that played on ous like fun and our men cood not get their guns to bair upon it and the rebs did send in the shells at a big rate. After the rebs was drove back on our rite they made a flank moove and the first we new they was on our left and they made a charge against our cavaly but they hill their row with them but neather side gain anything and it was not a grait while before the rebs had got in our rear and their we was intialy surrounded and we did not know which way to make a blow, but they sent the cavaly one way and they made the rebs get rite along and the infantry made a strite in another plais and they don a good pease of work we soon got it all cleared out in our rear the fite lasted untill nite and then we withdrew our foarses. We had to leave a good meny wounded men on the field and the artilary was plaised on a small hill rite in the centry of the field so in case that the rebs did make a dive at ous they wood get their fill we laid in the field untill our scouts com in and sed that they cood not find any more of our men. Their did not a great meny stragle away for they did not know wheir to go to. We got started to march at 100c in the forenoon and we got back to our old camp on the Norfork road that nite gust at dark and this morning finds me a sitting on som hay a writeing a few lines to you to let you know that I am allrite yet our lost in the fite is estermated at ten hundred in kill wounded & mising and we had about 14 hundred prisiners and we do not know how meny was kill & wounded but som of our men sayes that the rebs took them across the corn field wheir the charge was and that the ground was covard with the ded it is estermated that their kill & wounded is as much as our holl lost if not more. Their lost must com vary near 30 hundred,[1] as I am a writeing the men are all holaring there is about 60 of our men gust got in that we expected was taken prisiners they was out on picket and was left their so the armey mite com out and not get into a trap the rebs got all around the boys but they dove rite into the thick woods and brok the rebs cavaly line and they com out allrite and they brot som rebs along with them to. Well I must close by Biding you good By

From your husborn

Guy C. Taylor

Write often and I will as often as I can.

NOTE

1. Taylor's letter described the Battle of Hatcher's Run (aka Burgess Mill), which was fought October 27, 1864. Union losses were 166 killed, 1,028 wounded, and 564 missing. Confederate losses were unknown. Lee's thin ranks had held once more. The Thirty-Sixth Wisconsin distinguished itself during the action. The regiment captured more prisoners than it had men. George Fiske from Sparta, Wisconsin, was commanding the Thirty-Sixth Wisconsin Regiment at the time of the battle (Aubery, *Thirty-Sixth Wisconsin Volunteer Infantry*, 274).

Oct. the 30th 1864

My dear wife,

As we are laying still I thought that I wood write a few lines to you to let you know that I am well and am in hopes that theas few lines will find all of you at home injoying the same blessing. We are now laying in the rear of Foart Rise again we com hear last night but we do not know wheir we may be by tomorrow. We are a glad set of boys now I can tell you sean that we com out of the fite so well we did not know for one while as any one cood get out. We run around like so meny crasy men. We wood start to go one way and the rebs shells wood turn us to go another way and that is the way we went for as much as a hour and then we started rite threw a pease of woods and their did not a great meny shells com in their and we kept a working our way along and we hapen to be vary fortunate and struct the same road that we went up on and their was a lot of horses goine down the road as fast as they cood go and it was so dark that you cood not see a horse 4 rods ahead of you but we three that was togeather kept up a loud talk so we wood not get separated and went as so we was runing for our lives and when we got about 2 miles down the road we stopt and fed our horses and got somthing for ourselves but we did not have any to much time to eat for gust as we got the things pack up again the troop com along and sed that they was the rear gard and that their was nothing behind them so we started again in the rain and thick woods with a narow road threw and you can guess how dark it was. We got out of the woods and layed down in a field at about 2 oc in the morning and we found the Docter a little after sunrise and we then started for the reg. and was vary luckey we did not go more then a hour before we found them, and we got back to our old camp on the rear line gust at dark and last nite we com over wheir we now are, and we are in hopes that we will lay still for a few days for the boys have got soar feat. Their is to men agoine to be shot for desurten[1] they was rebs that com over and took the oath and then inlisted and got 1000 dollars bounty and then bot up a mess of blankets and in our raid the other day they tried to get into the rebs line but they got stopt and they will cross the line of death today at 4 oc pm I shell go and see them shot in case that I can leave the horses. It seams rather hard but they must be made a example of or their wood be alot more trying the same game. If they did not want to die let them do as a man shood. We are down hear gust for the purpas of shooteing gust such rebs, as they are. Well Sis I must close for this time by Biding you good By

   From your husborn

Guy C. Taylor

NOTE

   1. Approximately 500 men representing the North and South were shot or hanged during the Civil War with two-thirds of that number being executed for desertion.

NO. 23 [*NOTE:* TAYLOR USED THIS NUMBER ON TWO PREVIOUS LETTERS.]
RECEIVED NO. 18 & 19

In camp in frunt of Petersburg Va
Nov. 3rd 1864

My Dear Wife,

   I received a letter from you this morning and was vary glad to hear that you are all so well. My health is vary good. We are now laying in the frunt line as a suppoart. They suppoart batary 13[1] it is in Foart Haskell[2] it is about one mile to the rite of foart rise. It is a vary good plais for the boys and we never did have so good a plais before. We are rite in the rear of the reg about 60 rods and we have a bomproofe for ourself and one for the horses, and then we have got another that is about 9 feat squir we have got that fix up so we can have a plais to cook and write in. I went to work today and made a fireplais in the frunt of the tent and as I have bin to work the boys said that they wood get supper, so as I am sitting a writeing to you Marten is a cooking beans and talking with Whitney.[3] *Note,* he bothers me by asking if the beans are don and as they are vary near don I will stop writeing and eat my grub. That is the most that we do down hear. We have fort sevrals battles but their is one battle that we do fite most evryday and we do not make out much neather that is a fite with the gray backs, or body lise we cannot keep them off from ous. Well as I have got threw eating beans and hardtack and coffee I will try and write a little more but my eys are not hardly strong anough to write vary long by candlelite I received a letter from George today allso he is well he says that he talks of bying 80 acars of land up their.[4] I do

Fortifications near Petersburg, Virginia, 1865 (courtesy Library of Congress Prints and Photographs Division)

not know but he will make it pay but I dout it somwhat but he can act at his own pleasure about it. He says it is a grand plais to rais stock but in case he dos not do any better up their then he has don in Bristoll at stock raising he will not make a vary big fortune, but I do not know as it is all his falt for not doing any better, it wants sombody in the house that can save, and not onley save but to incurage in rume of discuraging one. Well anough of this. You say that Chipman has not paid you any yet onley that what you made a turn of. I wrote to him about it and I got a letter from them and they said that they wood pay you in a little while their little while is what I call a long while but I will wait a little while and see if he dos not pay you and if he dos not I will let him know that it must com or he will have to pay it to a lawyer for I will gust put it into lawyer Reaves hands and see if he can get it. How do you get along about your State money have you got that rite along & has Moses paid you yet or not, and how has he made out this sommer. You ask me if I tended meetings. I can say that I do we have had the whole of two surmons preach in our reg and I went and hurd them both. They was delivard by our Chaplain he is a vary smart speaker, but if he wood turn his surmons into temprance lectuars I think that it wood do more good. The 36 has got som good men for officers, but they are not agoine to be good vary long if they do not stop drinking so much now for a few weaks they have bin drunk one half of the time, but I must say that I never did see any better behaved men then what the officers was at our last fite. They was all sober men from the private up to the genral, but since that time som of them has not bin what you mite call sober since but their is one thing our regimental officers are men that do not abuse their men when they are drunk. You say that the Lodge has change their form a good deal. I do not cair how much they change their form if they will onley hold to the rite principal but if they try to turn the Lodge into anything but a temprance Lodge I hope that their is men anough in the sosiety to expose it and prosi-cute it untill the thing will be no more. Their is a great chance for all men and wimon to work for their will soon be alot of vile men to go home before long and as they find sosiety at home so will they before they have bin in camp and from home so long that they are agoine to take the vary stand that they find when they get home, so if the people at home wants to see good Sitison of Soldiers they must try to get themself such before they get home, for the soldiers are willing to do as a mayjoyity dos. Nov. the 4 as it was late last nite I thought that I wood wait untill today to finish my letter and Behold this morning brot to me another letter from you and one from Amanda. I have got the letter that had Charles picture in, it is a vary nice one to. I wish that I cood see him but I cannot at presant but the time will com (I am in hopes) that I can see all of you again and wonce more live in pease times but not untill the rebs are whip in good earnist and the clink of chanes & slavery is hurd no more in America. You say that their has bin a mass meeting in Madison and it was a grand afair. I am glad that the men are not all ded, their is a good meny men in the armey that cry pease, pease when their is no pease at least I hope that their is no pease untill we can have pease that is worth calling such, and when we do have such pease then we can com home and think that we have don our duty and have fot the good fite and univarsal Liberty is our reward. Well Sis I will write to Chipman again about that money and see what he dos inten to do about it and I think that I can fetch him to turm at any rate I can try but I must close so I will Bid you good By

From your husborn

Guy C. Taylor

NOTES

1. Union batteries were numbered consecutively, beginning with Battery 1 on the Appomattox River, which was east of Petersburg, and then running south and west around the city.

2. Fort Haskell was one of the forts built on the front line of Union fortifications at Petersburg. It became particularly important after Fort Stedman was successfully assaulted by Confederate forces on March 25, 1865. The Rebels were unable to capitalize on their early success, partially because Fort Haskell was successfully defended.

3. Pvt Selden H. Whitney, age 24, farmer, Union, Rock County, Wisconsin, Co. F, Thirty-Sixth Wisconsin Infantry (*Roster, 36th Wisconsin Infantry Regiment of Volunteers and Draftees,* 144).

4. Taylor was referring to eighty acres of land that his brother George eventually purchased in the town of Clinton, Vernon County, Wisconsin.

∾

NO. 24

In camp in frunt of Petersburg Va
November the 6th 1864

My Dear Wife,

I wonce more sit down in my little house (that is built of logs & durt) to let you know that I am still in the land of living. I wrote to you a few days ago and after I had got it most don, I got another one so I suppose that I must write a answer to each one, or the first that I shell know, you will say that I do not answer all of your letters, and in such case I am afraid that you wood flair up and say that you wood not write anymor (not much I guess). Well Sis the last letter I received was No. 19 in No. 18 I found a fine look-ing boy, and I can ashure you that I was glad to get it, for I know that it is a purfect picture of him. We are still a laying in the frunt line of works but it is a vary good plais for the men, for the works are so high that the balls cannot hit them. The boys all feal first rate and they all say that they think

that the war will soon close, and I am in hopes that it will but I do not want
to see it closed, with any compramice, with the trators. I had rather stay and
fite them for 3 or 4 years more and have a purment pease when their is
pease and it is my opinion that we will have pease that we may well call
pease, for in case that Lyncon is re-elected (of which their is no dout) the
South will see at wonce that they must fite for fore years more or surmit to
the turms that may be ofeard to them, and to fite for that leanth of time they
cannot, for they are now in a destitute situation and our armey is now runing over the best part of the south, that is Georga. Shurmen[1] is a striping
evrything slick and clean, and Georga, had bin the vary mainstay of rebeldom, and since Shurmen has taken Atlanty evrything in Petersburg has
risen to an orfull rate. Their was some Joners com in the other day and they
say that they cannot get sugar or coffee at any pryse, and they have to pay
5 dollars for one pound of cheas and vary poor at that, one pair of boots are
worth from 75 to 100 dollars and evrything elces in the same propotion and
still on the rise. They will give 20 dollars of their money for one dollar of
our money, so you can *see* that it must be vary hard for poor people to live
in the South, and their is alot of such ones, for our boys has strip meny a
famely from their homes. They com to a farm they do not go at work the
first thing to burn up the fences, but they go rite into the hous and take
evrything they can lay their hands on to, in case they are not willing to take
the oath,[2] wheir our last fite was their was two houses put under gard for
they was old men and they claim to be Union men and was redy to take the
oath then their was a good meny houses that they did not put on gard over
and it was no time before evrything was strip and good meny was set on
fire. Wheir the officers thought that we mite want a hospitol they wood not
let the boys burn them, but it was fun for the officers to see the boys get the
things out of the houses, you wood see som of them have on a nice bunet,
and another a dress, and som a Shall or Silk Cape, and finley evrything that
man or women wairs, and you go up to a house and you can hear the boys
talk, the dogs howl, the cats mew, the pigs a squealing, the calf a blating,
and the chickens a squacing and take in all in all, it makes a fine music
espesualy when the bellow of the canons & the rattle of the muskets are
intermingle with the rest of the music, (but such is war) and if that was all
that we cood see or hear war wood not seam to be such a horable thing, but
when you com to see the ded and dien laying around and hear the shreeks
and grones of the wounded, it is a diffrence thing alltogeather, (but such is
war) but man is born to indure hardship and to suffer and in case it is his

duty, to give his life to acomplish som great end, he shood freely give it, and their has meny brave men, gave up their lives in this strugle & God onleys knows how meny more may be call on to do the same thing, and it is the duty of evry man to go and fais the fow, that is not onley trying to brake up a noble govament, but are trying to crush the body and sole of their felow man, and try to lay aside all (as you mite say) the laws that is tort in the Bible, but I must close so I will bid you good By

From your husborn

Guy C. Taylor

Be of good chear for better days are a coming

NOTES

1. Taylor was referring to Gen Sherman's operations in Georgia, which included taking Atlanta on September 2, 1864, and culminated in the fall of Savannah on December 21, 1864.

2. Southern citizens were provided an opportunity to take an oath of loyalty to the United States when their property fell behind enemy lines. If the oath was taken, a guard was posted over the property; if the oath was not taken, the property was not protected.

∽

In camp in frunt of Petersburg Va
November the 7th 1864

My Dear Wife,

As it is a rany day and it not vary pleasant to be a runing about so I will try to pass away part of the day in writeing, and I do not know of any other one that I can write to with more pleasure then I can to you so I seat myself on a bag of oats in my tent with my feete to the fire, trying to scribble a few lines to let you know that I am injoying good health and am in hopes that you are all injoying the same. I expect that their is sturing times now in old *Wis.* as tomorrow will be election. Well their is som stur hear but not so much exsitement as I thought their wood be. I do not know the reason unless their is so few to oppose the genral mas of the people. Their was a speach handed me last even by a McClenon man the speach was delivard by hon. Mr. Arnold[1] in Milwaukee Wis. the man handed it to me to read and as I red it he wanted to know how I like it I told him that I did not agree with him and that I did not believe he did "oh yes I do says he" so it give ous a chance to examon the speach and to talk on and before we got threw with it he says that he dos not go in for any such thing at all, but then let the election go as it will their is no other way to settle this war onley to fite it out or to fite the south untill they are redy to seu for pease, and when they com to that then of coarse it is the duty of both sides to try and com to a understanding and stop the shed of blod but for ous to seu for pease is onley to caus thousands of our men to sacafice their lives for near nothing, no I cannot say that neather for it will be somthing, it will be a devided union a disgrase nation in the eys of all the world and not onley that but I do vareley believe that the curse of God wood rest upon this nation. Well Sis as the rain has stopt and I have got som work to do. I will close for this time did you get a letter from me with a cotton bud in it, it was I think No. 20 but I am not suar. Well good By for this time.

From your husborn

Guy C. Taylor

NOTE

1. Jonathon Earle Arnold was a lawyer from Milwaukee, Wisconsin. He ran for Congress as a Democrat in the 1860 election ("Dictionary of Wisconsin History," www.wisconsinhistory.org/dictionary).

∾

NO. 25

In camp in frunt of Peters burg Va
November the 8th 1864

My Dear Wife

I received a letter from you yesterday and was vary glad to hear that you are all injoying such good health. My health is vary good yet and I am injoying myself vary well as much so as anybody can in my plais. We are a having vary easey time of it, but it is not quite so pleasant hear as it is in Wis. but then we cannot expect it, and I am contented to stay hear untill the war coms to an onable setlement. The Lord knows that I do not want to see anymore of our fellow men layed ded on the battlefields, but neather do I want to see a patch up pease so in a few years that we have to see the same thing again. While we are at it let ous fite untill the thing is settled as it shood be, no matter how meny battle fields we may have to pass over. Let ous see the worse of it and in case that we do not live to get back home again our children can injoy the fruits of our labor. We had a little fite last nite on our left the rebs drove in our pickets a ways and we sent them out reinforsement and they charge on the Joneys and kill & wounded 40 and took 40 prisiners we lost 2 men killed and sevral got wounded but I do not know how meny. Today is election[1] and their was agreement made that their wood be no fireing for 2 hours and it seam like a calm after a hard storm but it is late in the day now and the storm of shot & shell is the same as usal and a little more so. It is anough to make any one dispise a surtian class of men to see them runing for som little hole so they can get into out of danger and then hear them cry pease, pease, but anough of this, you ask me to give my opinion of the Christian Commisionars. I do think, and know that they are a doing a vast amount of good. The men that is in the field dos not get the benifit of it nor do they nead it but you go to the hospitol wheir our boys are a suffering and then you can see what they are a doing. Their is thousands of our boys that are now healthy men that wood have laid in their graves if it had not bin for the C.C.L. I know that I was laying in my tent at Bells Plain in May that they don a good deal for me. Their I was left & no one to give me anything the docter that was in charge at that time wood not do anything for the sick & mite as well not for the wounded, and after I had layed their days with two others I got so that I cood not get down to the Senatory Com. to get anything to eat and I did not know but that I wood have to lay their and starve but soon com around som of the C.C.Lers and they see how we war and one of them that stop to our tent went down to their larg tent and brot up a basket of the vary best crackers and tea and then he brot ous som blackbary wine and he or som other one was their twise a day untill I was sent to Washington[2] and that is the way they are at work they hunt up those that is not look out for, and then they fine cloaths for all of the wounded in the *hospitol*, and evrything a wounded man has extra from any private coms threw the hands of the C.C.L. & S.C.L. they work togeather, no I do not think that they can have to much prais or be help to much for they are doing the work of a Christian and a Sitison, but I must close for this time By Biding you good By

From your husborn

Guy C. Taylor

NOTES

1. The Thirty-Sixth Wisconsin vote tally was 86 for Lincoln and 51 for McClellan (Aubery, *Thirty-Sixth Wisconsin Volunteer Infantry*, 187).

2. It was interesting that Taylor had apparently been very sick and in danger of losing his life at Belle Plain because his letters to Sarah from the Belle Plain Hospital did not indicate the severity of his condition. However, it is likely that throughout his service he had concealed certain facts about his health to prevent her from worrying.

∼

In camp in frunt of Petersburg Va
November the 10th 1864

My Dear Wife

As our Chaplain has made me present of a can of milk & sevral steel pens and as I have bin a trying the milk and find it is good I thought that I wood try the pens allso, so as long as I wanted to waist time & paper I did not know but what you wood like to see the paper after I have got threw scribling . I am well & this pen writes well or it wood if it was in the hands of one that new how to use a pen. Well I suppose that you want to know what I am about. Well it is the same thing take cair of two horses and lop around the rest of the time. I am guss now siting on a emty bag, and a bag of corn & oats to my back up against the brestworks. Well Sis their was another fite last nite the rebs tried to take our picket line but they got all that they wanted but they did not get the kind that they wanted for they wanted our men and in room of getting men they got balls & shells. It was a splendid site to see the shelling they look like so meny sky rockets and then when they burst to see the fire streak out over the works, som of the while, we throwed from 3 foarts, 12 morter shells, to a time and it dos not take them but a few minuits to load. Their was som of our men that got kill and som wounded but I do not know how meny but not but a vary few. I saw one this morning that was wounded but I will bet that the rebs had som work to do to bary their ded for I never see such strait shooting before. Somtime we cood see from 3 to 8 shells burst rite in the rebs work all at a time and then as soon as the shells began to go so fast they got sick rite away and stop fireing. I was up to the company while the fite was goine on and Capt Canon[1] com along and says "Boys look their do you not see the voats that we are a sending over to the Joneys" and as we look in the way he pointed we counted 10 shells goine over. The boys was all awaik, and redy for a fite but the picket line wood not let them threw so we stood a looking to see the fun but we did not have a hand in it at all but no one feals vary bad about it though. Well Sis I expect that we will have a big fite yet this fall for the weather is so fair for mooving troops, and then when the Joners find out that old Abe is to leed on the Yankes for 4 years more they will giv ous a hevy battle I am thinking, but I talk as so I knew that Abe was elected but I think that he is anyway. Well I must close for this time

By Biding You Good By

From Your Husborn

Guy C. Taylor

NOTE

1. Capt Austin Cannon, age 33, blacksmith, Marcellon, Columbia County, Wisconsin, Co. H, Thirty-Sixth Wisconsin Infantry (Aubery, *Thirty-Sixth Wisconsin Volunteer Infantry*, 348–52).

∽

NO. 26

November the 18, 1864

My Dear Wife

I wonce more pick up my pen to let you know that I am well and in hopes that theas few lines will find you the same. We made a moove nite before last we moove som 2 miles we are now laying in the rear as a surport but we do not know how long we may stay hear, but I think not a vary long time, for it is to good of plais for the boys, & then I think that we shell go on another rade in a day or to to the left. I cannot write you any noose except that our reg. had a new flag presented to them today, so we are a reg. once more. We lost our flag you know at Reams Station and we gaind it again at the fite on the 27 of Oct. Well Sis you must not get downhearted in case you do not get another letter for a long time for in case we do make a rade again on the left we do not know how long we may be gorn or wheir we may stop, but it dos not make any odds, if we are onley sucseffull. I am in hopes that in case we do start that we will go to the southside railrode[1] and tair that all to bits, and if we can onley get their it will not take long to rip it to peases you may be ashuared. Well Sis you sed to me in one of your letters that you did not want me to write to Chipman about that money so I have not writen onley that I wanted him to send to me five dollars in money & 2 in postage stamps. We have to pay 5 sents apease for stamps hear and run all over creation to get them at that prise and somtimes we cannot get them at that I have bin offeard 10 sents good meny times and I wood not let them go at that but I never paid onley 5 for them, and I think that is anough so in case that George shood pay you and in case he has sent them to me you can deduct it from the pay and I want you to write and let me know if he dos pay you or not and in case he dos not nor send me what I have ask for he will get a blesing that wont be quite so nice. Well Sis I must close for this time as it is late and I want to send this off tonite for we do not know what tonite may bring. We may be on the march you must not think that their is anything to mater with me in case you do not hear from me again for somtime. I think that I can write somthing more the next time I write

But I will close By Biding you good By

From Your Husband

Guy C. Taylor

NOTE
1. The Southside Railroad connected City Point, Virginia, on the James River to the agricultural area south and west of Petersburg. It was a major supply line to Confederate forces protecting Petersburg and Richmond. Ironically, the captured portion from City Point to the Union lines was also the major supply route for the Army of the Potomac.

∽

NO. 27

In camp in frunt of Petersburg Va
November the 21th 1864

Dear Wife

I wonce more take my pen in hand to let you know that I am well and in the hopes that you are all injoying the same. We are now laying back in the rear again as a surpoat to, two batareys and we have got a vary good plais to. My little house is in a barn and the horses are in the same bilding if we was in Wisconsin we wood think that it was not vary nice way to live with the horses but it is vary nice plais down hear, at any rate it is so nice that we are crowed all the time with som of the boys it may be that they com hear on acount of good company (over the left), well Sis I want you to write to me how things are agoine at home and what things are worth in Wis. Things do not cost anything down hear a pair of boots are worth 12 dollars and gloves are worth 4 dollars and vary poor at that but then we are not ablidge to bye boots but it is the choapes in the long run for it is mud and water more then ankle deep and it dos not pay to go with wet feat, it dont for me anyway down hear but their is som boys that can lay in the water day after day and it dos not seam to hurt them in the least but it is not me,

I have to be three times as carful down hear as I was in Wisconsin, let me lay in the rain one nite and the next day I cannot hardely stur, but as it is I do not have to be out in the wet. I do not know as you get my letters now for I have writen fore since I have got one from you the last one that I got was writen on the 30 of Oct. but then I expect that it is owing to the mail it has not bin vary reglar for somtime we do not get the mail for two or three days to a time the boats are not reglar from hear to Washington, but all their is about it I must be contented without mail if I cannot get it. I wrote to you a few days ago and I spoke about sending for som money. I have sent to Chipman for 5 dollars in money and 2 in stamps and when he pays you, you can take it out in case he sends it, and I want you to let me know wheather he has paid you or not and in case he has not I want you to ask him once more for a settlement and in case he dos not com to time let me know it as soon as you can and I will try and see if sombody elces cannot get it their is men that makes that their buissness and I had as live give it to a lawyer as to him and a little rather. I got a letter from Lydia that was writen on the 6 of this month and she seams to think that they have don vary well for this year and I am vary glad of it for they nead all that they can get as well as we do, and I got a letter from George Taylor he says that he likes up north vary well, Ada says that she is vary healthy now but she dos not like up their vary well but then I think she will have to stay their awhile. Well I must close I think this will do for a rany day and it is the third day that it has rain and the mud is deap and a little deeper, and all is still on the lines except the rebs make som stur they keep a gard on the go all the time by their desurating. They com in from 20 to 100 evry nite now But good By for this time

From your husband

Guy C. Taylor

NO. 27 [*NOTE:* TAYLOR USED THIS NUMBER ON THE PREVIOUS LETTER.]
RECEIVED NO. 23

In camp near Petersburg Va
November the 23rd 1864

My Dear Wife

I received a letter from you yesterday and was glad to hear that you are all so well. My health is good yet and I am geting so that I like *Va* prety well it is a much pleasanter plais in the fall then Wisconsin is for it is so warm last nite is the first time that it has froze any it was prety cold this morning the mud was stiff and tonite we can see som ise in plaises but it looks so that we was agoine to have som fair weather now and I am in hopes that we will for I want to hear or see one more fite this fall and then go into winter quarters and I want that to be rite between Petersburg and Richmon but I am afraid that I shell not see that this winter. I suppose that you wood like to know what kind of a house I have got well it is a vary good one for a Soldier to have it is in a barn fraim the roof is on so it dos not leak and then we have got up our tent and we have got a good fireplais in it so it is vary warm, the worst is our bed is on the ground but we have got som hay, so it is not damp but it is such hard work to keep the bed clean and then we cannot keep off the Gray Backs no way we can do, but then we aint the onley ones for it is gust so among all even to the Chaplain. It is no disgrase down hear to be lousey but if a man says that he is not so we set him down as a lier and wont believe a word he says. When I wrote to you before I was cooking for 3 of ous but now I do not, all that I do is to cook for myself and it dos not take me long to do my cooking neather. Well Sis the Hosifers[1] are agoine to have a Big dinner tomorrow the Chaplain has bin to Sity Point and got alot of stuff. He made me a present of a nice pair of drawes and a pair of socks & a can of milk, he got the stuff to the C.C. Society he brings up stuff evry little while and gives to the boys that neads it as I am takeing cair of his horse I get a little extry, he dos first rate by me. Well Sis I have sent for a little money from Chipman and it has not got hear yet but it may before long and I am in hopes it will, for in case it dos not com their will be somthing elces beside talk he must not think that I am out of the world becaus I am a Soldier for I am rite in hearing if not in site of him. Well Sis you must hold up good couradge untill I get back home and then I am in hopes that we may live in pease and our country be at pease also and I do think that will not be vary long from now neather at least I hope not for I have seen all the blodshed that I cair about seeing and tramp on the ded as long as I want to but then we cannot expect anything better in war times and on the fields of Battles, but then I must close By biding you good By

    From your husband

Guy C. Taylor

NOTE

1. Perhaps that was Taylor's term for medical officers.

NO. 28

In camp near Petersburg Va
November the 27th 1864

My Dear Wife

   It is with pleasure that I take up my pen wonce more to let you know that
I am yet in this world of Strife and am injoying vary good health. We are

Fortifications near Petersburg, Virginia, 1865 (courtesy Library of Congress Prints and
Photographs Division)

yet laying as a surpoart to two batareys and I do not know but what we are
agoine to stop hear this winter and I do hope that we may it did look as so
we was agoine to moove somwheir a few days ago but others has gorn and
looks now as so their was som prospects of our staying hear for somtime
and then they have sent all of the camps fixings that was left at Washington.
They are now at the depot about one mile from hear and the act Colonel[1]
says that he shell send for them tomorrow, he wood today but it is Sunday
and he is not in favor of working anymore then he is ablidge to on the
sabath. Well Sis we have had a thanksgiving dinner,[2] it was got up by the
Christian Commissions. It was quite a dinner. We had chicken (roasted),
blackbarys, tomatoes, pickels, apples, & well it was quite a dinner but it dos
not seam much like a dinner at home wheir evrything is taken rite from
the stove and put on to a table, but then we cannot expect the same hear as
we can get at home but we must try and make the best of it and hope that
the time may not be long heance, before this war will be to a close and then
we can go home wonce more to injoy the profits of our work. It has bin
vary still hear for sevral days. Their is som picket fireing as usal and som
canonadeing, but this morning it is quite noisey again. They are a fireing
vary fast today on picket and then we can hear the boom of the canon and
then the sharp deafing crack of the shells, and then the roaling nois of the
echo, it is quite charming sound, allthough we know that it means *death*
but then the soldiers do not think about death as a purson dos at home.
They are expose so much that they get so they think if they get hit it is allrite
and if not they think they are vary luckey and that is all they think about
dien, all they want is what they want to eat and drink, and then they are redy
to fite, and they do fite in good earnest, and they are redy to go rite into the
mouth of the rebs canons. It looks as though men was crazy to see them in
a fite but the thing of it is that men do not have any fear after they wonce
commence to fire. The noise drives away all fear and then let anyone breath
the smoke of gun powder they get reckless so they are redy for any kind of
work that is call on to be don. Well Sis as I am a siting in my tent the fifef
& drums are playing and the reg. is falling in for inspection, and evrything
is a stur down hear while I expect that evrything is quiet at home, and in
room of the people lisining to the armey music they are lisining to the
music of the human voice, and in room of hearing the command of the
officers they are hearing a man preaching the word of God, but such is war,
and when war is brot on by such a way as this one was, it is the duty of evry
man to be willian to leave his home and all of the injoyments of his home,

to lend a helping to cary on the war untill such trators will be glad to cry for quarters, and in case they will not hear to nothing that is reasonble then let ous fite them untill their will not be one left to write the history of their armeys, and then let the land wonce more be settled by men of principal with the stars & stripes for their flag and a Constitution that calls evry man a free man and that protets him in life & propety no matter what coller he is or wheir his burth plais was, but then I do not think that the people of the South is so fool hardish as not to lison to som turms of pease for they are geting tiard of the war as well as the North (and a little more so). Their is a wagon in frunt of my tent and their is a crowd of men around it and in the senter of the crowd the vois of our Comasary³ calling for each company in rotation and as somone of the companeys step up he gets his reglar wait of rations⁴ for his company and as I see that Company F has got theirs and gorn back to the Co. again I shell have to prospone writeing for a little while and get my ration or elces I will have to go without it and as I do like to have plenty to eat I think that I will go and get them. Well ration drawing is over and I wonce more commence to write I have said that we have had quite a good thanksgiving dinner but their was one falt and a great falt it was to they brot up a large amount of whiskey and large amount of men got beastely drunk but thanks God their did not one drop go down my neck and their has not any gorn down onley what the docters has given me when I have bin sick and not onley that but they will not get me to drink as long as I have my rite mind, they (that is som) say that I am a reglar old Preacher becaus I will not drink and swair as the rest do, but all I have to say to them is that I did not inlist to becom a mear bruit and to yield to evry little thing that com up. Why Sis if you cood gust be hear one day you wood say that you never thought that their was ever was so much Sin in the hole world as you cood see rite hear in one day. You cannot think any- wheir near the crureptness of the armey, and if any one shood tell you, you cood not believe it but one thing is surtain that their is no one that can tell you for their is no tongue that can speak it nor no pen that can express it on paper no one evry will know onley those that has witiness it them- self and well it is so, for if evry mother new the conduct of their sons they wood regret the day that they went into the armey & if evry wife onley new the treu caritor of hur husband and the vise that he is guilty of their wood be som sorafull times in the famileys curkle but then let time run on and when we get home again and can have the influance of good sosiety around ous again their is a large potion of the men that will becom good &

honest men, but then I must close for this time and I guess that you will not want me to write another letter for somtime as long a one as this at any rate. Well

Good By My Dear Wife From your Husband

Guy C. Taylor

(Take good cair of Charley)

NOTES

1. The acting colonel of the Thirty-Sixth Wisconsin was George Fisk from Sparta, Wisconsin. Fisk was in command of the Thirty-Sixth Wisconsin during the Battle of Hatcher's Run, October 27, 1864. According to James Aubery, "Special mention was made in all the reports by the commanding generals of the regiment and of Capt Fisk's 'Cool, daring, gallant conduct.' . . . Captain Fisk was one of the best officers in the regiment. He was admired and respected by every man" (*Thirty-Sixth Wisconsin Volunteer Infantry*, 337–39).

2. Lincoln first issued a proclamation of Thanksgiving on October 3, 1863. In 1864, Thanksgiving was celebrated on November 24.

3. The primary responsibility of the Commissary Department for both the Union and the Confederacy was to feed troops. The organization was responsible for purchasing, storing, and distributing food to the soldiers.

4. *Rations* refers to the amount of food authorized for one soldier or animal for one day. Rations varied throughout the war as circumstances changed.

CHAPTER 6

Winter Quarters

December 1, 1864, to March 23, 1865

In his December 1, 1864, letter to Sarah, Guy Taylor informed her that they had "got orders to build winter quarters." He then went on to share details about their shelter's location and construction. In various letters, he showed that he was very proud of their little dwelling—and especially fond of its fireplace. However, the arrival of the winter season did not completely bring an end to military operations. Taylor wrote about several moves, raids, and at least one significant battle fought; he also outlined his duties, which centered on his continued service to Dr. Woodward. In fact during the winter, his tasks of taking care of horses and cooking and his role as a medical attendant were expanded to serving as an orderly for the doctor as well as a temporary orderly for the colonel of the Thirty-Sixth Regiment. Then after the January 6 discharge of the chaplain of the Thirty-Sixth, Taylor actually shared the doctor's tent. Through his close association with Dr. Woodward, he had daily contact with the officers of the regiment and soon became the checkers champion of the unit after winning a series of contests with the colonel, doctor, major, and several captains of the Thirty-Sixth.

In this section of letters, Taylor continued his previous discussion concerning a soldier not knowing what to expect day to day. He described how he waited with anticipation for the official end of the 1864 fall campaign. He placed even more emphasis upon the expectation of Union success once the spring offensive of 1865 was underway. Taylor witnessed the plight of the Southern soldiers as more and more of them came over to the Union lines. It became evident to him that the Confederacy was near death and that the war would end after one or two more major fights.

Of particular interest in this section were Taylor's letters during the Christmas and New Year's holidays. His New Year's letter conveyed a humorous situation that he had experienced. His letter written on February 3 is also exceptional.

The letters during this period were usually quite long, indicating that Taylor had more time to write during the winter season. As a result, he could further develop and express his thoughts concerning war and peace, duty, temperance, and the like. Through his reflections, readers of his letters continue to learn about Private Guy C. Taylor.

∽

NO. 29

December 1th 1864

My Dear Wife

I take my pen in hand to write you and let you know that I am well and in hopes that you are injoying the same blesing. When I wrote to you last we was laying by the side of two foarts as a surport today we are somwheirs but I do not know onley they say it is on the exstream left at any rate it is som 10 miles left of our other plais. We have got orders to build winter quarters but it is doutfull wheather we stay hear all winter or not but I am in hopes that we will it is a vary pleasant plais and it is heavy timber all around ous. We are in an open field so it is free from any heavy wind and we can get timber to fix up with, and then it is not onley a little waies to a stream of water so it is vary handy for ous about the horses. It is now the first day of the winter month and it is so warm hear that a purson dos not want on any coat to keep warm with. We have not seen any snow yet and it has not froze any except to or three times. We have not seen any frost for more than two weeks and it looks now as though their was not much cold weather down hear. I got a letter from George the other day he says that he likes up north first rate and they are well and I got one from Amanda & one from Mart, the other day they (Mart) sent to me 5 dollars in money and 2 dollars worth of postage stamps and when he setles with you, you can deduct that out it will be 7 dollars in all. I wish that you wood send me som tea send ½ of a lbs., and do it up with brown paper and do not be to carfull how it is don up I see that thoes that dos not be vary purticular are the wones that get their things the most reglar. The boys are agoine to send

home for evrything they can think of that is (most of them) and I think that
they are vary foolish for it will cost them a large amount and then in case
that we have to moove they will have to throw evrything away. I do not want
you to send me anything unless I send for it for you do not know what is
wanted down hear so what I do want I will let you know as we have not got
setled yet and their is a good deal of fusing to do so I will close and write
again as soon as I get things straiten so good By for this time

From your Husband

Guy C. Taylor

My 2 letter

Dear wife,

As I did not send out the letter today that I have writen I thought that I
mite write a few lines more this evening. As Whitney is laying in bed I am
a siting up and a writing to you & to mother Taylor as I got a letter from hur
tonite I do not know but what you wood like to know what kind of a chance
I have got for writing well it is a vary good one tonite for a table I have got
a pease of a barel that has bin cut in two to make a tub that is turnd bottom
side up and then I have got a lantorn that I borrowed off one of the sutlers
and for a seat I have the hold of a handfull of straw on the ground so you
can give som little ide of my chance for writing but I will have a better plais
in a day or to for we have got our house pretty well along and if it is fair
tomorrow I think that we will finish yet and then for a table and a stand to
write on after we get our new house don and get it furnished I will gust
send you a invition to com and see me and I shell expect that you will com
for it is onley a short distance. You say that their is som truble in the lodge
it is a shame if the boys and girls to, cannot get togeather and agree well to
tell the truath it is a shame to let a sosiety like that be broke up by one or
two pursons and I cannot hardely think that it will be broke up at least I
hope not for I expect to be back their again in the coars of time and I want
to see that lodge and all of the lodges in good runing order. What dos
Brother Flint[1] say about it or is he afraid that he may get sombody vext if he
says a great deal. He is a man that ort to take hold of it and in good earnist
and not onley him but evry Brother & Sister ort to try and help the thing
along. Now is the time for the people to work at home if they want to have
a good sosiety for they will have a good deal more to conten with as soon as
the boys gets back from the armey and in case they go home and find that

their is a good sosiety and most of the folks around their homes belongs to it, a great meny will take rite hold and help them along while if their is no influance to throw around them onley what is to draw them into som grog shop you may expect to see a sorafull time of it, for their is a large amount of the boys that will act like so meny mad men when they once get loose if you had seen what I have by men drinking licker you wood not think strange of my wanting evrybody to work for the case of temprance and if a man tells me he is a trying to live a Christian life and throws one atom in the way of any society that is working for the cais of tempance I set him down as a purfect hipicrick and purson not fit to live in a cicilize community but ort to be kick out of the civilize community for he is not a purson fit to live in theas times. You tell the lodge members that I say if they let the lodge go down I shell think that they are not worthey to be trusted with anything for they are pledge to work for the order and if they work as they ort to the thing will com out allrite and the old saying is "all is well that ends well" I have supposed that the lodge was well and I want to see it end well but if it goes up in any such a way as that it dos not look to me as so it wood end well but I cannot believe yet but the thing will com out allrite after all, I hope so at any rate and the Lodge haves my best wishes and may God help them. You will see that I am crasy or foolish for I have made a orfull blunder when I had got two pages writen I see that I had got to sheats togeather and I thought that I wood not throw one of them away but I wood write in both and you can see by the number of the pages how they go for I do not expect you can pick out sence of it anyway so you cood not tell by that. You sed that you wanted me to send to you for what I wanted I shood have don so if Chipman had paid you but as he has not paid you what I want I meant to make him pay it, it is all the same for all what I can see but you have got a ide, that I am in nead of things and dont want you to know it, it is not so, I am in good health and have a plenty to eat and to wair and good anough plais to sleap so their is not anything except som clothing that I have bin in nead of and I have got them now, becaus I am a soldiering you must not get it into your mind that I am out of the world and in sombodys melon patch for I am not and I do not expect to go as long as I can help it. Their is one thing that I wood like to have you send to me that is a buget of tea that is somthing that we cannot bye hear at any rate. What evry the girls wrote to me and I was vary glad to get a letter from them and I wood try and answer them tonite but I have bin at work all day and I have writen one letter tonite to Mother Taylor and it is now nealy 11 oc and it is time that I was at bed But I will write to the girls in a day or two I began to write a letter to them gust before we made our last moove and I have not finished it yet. Well I must close so I will Bid you Good By

From Your Husband Guy C. Taylor

Take good cair of Charley but do not make to much of a pet of him for if you do he will get so he will try to be boss in a little while.

NOTE
1. Mr. Flint was a prominent citizen of the town of Bristol.

NO. 29 [*NOTE:* TAYLOR USED THIS NUMBER ON THE PREVIOUS LETTER.]
RECEIVED NO. 25

Dec the 4th 1864

My Dear Wife

I received your letter this morning and was glad to hear that you are all well my health is vary good we are now camp way round to the left near the southside railrode and we are at work putting up houses for winter we are agoine into winter quarters and it will take somtime before we get our camp fix up but when it is don it will be a vary pleasant plais it is in a large field (I say large not like Wisconsin fields) and it is vary hevy timber all around it so it is not but a short distance to go for timber the boys fetch it on their backs but we cannot build our house yet we have got to wait untill all the rest gets threw and then the officers will deside on som plais for a barn for the horses and wheirever that is their we will have our house but the act, Colonel says that he will have a team hall ous stuff for a house so we are fixing ous up a shanty to stay in for a little while we will have a gay time of it this winter all that I will have to do is to see to two horses and then the docter & Chaplian both says when I want to go anywheirs to gust take a horse and you may bet that I do not go a foot a great deal. I went out in frunt of our works yesterday about two miles and cross one picket line and went most to our frunt picket and got a load of straw I got as much as the little horse cood cary with me I devided it with the docter and he said that he wood not cair if I took a ride evry day if I wood do as well as I did that time. We think as much of a hanfull of straw as you wood of a good feather bed and it is a good deal harder to be got this is the first bit of good straw we have had this fall. I am agoine out this afternoon to see what I can find. You say that you wish that I cood be at home this new years day. I wish that the hole armey mite get home this winter I shell not try to go home this winter for it will cost so much and then I cannot get any longer then 20 days furlow and then it will not do to over run a furlow more then 5 or 6 days, so in case I shood get one I cood not be at home any more then 15 or 16 days and it wood cost surtain 75 dollars and that money will do you more good then what my goine home wood to stay so short a time. I am in hopes that we may all get home this coming spring and get home to stay for a longer time then we can on a furlow. Well Sis as I want to go away I will not write any more now but I will write again in a day or two so good By

　　From your husband

Guy C. Taylor

　　Pleas send me Som tea, I want father to plant som Va Sugarcain and see how it will do

ᔑ

NO. 29 [*NOTE:* TAYLOR USED THIS NUMBER ON TWO PREVIOUS LETTERS.]
RECEIVED NO. 26

Dec. the 5th 1864

My Dear Wife

　　As I received yours of the 27 and was vary glad to hear that you are all vary well my health was never any better then it is now and we are now fixing ous our winter houses, you say that you feal vary uneasy som way or other you must not worey any about me for I am in a nice plais now and I am as fat as a hog & gust as lazy. The reason that I wrote to you that you nead not worey if it was a good while before you hurd from me again we expected to go on a raid but we did not go but we struck camp on the 30 of November and march to the left about 8 miles and have gorn into camp on the extream left som 5 miles from the Southside railroad. You said that you wish that I had not writen to Chipman for any money or stamps the reason that I wrote to him for them was that he did not pay you and you wrote to me that you wish that I wood not write to him to get into any fuss about that money so I thought that he wood not refuse to send to me what little that I wanted and it wood be as well as so he paid it to you and then you sent it.

The money that you sent to me will not com in miss but then I do not nead anything now but what I have got. I have run in debt to the sutler for a pair of boots & a pair of gloves the boots was 10 dollars & the gloves 2 dollars totle 12 dollars you say that Mr. Wilder[1] talks of Breaking up the Lodge I want to know if Mr. Wilder runs that dristrict and in case he dos, why of coarse he can break up any kind of meatins and in case he dos not, I think that the members of that sosiety is not what they ort to be. What if their is two or three that is apose to them they have no rite to surmit. Suppose we wood say that we wood not fite for govment for their was one or two that was appose to it you wood say at wonce that we was not fit to be call men that wood not stand up for our rites it is the same in the Lodge if that Lodge goes down you may be ashuared that their is one that will think that you have not done what you ort to or what you have pledge yourself to do but then I cannot believe that the people of Bristoll is goven by Rood or Wilder if the majoyity of the lodge says giv it up why then giv it up and start another if there is anough to start one and be carful and get men in it that will stand to what they pledge themself to. If you ever neaded a good sosiety it is now for it will not be long before that country will be fill up with soldiers and they are as reckless as men can be let me say to the members of the lodge stand fast to your work and by the help of the Devine Provadence you can run a profetable sosiety in that neighborhood, but I must close By Biding you good By

From your Husband

Guy C. Taylor

Write often and Be of good chear for good chear is what makes life pleasant (all is well that ends well)

NOTE
1. Mr. Wilder was a prominent citizen of the town of Bristol.

∾

To be read in the Lodge
Mrs. Leuwis was vary much pleased write to[1]

Dec. 5, 1864

My Dear Wife

As I did not send the letter out today that I had written I thought that I would write a few lines more tonight. Whitney is in bed and I am writing to you and Mother as I got a letter from her tonight. I do not know but you would like to know what kind of a chance I have for writing. Well it is a very good one tonight, for a table I have got a peace of a barrel that has been cut in two to make a tub of, than is turned bottom side up and then I have a lantern that I borrowed off one of the Sutlers and for a seat I have the whole of one handful of straw on the ground, so you can give some little idea of my chance for writing but I will have a better place in a day or two for we have got our new house pretty well along and if it is fair tomorrow I think that we will finish it, and then for a table or stand to write on and after we get our new house done and get it furnished I will just send you an invitation to come and see us, and I shall expect that you will come for it is only a short distance. You say that there is some trouble in the Lodge. It is a shame if the boys and girls too cannot get together and agree, well to tell the truth it is a shame to let a society like that be broken up by one or two persons and I cannot hardly think that it will be broken up at least I hope not for I expect to be back there again in the course of time and I want to see that Lodge and all of the Lodges in good running order. What does Brother Flint say about it . . . he is the man that ought to take hold of it in good earnest and not only him but every Brother and Sister ought to try and help the thing along. Now is the time for the people to work at home if they want to have good society to live in for they will have a good deal more to contend with as soon as the boys get back from the army, for in case they go home and find a good society and most of the folks belong to it a great many will take right hold and help them along. While if there is no influence to throw around them only what is to draw them to the grogshop[2] you may expect to see a sorrowful time of it for there is a large amount of the boys that will act like mad men when they get loose if you had seen what I have by men drinking liquor you would not think strange of my wanting everybody to work for the cause of Temperance and if a man tells me he is trying to live a Christian life and throws one atom in the way of any Temperance society I set him down as a perfect hypocrite and a person not fit to live in a civilized community but ought to be kicked out of the society for he is not a person fit to live in these times. You tell the Lodge members that I say if they let the Lodge go down I shall think that they are not worthy to be trusted with any thing, for they are pledged to work for the Order and if they work as they ought to it will come out all right and the old saying is "all is well that ends well" I have supposed that the Lodge was well and I want to see it end well but if it goes up in any such a way as that it does not look to me as if it did end well but I cannot believe yet but the thing will come out all right after all I hope so at any rate and the Lodge has my best wishes and may God help them, and let me say to the members of the Lodge stand fast to your work and by the help of Divine Grace you can run a profitable society. But I must close by biding you Good Bye

From your husband

G. C. Taylor

PS. Write often and be of good cheer for cheerfulness is what makes life pleasant.

(All is well that ends well)

NOTES

1. Apparently Sarah rewrote Taylor's December 1 letter and corrected most of his spelling and grammatical errors (see Appendixes C and D). This is the only letter in the collection in Sarah's handwriting. It seems she then read her version to the lodge. Her note concerning writing to Mrs. Lewis was probably a reminder to herself.

2. *Grogshop* was another name for a tavern or saloon.

NO. 30

In camp December the 6th 1864

My Dear Wife

We made a moove yesterday and went one mile and went into camp wheir the 5 Corps was laying and it is a vary nice plais and I was in hopes that we wood stay hear this winter but the order is now to be redy to moove at a minute warning so it looks as so we wood not stay hear any longer then morning at any rate, I was a writeing a letter to Amanda when the order com and I closed my letter in a hurrey for I thought that I must write a few lines to you for I do not know when I shell get so to write again for we do not know which way we are agoine som says that we are agoine to follow 5 Corps but then we do not know as we shell and we do not know wheir that has gorn so we do not know nor do we cair wheir we are agoine it is a Soldier buisiness to march when orded and not ask which way ore wheir abouts they are agoine when we stop at a plais we can tell then wheir we went to (that is after we have inquired wheir we are). Well Sis you will have to pick this out the way that you can for I am in a hurrey or I cannot mail it tonite and then if we start earley in the morning I cannot send it untill we stop. Tell the girls that they may expect a letter from me as soon as we get settle down so that I can get a chance to write. Well Sis this is not a letter it is onley a few lines to let you know that we are agoine somwheirs and if it is sevral days before you hear from me again you must not think strange but I will write again in two or three days if I can get a chance. Well good by for this time

From your husband

Guy C. Taylor

Have you got the cotton that I sent you or the cain lead.

NO. 31

In camp Dec the 8th 1864

My Dear Wife

I pick up my pen wonce more to write to you a few lines to let you know that I am well & hope that theas few lines will find you all injoying the same blessing. I wrote a few lines to you yesterday to let you know that we are expected to go on a rade we was all pack up and redy for a start at any minute all nite but we have not gorn yet and I do not think that we will but I cannot say for we are now under marching orders so we may have to start in a little while but I hope not for our boys have bin in so meny rades they are most all gorn we have now about 200 men in all and a few more rades their will not be anough to make a show but in case we are neaded away we go in good spearts and in case we com off allrite we are not sorry that we went and in case we do loose a good meny it cannot be help and their is no use to cry about spilt milk. We com down hear to whip the rebs and we cannot do it unless we have fites so let the fites com while it is cool weather and not wait untill another sommer when it will be hot anough to kill men when they lay in camp. Now is the time to fite and they are a fiteing I expect the 5 Corps it is repoarted has met the enemy and they are trying their guns wonce more we can hear the repoarts of this artilary but we have not yet hurd the result of the fite.[1] It is my opinion that they will try the southside railrode in a few days if the weather holds good. All of the armey around hear is under marching orders and then the train has got orders to be redy to go at any time so it looks as so we was agoine to have warm times somwheirs but we do not know as we will have a hand in the mess or not we hope not but if we do we will do the best that we can the boys of the 36 have don som orfull fiteing and their is a good deal of fite in them yet they will not be the first to run unless it is towards the enemy. At our last fite I thought that the 36 had gorn up when I see the rebs get in their rear but with a yell and a charge they made for the rebs lines and they did not loos onley one man and they kill a good meny and took 200 prisiners and com out allrite. Well we have got to have evrything in redaness to moove at any minute tonite but then we may not stur after all if we do not go on this rade we will be vary likely to stay wheir we are now all winter and it is a nice plais to stay we have got a good house and a good fireplais in it all the falt that I find with it, it is to warm for this kind of weather but it will not be so warm all winter at least I hope it will not for I shell not know how to live all winter without seeing som snow and eise. Well Whitney has gust com in and he sed he wanted to have a fire and he has got one that will make ous eather sweat ore go outdors and stay. Well I must close By Biding you good By

From your husband

Guy C. Taylor

NOTE

1. The Fifth Corps (a cavalry division) and a division of the Second Corps, totaling 4,200 cavalry and 22,000 infantry, were sent south on Jerusalem Plank Road. Their objective was to destroy additional track on the Weldon Railroad. At an expense of around 200 casualties, sixteen miles of railroad track were destroyed (Trudeau, *The Last Citadel*, 264, 284, 285).

NO. 31 [*NOTE:* TAYLOR USED THIS NUMBER ON THE PREVIOUS LETTER.]
RECEIVED NO. 27

In Camp December the 10th 1864

My Dear Wife

I have gust red your letter no. 27 and was vary glad to hear that you are all injoying as good Health as you are my health is vary good and I am getting to be vary fleashey you wood not hardely know me I guess that I am 15 lbs heaver then I evry was before. I am yet staying with the horses but I do not know but what I shell go back to the company again, for their has a new order com that evryone in the ranks must cary a gun and if I cary I shell go rite to my company, but I think that the docter will have me give it up in case that I do have to draw one I have drawn two and they have both have gorn back again and may be the third will do the same but then I do not cair vary much anyway. This new order is on acount of so meny of our men goine off on a rade. You see the 5 Corps and 1 div. of the 6 and 1 div of the 9 and 2 division of the 2 Corps, the hole armey that has gorn on the rade will amount to about 60 thousand men so you see that it has left our armey on the line rather weak but they wood find that they wood have somthing to do to com across our works but then it is necassary for evryone to have a gun so in case that the rebs do make a dash at ous we can all have a chance to fite but when we do not have a gun we are in the other mens way and do no good but then they soon get to the rear with their horses, but let things rip all I want to see is to see the rebs a coming across the field to make a charge on ous. We mite loos a few of our picket but then they wood not get any nire to our works then 8 or 10 rods and by that time that they got out of reach of our boys guns their wood be a lot of them left on the grown for ous to cover up. If we have sent off 60 or 70 thousand men they wood find out that they have not got men anough to brake our lines for the foarts are in such a way that they can sweep rite up the works and when they get into the ditch they wood meet nothing but death for they wood let the grape & canaster fly all a long the line and then the little balls wood do their work to. You say that you had not got your pay yet from Chipman, but that you are agoine to write Mart about it well you can write to hur and in case they do not pay you I do not want you to say anything to them again but write to me gust how much you have got from him and be shure that you send me gust the amount so their can be no flow pick for I shell write to a lawyer and have him see if he can get it, and I have not got any dout but what it will com. If a purson wants to be mean I think that I know how to be gust as mean as the next one. You ask me if I new that Mr. Marr was ded I hurd of it rite away after his death you see they have to send the repoarts from the hospital of any deaths or any furlows or any cloathing to each Company so they can put it on the company Books for evrything has to go gust as the book says for it is the headquarters of all the proseedins of all cloathing and money matters, so you see we hear of any such thing rite off after it hapens. I expect that Mrs. Marr feals vary bad of coars she must but then we have got to die somtime anyway and if it is our lot to die in the armey it is all rite, and the folks at home will have to content themself the best they can. Mr. Marr was a farther to me when I was sick when I was at

Bells Plain he found my napsack and got it out of the boat and took out the things and dryed them and brot them to me and when he found out how I was he went and got me stuff to eat and fix up my tent in vary good shape and that day was the last time that I see him when he shook hands with me and Bid me good By little did I think that it was the last time that we was evry to meat on this earth, but then we cannot tell today what will hapen tomorrow, but then such is life. Well Sis you say that farther is agoine to kill his hogs next week I think that it is a little colder their then it is down hear or you wood not keep much fresh meat. Allthough it is prety cold hear gust now it was vary warm yesterday untill about noon and then it began to clowed up and grow cold and it rain & snow all nite last nite and this morning evrything was covard with snow & eise but it is most all of now gone and By nite the ground will be bair again. I have writen to you once or twise that their was a rade goine on, and it is agoine on a good wais the repoart that has gust com in is that they are somwheir about 50 miles south[1] of hear and the rebs have got in the rear of them so it is most likely that we will not hear from them again untill they cut out somwheirs. We did expect to go to but then we are hear yet and we do not expect to go now but then we are under marching orders yet but if we do go we do not know wheir we will go to but I am in hopes that we will not have to go out of hear for we are in a good plais it is in a pleasant plais and then the watter is good and that is somthing new for ous to have good watter and then wood is handy to, so evrything that we want is rite hear we are in one half mile of the depot it is the last depot on the left but I shood not wonder if that rode was a runing sevral miles further before next spring. The rebs are a faling back prety fast but I expect that their will be a big fite before we get the southside railrode but then it must com anyway. You said in one of your letters that farther wanted to know if I cood not be at home on new years day I wood like to be at home vary well but then you can eat the good things and gust think of one that is in old Va and it will do gust as well. You say that Lydia is not well I am sorrow to hear it for the hart complaint is a vary bad complaint and she will have to be vary carful or she will see hard times yet. You must write and let me know how they get a long in the Lodge I am in hopes that they will keep the thing a runing for I think it is a good sosiety and they can do a good deal of good. Tell the girls to write to me often I wrote to all of them in one letter and sent it in your adress so they cannot say that I wrote it to any surtain one. I wrote to you for som tea if you have not sent it you may not for it cost so much and then I can do without it as well as not. We have a plenty of Coffee and sugar so we have warm drink anough. As for that money that I sent to Chipman I have got 5 dollars in money 2 dollars in stamps and one dollar that I got in one of your letters it has cost me somwhat more my being back with the horses but I have no dout but what it has saved me from a good meny sick days but now I am able to go at work at most anything. I am as tuff as a horse I wish they wood gust bring this war at a close and let me see if I cood go at work when I get home. They all say that the Soldiers will not be good for anything when the war is over. I think som so myself I have not got any dout but 8 out of evry 10 will be laying around som sallon one half of their time but then a good meny will soon see that they have not got money to spend in that way after a little. Well I must close By Biding you good By

From your husband

Guy C. Taylor

NOTE

1. The six-day operation was referred to as the Weldon, Belfield, Hicksford, or Applejack Raid (Trudeau, *The Last Citadel*, 285). It succeeded in further disrupting Lee's supply network.

⁓

NO. 32 RECEIVED NO. 28

Dec. the 12th 1864

My Dear Wife

I received your No 28 day before yesterday and was glad to hear that you was all as well as you are. You say that Lydia is not at all well, she had ort to try and see if she cannot get help rite away, for hur complaint is one that had not ort to run at its own will my health is vary good we are rite in the same plais yet that we have bin since I wrote to you that we was under marching orders. We do not think now that we shell go away this winter anymore then to moove along the lines. We have not got orders yet to fix up our houses again so we are a waiting to see wheather we are agoine to stop hear or wheather we have got to go to som other plais to put our little house but then Whitney and myself have got a good house now but som of the boys have not got any at all their is 3 of our Company that are now staying with ous a waiting to see wheather they want a house hear or not we are under marching orders so we have to keep evrything pack up onley what we are ablidge to have to keep from goine hungry & cold, but most likely we shell get orders in a few days to do somthing if it is nothing more then to march. You say that you have not drawn onley 15 dollars of your money from the state yet. It looks to me as though you are trying to be a little to saveing I want you to look out for yourself but I do not want you to go pinch to save money for if you do it is your own falt, but then look out for health first and then it is time anough to look out for saveing money. I wrote to you about the 5 Corps and som others with them agoine on a raid. We have not hurd from them yet but then we are all in hopes that they will meet with success for we think if they do that their will be a prety good show for ous to get home by next spring. Their object is to take the railroad wheir the Junction is from the southside rode to the Welding road so you see if they get that point they will not onley distroy the onley road that runs into Petersburg but they will distroy a large amount of stoarge propaty. The 1 & 3 divisions of our Corps went out on a rade and we thought that they went with the 5 Corps but we was misstaken for they have partly got back. It seams as though the rebs was a runing troops at the southside rode to try to hed our armey so they sent out theas two div. to make a rade to call the rebs another way they made a rade on the same ground that we did on the 27 of Nov. and they went som farther then what we did and the rebs com against them with 3 lines of battle and our men fell back a wais and then they got behind som brestworks and they gust told the Johneys to com on and on they did com and our boys sent them back again in hot hast but for all that we yet hold the ground we have met with a large lost of men when they made our men fall back they was slaying our men at holesale their was 130 ambalances com back the next day after the fite loaded with wounded their must bin not fur from 300 wounded but we do not know how bad. The rebs was cut up but they must have lost vary hevy when they charge on our works with 3 lines for they cood not got out of reach before they wood receive som 30 to 40 rounds and when there is som two thousand musket leting into them as long a time as that their is sombody agoine to get hurt, know dout but what our totle lost is nearly 500 men and if the rebs, have not lost as meny they are vary lucky and our men did not shoot vary strait But then I must close By Biding you good By

From your husband

Guy C. Taylor

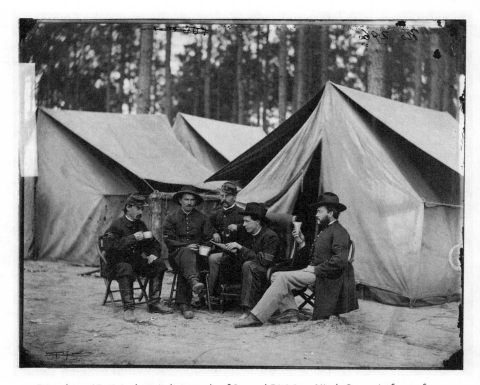

Petersburg, Virginia, hospital stewards of Second Division, Ninth Corps, in front of tents, October 1864 (courtesy Library of Congress Prints and Photographs Division; Timothy H. O'Sullivan, photographer)

❧

NO. 32 [*NOTE:* TAYLOR USED THIS NUMBER ON THE PREVIOUS LETTER.]

In Camp Dec. the 15th 1864

My Dear Wife

   I take up my pen to let you know that I am well and hope that theas few lines will find you injoying the same blessing. We have moove since I last wrote and I shood have writen before but we have bin at work pretty buissey a fixing up our houses again. We mooved about 1½ miles further to the left and we now think that we have got to the plais wheir we will stay this winter, but then it may be as it has bin hear before, by the time we get all fix up we may get orders to pack up and get redy to moove again.

I will try and finish my letter now as I have got som what tiard, and I am agoine to wait untill after dinner before I do any more work. We are agoine to have a nice house when we get it don. Mr. Miller and myself have bin at work today will make two days at a fireplais and all of the officers say it will be the best shape one in the reg. We will get it prety near don today and som are at work at laying up logs and banking up. Their is 5 of ous that is togeather now Whitney & Duch Jo and myself as horslers and Miller the stuard and Heart the Docters ordaley. We have a large famley for a small log house but then they are all prety good naturd except myself and you know vary well how I am so their is no use in my writeing anything but the truath. Well Sis I wood like to have you gust run in and give ous a call when we get our house don. We will give you as good a meal as we can get up and we will let you have a seat on the ground. Well we will get our chairs & table bime by, when we get other things fix. Our Chaplain has had vary bad luck he lent his horse to Capt. Wicks[1] and he was stold so it leaves me with one horse again, but I was not to blaim this time. Well Sis I must close I will write again Sunday for I will not work on Sunday anyway and today is Fryday well good By my dear wife

From Your husband

Guy C. Taylor

NOTE

1. Capt Wicks was probably Capt George Weeks, York, Wisconsin, Co. B, Thirty-Sixth Wisconsin Infantry (Aubery, *Thirty-Sixth Wisconsin Volunteer Infantry*, 296).

ᵒᴥᵒ

NO. 33 RECEIVED NO. 28

In camp Near Petersburg Va
Dec. the 17th 1864

My Dear Wife

I wonce more sit myself down to pen a few lines to you to let you know that I am in the best of health. I got a letter from you last nite and glad was I to hear wonce more that you are all injoying such good health for health is the staff of hapiness. I wrote a few words to you yesterday to let you know that we war not all ded down hear. We got hear (wheir we are now) last Tusday nite and Wendsday we went at work to fix ous up a house and we work untill last nite prety hard and we have got a prety good house, but then

Officers in front of winter quarters at Army of the Potomac headquarters, February 1864
(courtesy Library of Congress Prints and Photographs Division)

it is not don yet but then we thought that we wood lay still today and tomorrow and then we would be redy for work again on Monday. We have got
gust the nices kind of a fireplais. We have not got the Chimney don yet but
it is so we can have a fire in it. It seams as so we had got back home last
nite, it is the first time that we have bin so to take our close off for 3 months,
so you can guess that we have got ous a bed & a house as good as we ever
hed in the armey. Our bed is made of small round poles and then we rob
the horses of their hay, and it makes a nice plais to sleap all that we want to
see now is one hevy storm and then we will be shure of staying in our house
this winter but if the weather hold good it is doutfull about our staying hear
meny days, for it is a good time to make rades. Colonel Warner has got back
hear again he will take the Comand of the reg. now. Docter Miller we hurd
last nite by mail was gust at the point of death (he is at home) it is a sorfull
thing for this reg. We will have onley one Docter, that is Woodard and their

is plenty of work for two to work and then som of the men will not get any to much cair. We have met with another lost in horse flesh. The Chaplain lent his horse to one of the Capt. to go to a coart martial and he hitch him and when he went to get him again he was not their and they cannot get any track of him at all, so it leaves me wonce more with onley one horse to take cair of, and I do not do much about that one, for I do the cooking and the other boys take cair of the horses. Well Sis you must not let evrything truble you that is not gust as you wish it was. You say that Father says that he thinks that Chipman will not be willing to pay you more then 75 cents a acor for the plowing. If he will pay you that and will pay you for the drawing of the wood I think that you had better take it for we do not know how long it may be before I get back home again and the money now will be worth as much as it wood be in two years from now at 1 dollar per achor, and if he will not pay you any more then that I think it will not pay to have any fuss about it. If I new that I shood get home next spring it wood Be a diffrance thing but in case he dos that he must never get in my way if he dos he will pay dear for it now that is surtain, if it not for twenty years from now, but then anough of such talk. I got a letter from George nite before last they was all well and they write as though they like up their pretty well. Well I must close for the Docter wants me to go and put the Saddle on his horse. Well Sis you must hold up good courage and hope for the best and prepair for the worse so you are redy to stand any kind of nuse wheather it is good or Bad. Well I will close for this time By Biding you good By

From your husband

Guy C. Taylor

Take good cair of Charley

NO. 33 [*NOTE:* TAYLOR USED THIS NUMBER ON THE PREVIOUS LETTER.]
RECEIVED NO. 30

In camp near Petersburg Va
December the 20th 1864

My Dear Wife

I got your letter day before yesterday and glad was I to hear that you are all well. I shood have writen before but we have bin at work a making our

cabben som larger and we have got it so it dos vary well now. It is a good
deal better then the officers tents are, but then it is not don yet, but we all
wanted to write so we thought that we wood take today the pen in rume of
the shivel & ax. You wrote about a pair of boots. I have got me a good pair
so I do not nead anymore so you may *not* send them. Well as for that acount
of Chipmans I will see if I can get it and if he will not settle with me he will
have a good time of it. I rather think I shell send word to him to send it to
me rite away or I will make cost on it and if he sends it to me, I shell send
it rite to you so you will get it anyway and if Mart is mad about it I do not
cair I ask no odds of any such folks as that. I think that they have bin mean
long anough so I will see if I cannot be gust as mean as they can. If I have
the devel to work with I will take the devels own way to work and then their
will be no chance for anyone to find falt you see. I expect that you will have
som kind of a time eather Christmass or new years. I wood like to be with
you and pick som of the chickens bones but then as it is not posable for me
to be with you, it will not make any diffance with you (at least I am in hopes
that it will not) for I can content myself gust as well with a pease of raw
porak and a hard tack as anything elces. You say you wood get the start of
me this year by wishing a mary Christmass. I will give up that you have got
the start of me this time, but then I can wish you the same and a happy new
year, not gust for the few new days in the year but may it be a happy year to
you all threw. You say that you want me to let you know what I want in case
I want anything well their is one thing that I want but then you cannot get
it for me. That is I want this war to com to a close, but when I say com to a
close I do not mean that I have got tiard of the war, but I want to see the
south com back and ask for pease and let ous have a pease that our children
will not have to fite over in a few years again, and if the people will onley be
trew to their selfs, and to their country, we can soon com back home with
such a pease established, and we can then say with thruth, that our land is
the land of the free, and the home of the brave, but dear wife, it is not for
you or me to say how meny may have to sleap that sleap that knows no
waicken on this earth, before such a pease is establish. We know that their
is meny a one that will be left, to moarn over the lost of the one that they
long have loved, but then when they know that they fell in a noble caus, and
they can see the fruits of their labor riseing up to bless the land, it will be a
great comfert to the moarning heart. You must rite and let me know how
they got along in the Lodge. I am in hopes that we will soon get fix up hear
so we can have a good plais to write, and then I will try and see if I can write

a few lines to the Lodge, but as we are now all in a mess, I cannot think of anything to write at all, and then they wood want sombody that was prety use to my stile of scribling to pick out the words, and then they will want a set of lawyers and a mess of ministers to make out any sence of it. I got that note that you sent of Marrs death. It was the first that I had hurd of his being wounded[1] I was not up with the company at the time he went back, but the boys all say that he was not wounded, but that he was vary sick but then that dos not make any diffance at all. He was at his regler duty as a soldier shood be he died for his contrey, and when he left this world he left all trubles behind him and now is injoying the hapiness of Heaven. He leaves a wife & child to moarn over his lost but then they cannot but think that he is better off wheir he is then he cood be hear on earth. You wanted me to write somthing about comeing home well Sis if you will write and let me know when the war is agoine to close I will let you know prety near the time that I shell go home, but then I think that is a hard thing for you to find out but then we will all know it after awhile and if it is a good while that we are away from home so much the more charm will their be about home when we do get back again. I expect that you are a making a regler pet of that boy of ours but you must not let him get to be boss for if you do the pet will be a heap of truble to you but then I do not worey any about it for I think you are old anough to know how to train up children. Well I will close for this time By Biding you good By

From your husband in the armey

Guy C. Taylor

NOTE

1. Pvt John B. Marr left his company June 12, 1864, because of sickness. He died of chronic diarrhea October 29, 1864, at the U.S. Army Hospital in Philadelphia, Pennsylvania. He was buried in the cemetery there as John B. Man (*Roster, 36th Wisconsin Infantry Regiment of Volunteers and Draftees*, 135).

In camp near Petersburg Va
December the 24th 1864

My Dear Wife

I reccon that you wood like to know what I am up to now days, so I thought that I wood try to write to you a few lines to let you know that I am aloping around. Well we have bin at work by add shells on our house. This morning we made up our minds to do somthing today so I took a horse and rode som fore miles to find som boards for a table and the other boys got things redy for mudding up the house, so Miller and myself don the plastering and Whitney and Jouph mix the morter and we made the mud fly when we got it started, and I am a setting up to keep fire tonite so it will dry out it is rather damp but then it will soon dry out for we have got pitch pine to burn and it keeps evrything so hot that you cannot hardly tuch it. It is now about 11oc at nite and I am a siting on a box in frunt of the fireplais a trying to pen a few lines to you, but the fire makes me sleepy so I will wait untill morning.

Dec. 25 Christmass morning,

I again take my pen to try to scratch a few stray thoughts to you. It is a vary pleasant day down hear it dos not seam much like Wisconsin it is warm and pleasant it is frozen a little but one warm day will make it all mud again. You may think that we are way down in south in the field a camping and we cannot get anything for Christmass but then we can we went yes-terday and bot fore vary good pies they do not cost anything onley thirty five cents apease, and we got one for our Leautentant he is out on picket and I am agoine out to take it to him they are about one mile in frunt of ous. I went out to the line yesterday but I did not find our boys they do not lay wheir they did a few days ago their are further to the rite and the third divi-sion is wheir our boys was so I will know this time the coarse to go and I can soon find them, and let anyone that is not use to the armey cood not find anybody they want to. We can tell by the badges[1] what division they belong to and we know how the divisions lay so let ous get into any plais in the corps and we can soon find the brigade that we want to and then it is no truble to find the reg. Whitney is redy to go out to the picket line with me so I will wait untill we get back. Well Sis I sit myself down again to write. I have gust got back from my walk we did not see anything worth mentioning out on the picket line. We had no truble in finding our boys they have got a vary good plais out their they are in a vary heavy pease of woods and they have fix up their tents pretty warm they do not take the pains to fix up their as they do at camp for they do not stay their onley two days at a time and one waits for the other to fix up their tents. Well Sis I got a letter from you this morning and was glad to hear that you are injoying such good health. The letter was No 31 you say that you got one dollar from your Friend Chipman (I shood not cair about having such friends) but then never mind I have wrote a letter to him and I think he will take som notice of it and if he dos not I will try and see if I can make him do somthing toards setling up. Well Sis you say that you are agoine to take twenty dollars of your state money and put it with that money that I sent last in plais of that money that I sent last spring. You know your own buisiness best but I do not want you to pinch yourself to save money, money is a good thing but good health is a better thing. I shood think that you had better take the state money and make use of it for yourself. You say you want me to have somthing if I live to get out of the armey. If my health is spaired I can earn my living when I get home, and so you nead not save money for me but look out for yourself I do not mean that I want you to spend evry sent that you get but be prudant of money & of health for we cannot tell what may turn up yet no man can tell how long he may live, nor no one knows how soon he may die espeshley hear in the armey. Well Sis I got a letter awhile ago with som thred & nedels in it and the one that I got this morning has got som tea in it. You nead not send me anything of any acount for we can get what we want hear great deal cheaper then you can send it and then you do not know what we do want down hear you seam to think that we are short for evrything but is not so we are better provided for then the men are at home that is with what a soldier wants. Well Sis I will stop for this time so Good By My Dear Wife & Child

Guy C. Taylor

Afternoon

Dear Wife

As Christmas is a day of rest to me I do not know of any better way of spending time away pleasantly then by writeing to you. You say that the Lodge is agoine to try to have som kinde of a doings new years, well I am in hopes that they will, and if they do, I am in hopes, that it will be a party of peoples that has com togeather to injoy themself and the pleasure of this world, and not onley injoy it for amusement but may it be conducted in such a manor that they can injoy it for improvement. I wish it was so I cood be presant at the meating to injoy it with you but then I am contented to stay hear untill this wickard rebelion is put down but then it is a pleasure to me to hear that the folks are not asleap at home. We as soldiers have a duty to do hear in the field, you allso have a duty to proform at home, while

we are in active servase a trying to overcom our Country fow, it is your duty
as friends of temprance and Good Templers to be in active servace against
thoes enemys that has for their leader King Alcohall. I can say for one that
I know that we cannot take to much pains nor do to much for the caus of
Temprance, and let me say if you had seen one half of the horable deads
that is caused by the effects of licker that I have you wood say that we cood
not do anough for the Temprance caus. I have seen men made to cary a
heavy stick of wood untill they wood fall under the wait of it, and seen them
punished in all maners of waies, but iev seen officers lay beastely drunk in
the mud and water but that is nothing for they are men of som importance.
Yes it is alrite in the eyes of som for officers to go into battle and lead men
into all kinds of danger when their is no use of it, meny a brave boy have
fell by being lead on to battle by whiskey, but thank God som of the coman-
ders get their pay for their conduck we lost one Genral by his being so brave
he was agoine to send the picket line out to see wheir the rebs was and as
he was trying to make the men obay his order he had a ball put threw his
arm it wood be a great blessing if evry drunking officer wood get the same
(I cannot call any names for I am onley a private), but I am in hopes that I
may live to see the time that I can be alowed to speak what I think, and if I
am promited to live to see this war at a end and to return home wonce more
to injoy domestic life I shell be better prepaired to stand the strife of the
world. Well I will have to close this for it is geting to be lait and I want it to
go out tonite.

So I will close By Biding you
Good By

Guy C. Taylor

NOTE
   1. The use of badges was first attributed to Union Maj Gen Philip Kearney who supplied them to those in his division. Later, Maj Gen Joseph Hooker adopted the idea after
he assumed command of the Army of the Potomac. The badges were very useful for unit
identification. They were originally worn by soldiers on the top of their kepi, on the left
side of their hat, or over their left breast (Faust, *Historical Times Illustrated Encyclopedia
of the Civil War*, 184).

In camp 5 miles South west of Petersburg Va
December the 28 1864

Dear Wife

As todays mail brot me good nuse from home I thought that I wood be prompt in answering it so I sit myself down to write a few lines to you to repeat the same sed words (that I am well) I am vary glad to know that you all are injoying such good health. I expect that you are now a having nice slaying while we are a walling in the mud it has raine evry little while gust anough to keep it all splash. Today it was vary pleasant but tonite it rains again and it looks as so we was agoine to have a long rain, but we cannot tell for one day it is rainey or cold and the next day it is plesant and vary warm.

Dec. the 29

Today it is quite cold and a few flaiks of snow is seen falling but onley now and then a flaik. I do not know of any nuse to tell you except the Sad nuse of the death of Docter Miller. He was our head docter he died on the 20 at his own home it is a sevear lost for our reg. He had the confident of the men and the men did of him. I expect that Docter Woodard will com in head Surgant now of the reg. You sed that you had received $10.28 from Chipman now I want you to let me know now what was don with that lumber that I had up by the well in a crib wheather it was got by any of your folks or wheather Chipman made use of it or not for if he made use of it he will pay for it. I have written to him and it was a rather plain letter but he will get a plainer one if he dos not send me that money. He may think as he pleases about it, if he dos not pay it to me he will pay it to a lawyer. I do not want you to take a sent from him now. If you get short for money take that you have and use it. I think that I can send you som bime by for most likely Chipman will pay me before long. Day after tomorrow we will muster for pay again and they most all think that we will get our pay by the middle of next month and I am in hopes that we will for I have rather that you wood have the money then to have it in the hands of the govarment for if you have it you can have it to use when you do nead it. Well Sis I must close for this time and go to work about the horses so good By
From Your husband

Guy C. Taylor

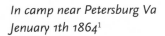

In camp near Petersburg Va
Jenuary 1th 1864[1]

My Dear Wife

As today is the first day of the year, I thought that I wood write a few lines to you to let you know that the new year found for me to do the first thing was to get up about one oc in the nite and catch a horse that broke loose, after that I had a good sleep and gust at the Braik of day in com the Docter and says that he has got to go out on picket and that he wanted me to go with him so up I got and fed the horses and saddled the Docks horse and he sed that I wood have to take the mule so on went the saddle and he com down and sed that we had got to go up to the Bregade headquarters to be inspected so on we went and you can guess how I look on a old mule goine to be inspected but then it was allrite it was gust what I wanted, anything for fun, so when we got started I put spurs to my long eard animel and swung my hat and call out for the Docter to com on. Their was men all around and it made a purfect rore break out among the men. Well we got threw the inspection and started for the picket line, and got their at 10 oc and I returned back and got the Docters dinner and took it to him, and now I am with him. We are in a house in the rear of the pickets wheir the resurve lays the house is quite a large building the Famley that owns the plais is living in it their is a old man and two wimmen and one little girl. They appear to be prety smart folks the wimon in purticular the old man he dos not seam dispose to talk much. I do not know but you wood like to know what sort of a room we have to stay in well it is a large squir room with one bed in it vary nice one, one beaurow with a large revolving looking glass on it, one Secutary with two com on glasses on two tables, good meny books, sevral picturs haning up, a large fireplais and a good roaring fire in it now you have the apperance of the room made, if you can gust immagen how I wood look sitting by the table a writeing you wood have a correct Ide of my situation. The Docter and one Leeutenant, one Caption and the old Sitison are a sitting around the fireplais and talking about the war. The men and officers all agree on one thing that is that war is most at a close, but then we cannot tell when the last battle will be fort but I hope before long. Oh . . . I guess you wood like to know how long I have got to stay on picket we have to stay 3 days but I wride to camp 3 times a day for my grub and

the Docters. We will have a jolley time of it down hear. I wood not cair if
they wood let ous stay hear all winter. Well I must close for this time so I
will Bid you a happy new years and good By

From your Husband

Guy C. Taylor

NOTE
1. The date "1864" should be "1865."

⌒

NO. 34

In Camp Near Petersburg
Jenuary the 4th 1864[1]

My Dear Wife

I have received two letters from you since I last wrote but the reason that
I did not answer the first one was that I had gust sent one to you. I was vary
glad to hear that you are all well. When I wrote to you last I was out on the
picket line and we have gust bin releived so I thought that I wood write a few
lines to you to let you know that I am well and had a good time on the picket
line. We was in a hous wheir their was a famaly in it. The ladyes (if they cood
be call so) was great hands to talk but you know that I had nothing to say for
I am afraid of wimmon kind. Well Sis you say that it dos not look as though
the war was vary near the end by their calling out the 300,000 more men.[2]
I think that will be one of the greatist helps that we can get for they will get
into the armey before spring and it will let the rebs know that we can rais
men yet when they are cut short. You cannot find a officer but what thinks
that we will all be home by next fall surtian and most of them think that they
will com to turms by spring, for they will see that we have filled up our ranks
again and they cannot get any men to speak of to go into their armey for they
have got them all now, and they are getting whipt on all sids and are not
gaining anything in anything whatever. They have had all their best land run
over and all the produse distroyed that was laid up for the armey now flower
is $400 dollars a barrel in Petersburg, and good meny cannot get it at that
prise. The man told me, wheir we was on picket that 8 weeks ago he solt
potatoes at 60 dollars a bushel tea sugar & coffee they cood not get at any
prise, but they can get all they want now but not at Petersburg but at Unkle

Sams depot for they have com into our lines by our lines being advanced. It seams rather hard for a little girl that is their it is the old folks grandchild. The childs parrents went into North Caralina to see some of their relations and before they got their viset out they found that their plais had com into our lines, and they cannot get back again but the child seams to be gay & hapy. She is 6 years old and she is as smart as a whip allmost evry time that any of the officers com in that has bin their before brings hur somthing. I ment to have written you a new years letter but my being down on the picket line I cood not get any time to write but I will try and a little diffrance one from this in a day or two, so you will have to wait untill next new years for a new years letter. Well I will draw this to a close By

    Biding You Good By
    From Your Husband

Guy C. Taylor

NOTES
    1. The date "1864" should be "1865."
    2. Lincoln's last call, made during the winter of 1864–65, was for one-year men.

In camp 5 miles south West of Petersburg Va
Jenuary the 6th 1865

My Dear Wife

(Seat by our little writeing stand) I once more take my seat by our little writeing stand for the purpose of writeing a few lines to you to let you know that I am well and am injoying myself as well as I can being away from home. I got a bugget from you last nite and som of the thing com vary good to me, as I am most out of hanchiefs & towals and the needle book is gust what I wanted, but the Scarfe is not of any use to me and I will send it back by mail again for it is worth paying postage on and in case we had to march I wood have to throw it away. You thought most likely that we had to bundle up to keepe warme but it is not so, the most of the time we have to leave off our coats, we are not in Wis. we have not seen as much as one inch of snow yet and it dos not look as though we shood see any eather, for it is a raining like fun now, and as warm as summer is in Wisconsin. I have gust got back from seeing a man shot for desurting from his post on picket.[1] It is anything but a pleasant site to see, but then it is natral for me to want to

see evrything that is agoine on, but I do not think that I shell go to see
another man shot but then I shell go and see one hung if it so that I can.
Their is one or more hung or shot evry Fryday at the Corps headquarters.
Well Sis I do not know of anything to write about it is all one thing hear we
are in winter quarters now and all that we can see is the men and the tents
and teams their is about 100 teams go past hear twise a day to draw wood
and it makes nice roads now I can tell, mud gust about one foot deap all
along the road and then wheir their is a little hollow the mud has not got
any bottom to it. You have written about that money of Chipmans you say
that he has not paid you yet. I do not think the he will eather for I have
wrote to him to send it to me gust as quick as he cood after he got my letter
and it is most time for me to get a answer from him. I give him to understand that he must pay what was rite for the plowing and pay for the wood
that I drawed up their, if he dos not send it to me before a great while I shell
write to him again and then if he dos not send it I shell write to somone
elces and see if it can be corlected, but then I am in hopes that he will pay
it without any fuss but if he dos not, fuss it is and we will see who will com
out the best in the end. Well Sis I guess that you had not better try to send
me anything unless I send word to you what to send you seam to think that
we are a suffering down hear it is not so, you cannot tell what we want at
all you mite put up a box of stuff and send to me and I wood have to throw
it all away if we had to march if we did not go over two miles. We do not
want for anything scursely. We can get evrything that we want hear but it
cost som more. Now thoes hanchiefs wood cost $1.50 apease. They com
vary good for I had not onley one and that is pretty well woren, but then I
know you thought that what you sent wood com good to me. Well Sis it
is gust as well it will not cost much to send that scarf back again, and I
know that you had rather have me send it back then to throw it away. Well
you must be vary carfull of your health and not go to work roaling logs ore
piling up wood for if you do I am afraid that you will pay dear for it well
must close for this time write soon from your husband

Guy C. Taylor

NOTE

1. According to James Aubery's history of the Thirty-Sixth Wisconsin, the soldier
who was executed was from the 184th Pennsylvania Infantry. Aubery states, "The whole
division was ordered out to see the execution so that they might see the penalty for desertion" (*Thirty-Sixth Wisconsin Volunteer Infantry*, 204).

❧

In Camp Near Petersburg Va
Jenuary the 8th 1865

My Dear Wife

I once more take my pen in hand to let you know that I am injoying the vary Best of health. We are a having a vary good time of it this winter. We have got a vary nise camp the tents are fix up in the vary best of way. They are bilt of log and plasterd up in good shape and evry tent has got a good fireplais in it. You may think that it is owine to the cold weather, the reason that we go into winter quarters but it is not so, for it is not cold anough to do any hurt about marching or laying on the ground, but the truble is it is rany weather and the soil is so that they cannot draw any artilary, the wagons wood sink rite down to the hub on the dryest land, so you can see by that it wood not be vary nise in hollows and on low land and they have to go threw swails and cricks when they go out on a rade, for it wood not look well to go rite on a main road to make a rade, for the rebs wood soon stop your advance, but by goine on a by-rode they do not know what way to look for ous. Well Sis their has bin a order sent to our Divison headquarters to have me detailed by the div. Docter and if I am I shell be allrite. If I get the plais it will be threw the influance of our Docter. Woodard was the won that sent my name their. Woodard has don the fair thing by me evry since I have bin in the armey and it has bin a vast amount of help to me, for I am surtain that I cood never stand it to cary a gun and all the rest of the luggage, and what is the reason I do not know unless it is owine to the climet but let me march with the belts and the knapsacks on I cannot hardely breath but I am allrite when I do not have any load to cary. I am getting to be vary fleashey and I somtime think it wood be a good thing to go at work and wair off som of my flesh. I never was as fleashey as I am now I guess that I will way as much 165 lbs. Well Sis we have lost our Chaplain[1] he has got his discharge his wife is sick and his Son has inlisted since he com into the armey, so it has left his famley without anyone to look after them so he thought that he wood resine and go home and stay with that women of his she cannot bair to hav hur man out in the field poor delacot creather she must be but other wimon can part with their husband & son and that is nothing but then anough of that so I will close by Biding you good By from your husband

Guy C. Taylor

NOTE

1. Chaplain Peter S. Van Nest from Geneva, Wisconsin, was discharged January 6, 1865. He was honorably mentioned in the official report of the Battle of Hatcher's Run, Virginia, October 27, 1864 (Aubery, *Thirty-Sixth Wisconsin Volunteer Infantry*, 293, 393).

NO. 35 RECEIVED NO. 35

In camp near Petersburg Va
Jenuary the 11th 1865

My Dear Wife

I have received two letters from you since I have written and one from Mother Thompson but they all com in a heap togeather with two from Chipman makeing 5 at one time. You may be ashuar that it was a pleasure to me to get such a mail, and what made it more pleasant was to hear that you are all well, my health is vary good and I am injoying myself first rate. I wrote to you in my last that I soon expected to be detaled by the Commander of the Divition.[1] The papers got back to the docter in fore days after they war sent so I know now what my reglar buiseness will be the other one that was detaled is acting ordely or clurk. He is a vary good pensman but then he is vary carless and forgetfull and in case he is not more carfull he will have to go back into the ranks and if he dos it will fall on me to pick up the pen. It will not be a vary bludy weppen but it may be a vary sharp pointed one. I have got into a good plais now and I am vary much indebted to Docter Woodard for it, he has bin a friend to me that is worthey to be call a friend, and I am bown to do the duty that he wants me to do in such a shape that he will be satified with it. It will not be onley a pleasure to him but it will be a great help to me far better then money to, for it is gust such a school as I had ort to go to and I mean to make it pay me well. I think that this war will com to an end in the coars of time and I am in hopes that I may be premited to return home again and if I do I want it to say that the armey has bin a great help to me in room of a curs. I think that I have not lost anything yet by coming into the armey, to be shure it has bin pretty losom by spells for me, and I know that you have seen prety sorfull times, more so then what I have. I have not seen the day yet that I felt sorrow that I inlisted on my acount when I hurd that you was sick I did wish that I had never sined my name to any armey book but it was on acount of my wanton to be at home with you. You have got along and I do not know but what you got along as well as you wood if I had bin at home, allthough it wood bin a great pleasure to both of ous if it had bin so we cood have seen one another and it is so in evry state yea in evry town that their is thoes that wants to see their loved ones at home again but then we must think that we have got a duty to do and we shood be willing to do it let it be evry so hard. Well sis you say that H.L. has fell in love with a girl and he is vary unhappy becaus his mar dont want him to marey hur prehaps his mar has not ween him yet, and if such be the case I do not blaim hur any for it must be vary hard for a mother to nurse two at a time. Well sis your pa did not feal vary happy when we was mared but I do not think that made much diffance but then he has not had to nurse both of ous vary much yet and my plan is that he will not have to. Well good By

From your husband

Guy C. Taylor

Chipman has written to me about that money and he is agoine to send me som of it rite away I expect that I shell get it before you get this Mart is afraid that I am a little mad and she well mite think so for so I was.

NOTE
   1. The commander of the Second Division, Second Army Corps was Maj Gen John Gibbon.

NO. I DONT KNOW I GUESS 37 [*NOTE:* TAYLOR SKIPPED NO. 36.] RECEIVED 38

Laying around in the woods in VA
January the 11th 1865 [Note: Taylor used this date on the previous letter.]

My Dear Wife

As we have gust stop for a time I do not know for how long, but at any rate I thought that I wood scrible a few lines and in case we had to moove again before I cood get threw, I wood have so much don anyway. Evrything is all still except the axes they are laying down the timber at a fearfull rate. Since last Sunday their has bin a good meny miles of works built and hundreds of acors of heavy timber layed low, wheirever our armey goes evrything is stript not a schrub left to show that any human man ever dwealt their unless the folks stay on their farms and take the oath of alegents and then they will have their house garded but all of the fences is made into wood to keep the boys warm it burns so much better then green pine and then it is easer to be got. Well Sis as I sit hear a writeing the little fires that the boys has built to cook their coffee is filling the woods with smoke, and as for my situation it is a vary pleasant one my seat is the ground which makes a vary stoute seat, the Back is one of the principal things in Va that is a large pine tree, and for a writeing table I have a narrow pease of a board (part of a cracker box) with my paper in my lap my ink stand sets on the same seat with me, and in frunt of me is one of our boys coffee fires. Well Sis we have had rather a hard time since last Sunday but then thoes that has got along untill now all saft and well has not a word of complaint to offer allthough our reg. has not bin in any fite eather we have not lost onley two men they was eather killed or taken prisiners on the picket line. They was out their and the rebs drove them in they let two heavy volleys into our boys but they shot at random and when our boys avanced again they cood not see any sines wheir their had bin any killed but then it is most probale that they was taken prisiners at least I hope so for if they are in the hands of the rebels they will stand som show for their lives, but then I wood try my luck at runing before I wood stop and give up, for I do not cair anything about goine to Richmon to try my hand their but then their is not much danger of my bein taken for in time of battle I have to go back to the rear wheir they cary out the wounded, so all the danger I am in is the shells that somtimes burst all around ous the shells dos more harm in the rear then they do in the frunt for they go to the rear so in case we are driven back that we cannot get back without geting orfulley cut to peases by them. We have made another moove we went som 10 rods and the boys are all at work falling timber. We are agoine into camp hear we have got a fine line of works to lay behind and then their is any amount of timber so it will not be onley 4 or 5 days before we will have another camp as good as the old one was but it is on the frunt line[1] now and before it was on the flanking line,[2] but then it dos not make much diffrance for our picket line will be som ¾ of a mile from the works and then we are so far from the town that their is not any Picket fireing goine on, and then the boys has got so they do not cair about shooting one another. Well Sis I suppose that you have hurd all about the fite before now and you will know a good deal more about it then what we will down hear for a while that is how it com out in the end of coars we know more about how the battle was conducted then what you can know. I know that I have seen all of this fite that I caired about seeing and I know vary little about this fite. I see som 80 or 90 wounded and sevral that was killed. I help fix up one grave he was a man in our Bregade and he has the name of being a nice man and splended soldier he leaves a wife and two Children he belong to the 69 NY. We are a having vary fine weather hear now it is vary warm and pleasant but then fine weather dos not write fine letters I know and you will think so to when you read this. I have had to gump up and run to another plais as much as a duzen times on acount of the trees a falling. Well I must get again.

So good By for this time
From your husband
In the woods

Guy C. Taylor

NOTES
    1. The main battle line of a military unit.
    2. The right or left battle line of a military unit.

◞

NO. 40 [*NOTE:* TAYLOR SKIPPED NO. 38 AND NO. 39.] RECEIVED NO. 39

In Camp on the Armstrong farm
January 13th 1865

My Dear Wife

I received your long wished for letter yesterday and was glad to hear that you are all well. We have seen som rough times for a few days past but then it is all over with now and we are in camp again, allthough it dos not look vary nice yet but in a few days it will be a pleasant camp. The officers tents are all up and a good meny of the mens tents, as I stop with the Docter I am allrite as soon as any of them but then we have to have a house to cook our grub in and for the others to sleap in so it takes me quite a spell to get threw fusing about fixing up. You say that you have not got a letter from me for a week. I have writen reglar but then the mail has not bin reglar for evry little while. The mail boat will get stop by the eice in the river. I get two of your letters to a time somtimes I have had them com so sevral times. You say that you have bin to the lodge sevral times when their was not any I do not think that it will pay to lug that boy down to the School hous meny times for nothing it wood not pay me I know but then you know better then I do wheather it pays you or not, but let me say look out for health for all of anything elces, and injoyment the next thing. I wood like to discribe our lines of works and our Camp but I cannot do it for I do not know how the lines run onley rite in frunt of our bregade but it will not be meny days before I shell have plenty time to run around and then I shell think that I am at home again. I am geting so that I like soldiering first rate but then I wood prefur to be at home. I do not think that I will enter the reglar armey when the war is over allthough they are paying a large bounty 1000.00 dollars in gold 6 hundred down, but gold has no charm for me, in that way at any rate. I wood like the gold well anough but then I do not want to be bound out for know five years, it is most to long to suit my fancy. I think that when my 3 years are up I will try to work under another boss allthough Unkle Sam is not a vary hard master but then I do not take a fancy to the word master for I have seen a plenty of that down hear and if I live to get back north again I am in hopes that I shell not hear the word again, for the vary word is anough to curs anyplais I do not cair how holey a plais it is. I got a letter from George today he is well so is Add.[1] She is rather fleashey I guess, for she says she can roal one way as well as the other. It may be that the climate agrees with hur up north. The climate may be better but the soil I do not think is any better. I have hurd from all of our folks except from Williams and I hurd from them by the way of Amandy. They are all well all around the sap bush except down in old Va. I am trying to write and the docter has punched the fire untill it has all gorn out and my fingers are so cold I cannot scarsely write and I guess you cannot read it eather, but then I do not think but what I will be well again after holding my fingers to the fire for a little while, so I will stop writeing and try that kind of medison to see if it will not cure me.

January 14

I again will try to pen a few more lines. I have got well again you may think that it took me a long while to warm my fingers but when I had got warmed I had to go away and I did not have any more time to write, but I am well today and I will try to finish this sheat of paper. You say that their was a party at your plais and it give you a sick headache. Well I do not know what you will have to do unless you gust take hold and play your part in the plais. That will be as good medison as you can take. You must gust go to all of the parties that you can it will not hurt you in the least and see if you cannot be as smart as any of them. I well know how it is with you becaus I am not with you, you think that it will make talk in case you go

around much but who cairs about a little talk if folks has nothing elces
to do let them talk about ous for a while they will have to let somone elces
have a resting spell if they do. Their is nothing more unhealthy then to gust
settle down in one house and not stur out of it wonce a month, but go
whenever you can get a chance to, and you will find out that you can injoy
yourself better and you will feal Better. Well I will not scold any more at
present for fear you may get snuffey at me and that wood be a bad go. You
say that you wish you had som papers to send to me as for papers we get
them reglar now their is a nuse boy threw evryday and then we can get all
of the religest papers that we want at the Christian Commisioners so we are
well suplied with reading matters. It rather looks now that we have got to
fite som more yet before we have pease. Well I was in hopes that they wood
settle the thing up so to stop fiteing but it looks as so the south was not redy
to com back yet but then they will soon find out that they have got more
then they have bargin for, for our armey was never any stronger then it
is now and the southern is groine weeker evryday. They are loosing men
now vary fast by their coming over to our side of the lines they say that
they know that their is no pease yet and they have made up their minds
not to fite any longer. The south have got into a hard state their is no show
for them but to give up and the soldiers want to give up. Their is no hard
fealings between the southern soldiers and our soldiers they all are alike
that is on the pease qustion but the leaders in the south is the rooling
power. The private south dair not say a word to have it get out to the
officers. You may think it is a big story but the boys has bin out for wood in
frunt of the videts² on both sides and our boys have lent their axes to the
southern boys and they have borrowed & lent on both sides and have sat
and talk togeather for hours on frendley turms. Well I am in hopes that this
coming summer will bring the thing to a close and I think it will and without much fiteing to. We have got to whip them a few times and they will
then try for pease on a difrance scale from indipendents. Well Sis I must
close and go to work and build my fireplais so we can have a diffrance plais
to cook So good By

From your Husband Guy C. Taylor

NOTES
1. "Add" referred to Taylor's sister-in-law, Adaline, who was married to brother
George.
2. A *vidette* was a horse-mounted picket.

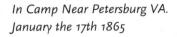

In Camp Near Petersburg VA.
January the 17th 1865

My Dear Wife,

I received your kind letter last nite and was vary happy to hear that you are all well and after takeing a long Ramble this fore noon I thought that I wood write a few lines to you to let you know that I am injoying good health. Well Sis, I have bin out on the picket line this morning, and went along the line about 4 miles, Mr. Heart, was with me. We did not know wheir our boys did lay and it made us a long walk before we found them but we did not cair for that, for we went out gust to see what their was to be seen, and we was well paid for our ramble for we went wheir we cood see how the armey was laying. We went upon a foart and look around and it was a site to behold, to look upon the Soldiers Sity. It is a great sity to and it is laid out in vary neat form it is laid out in one main body and then wings all around it and each wing consist of one bregade containing from 9 two 12, reg, and each reg. is laid out by its own commander and they are laid out in streats each Company by themselves as the barrets are at Madison, onley in room of barrets we have little log cabins 4 in each and they all try and see how neat they can make them, and rite in the rear of the compern-ers are the officers quarters they have large canvass tents and the streats are all set out with roas of little pines on each side both by the officers and private streats. Their is some 4 corpals that think they are the ruler of the euniverst and they will get men punished for nothing at all and they get prety badley punished for it to somtimes. Their was one sargent in our reg. that was to big for his own good he began to insult a man that stood on gard and the man did not give him any caus for so doing at all, and as the man was walking his beat the man stept up towards him a little to clost for the gard brot around the but of his gun and took the sarg. rite over the Skull plait and he fell like a ded man on went the gard gust so he knew nothing of it at all some of the boys pick him up and took him into a tent and they soon brot him two but the joke of it was he did not dair to arrest the gard he was afraid that he wood get a harder nock another time so he let it drop, and bore the pain of a soar head. You say that you will do as you have got a mind to about sending stuff to me, well I know that wimmon will have their own way when they can get a chance but then you nead not send me any more tea unless you want to for we now are a drawing tea evry little while and we keep som on hand all the time now. I think we will get tea the rest of the winter evry few days. I am vary much ablidge to you for what you have sent for it has com vary good to me and not onley that it com vary good to one of the boys that was sick. I like the tea but then I had rather give it to a sick boy then to drink it myself so I give him almost the hole of what you sent in fore letters. I am a going to have me a good cup of drink from that you sent in your last letter. Well sis you nead not think anything strange if Chipmans folks are mad at you but then I do not think that they will be mad at you. They are vary foolish if they are, allthough Chipman and I have had som prety hard words by letter and he has com to the conclusion that it is best to send what he owes ous to me I have got 7 dollars in one letter and I think that I will get another letter from them before you get this. Well sis I must close by bidding you good by.

From your husband

Guy C. Taylor

❧

NO. I DO NOT KNOW I GUESS 38 [*NOTE:* TAYLOR USED NO. 40 ON THE LAST NUMBERED LETTER; HOWEVER, NO. 38 WOULD HAVE BEEN THE NEXT NUMBER IN SEQUENCE.]

In Camp near Petersburg Va
January 21th 1865

My Dear Wife

It is with pleasure that I sit myself down, to while away a part of this stormey day in pening a few words to you to let you know that you are not forgoten by one that is far away from home . . . and from the ones that he loves. Allthough we are not promitted to see one another at the presant time, we can make time pleasant to ous both by the use of the pen. If it had not bin for the meny good and incurageing letters that I have received from home I cood not have pass away this last Season as pleasantly as I have. As long as I know that you are all well at home, and are injoying yourself as well as the ocation will purmit, I am contented to stay in the field, and can injoy myself I do not cair so much about the hardships of a campain. I was not blind when I inlisted. I expected to see hard times and I have not bin at all disappointed for we have seen that which trys what a man is, but for all that, I say and I know it to be a fact, that men can injoy life, and pass away time pleasantly in under the sirumstances that we have bin under this last campain it is in the power of man to make heaven of Hell or Hell of Heaven, so their is no use of men growling about a little hardship as long as they and theirs are injoying good health. I am in hopes that it will not be long before the armey can be disbanded and the men return once more to their peaseful homes, wheir they can injoy the comferts of private life. Well Sis you had som trying times but you must try to hold up good curaage and look forward for better days to com.

Jan. 22

As I did not have time to finish my letter last nite I thought that I wood write a little more today. The Storm has seased and it is vary pleasant this morning overhead, but rather mudy under foot but then it is vary good a getting around. You say that I have sent som letters that I did not number if so it was missake in me. I have a good deal of writeing to do and when I write a letter I am in a hurrey for I do not know but what I may be call on to do somthing elces, so I write as fast as I can and do not hardely know what I do write half of the time, last week I received ten letters I write one evry day and somtimes two & three. Well Sis have you had 2 dollars off Father Taylor, Chipman ses you have, he and I have had som words about our setling and I want you to let me know gust to a sent the amount that you have received in money and what has bin turned he has sent me the amount and I want it from you to. I think that it is allrite but then I will be better sattified with his account after hearing yours. He may think that he can send me any word that he has amind to and that I will beleive it and I shood if we had had a fair understanding about evrything, but if a purson tryes to play a mean trick on me once I do not know but what he will again if he can get a chance to. As I sit a writeing to you, the Drums are a beating to call out the men on inspection. Well Sis I have had to stop writeing for a few minuits and let the docter have the chair for a man to sit in to have a tooth pulled but it was quick don (and he did not hollow one half as loud as you did when you had one pulled at the crick) but then I presume it did not pull as hard. Well Sis I have sent back that scarfe for it is no use to me and it is worth more then the postage will be, so you can do what you have a mind to do with it. You say that you will send gust what you have a mind to, well if you do send me anything that I dont want I will send it back again and you will have to pay for it (now that what is the matter) and I guess that you will soon get sick of that dar. Well you must not scold me for not writeing oftener for I have not had time this last week to answer all the letters. I have bin a runing around a good deal partely for my own amusement and som for the Docter. It is gust good healthy work that I have to do when I go anywheirs I can ride or go a foot gust as I pleas when I take a ramble I go a foot and go wheir a horse cood not go on acount of works and brush. I think that I shell take a tramp again tomorrow or nex day down on the picket line again to see what is goine on down their. Their is more or less rebs coming in evry day they are sent north by the hundreds evry week this last week it is reported that their was 6 hundred com into sity point to go north their was 15 com in our bregade day before yesterday and som com in yesterday I do not know how meny I see two that com pass hear and they all tell one story that is they are whiped and their is no use in the south trying to hold out any longer the boys are deturmen to desert as fast as they can and then the famleys are allmost starving, flower is worth 5 hundred dollars per barrel and it is hard to be got at that potatoes 100 dollars per bushell so you can see that poor folks must suffer for want of food, but then it is the south own falt for being so redused, but then it is vary hard to see little Children crying for bread, but such is war and we cannot expect anything elcse.

Well I will close By Biding you good by

From your Husband

Guy C. Taylor

Excuse this small sheat of paper for I cood not get one any larger but I will try and get a larger one next time. Take good cair of our pet Charley.

∽

NO. 39

In camp Near Petersburg Va
January the 24th 1865

My Dear Wife

I wonce more will try to scratch a few lines to you to let you know that I am well, and I am in hopes that theas few lines will find you injoying the same good Blessing. I have not much to write for I have not bin anywheirs to see anything nor have I hurd much, I write this mealy to let you know that I am well, & to let you know that I have written reglar but, I do not know as you have got them or not. I have not got a letter for a week now. You see their has bin a hard storm and the boats cood not cross the Chestipeek Bay,[1] so it stops all of the mail, and then it is rumard the mail boat that was coming this way was sunk by the storm and if that is the case we will not get what mail their was in the boat I am afraid untill it gets wet, (if we do at all) you see the watter is rather deep in the sea. Well Sis their was a orfull nois last nite the rebs run down the river with 3 gun boats and their was a orfull Canonadeing, it has bin repoarted that all 3 of the boats was disstroid and then another repoart is that one of them was sunk and the other 2 got away so we do not know yet what the result of the fite is, but we will be apt to hear by twomorrow, we have had a vary hard rain and it has made it prety hard a getting around with a teem but then it has cleard off and the wind blows prety hard and the son is vary warm so it will not be long before the sand is a flying again. Well Sis I have bin a casting up the amount of money it cost to keep our reg. in whiskey & tobaco and I call the reg. 300 men it has gust about avage that, that has staid in the field, tobaco for 300 men for one year 3,760.00 for whiskey, 2,907.48 making $6,747.48 cts. dollars for one year. At that rate what dos it cost the hole armey, and then they all say that I put the estermate 2 cents per day to little, but then I have got it high anough to satify me, that I do not want eather artical to youse. I can spend money fast anough and not bye stuff that will do me more hurt then good, their has som of the boys, spent $50 dollars and run in debt to the Sutlars from $35 to $50, since they was paid off, it seams to me as so I had paid out a large amount of money but I am not quite so bad as that allthough I have run in debt $18.40 for a pair of boots $2 for gloves and the rest is for paper and invelops and eatables you can guess wheather I have wrote any letters or not. I have bot 3 and ½ quire of paper 3 bunches of invelops since we was paid and I am most out again but I think that I will go over to the Senatores and get a mess of such stuff. I can get it their by goine for it, it is not vary good paper but then it dos not pay to give 50 cents a quire, when I can get that for nothing. It is late and I will close and finish this tomorrow so good nite my Dear.

January 25th 1865

Well Sis I once more seat myself to write a few lines more. I have gust bin a choping wood for the tent and have got anough to last ous two days so I will not have any more to do, except to write, I do not know as I shell

do much of that for I do not get any mail and I will not write when I do
not get letters except to you so you had better be carfull and write often or
I may say the same to you (but I guess not) well Sis I wrote in my last that
I was agoine to go down on the picket line again but it stormed so bad
that I have not bin but I now think that I shell go tomorrow if the weather
is fair it is warm and vary pleasant today and it is geting pretty good rodes
again except in low plaises. It dos not take more then 2 or 3 fair days to dry
up the worst kind of roads, the soil is all sand and the watter goes rite down.
Well I do not know of anything new to write we had a vary noisey camp last
nite but that is nothing new, for men will get drunk if they are officers and
when drunk they are nothing more then any other drunken man, and they
vary often find it out to be so to, the other day one of the Captains of the 36
reg., was in the Sutlars shop and their came in two boys from a new york
reg. and the Capt tryed to put them out of the tent they went out without
any fuss and then they daired the Capt to tuch them, so out com the great
Magnificent Officer, and went to draw his swoard and one of the boys steps
rite to his side and told him with an oath, if he drew his swoard on him he
wood kill him and Whiskey shrunk away like a whip dog, and took the
officer with it I wood like to have seen him drawn his swoard for if he had
he wood bin laying on the ground the next he new and the swoard in the
hands of another with the point clost to his brest, if not clost to his heart,
if we had two or three of the officers shot when they was in a spree it wood
be a blessing to the 36 reg. and it mite save the lives of a great meny men
the most of the men that has bin kill in the 36, has bin don by whiskey and
it is a good deal so with other regaments. I have gust seen two boys that
belongs to the 37 reg. they say that James Spencer[2] is well I shell try to go
down their in a few days they are about 6 miles from ous. They are in the
frunt line. They are wheir we was awhile ago by Foart Rise. Well Sis I wrote
in my last about your sending me the amount of money that you have
received from George Chipman and I will say again for fear that you have
not got my other letter that I want you to send me the whole amount that
you have received in money or any other way. I have writen to Chipman
about the pay and I have got som from him and I think that he will send
me som more after a little. I wrote a vary plain letter to them and Mart was
orfull afraid that I was mad and the next letter that I wrote I guess that she
new that I was, at any rate I ment that they wood knowit. I give him to
understand that I was not ded if I am in the armey and that I am not afraid
to talk neather. Well Sis I am in the best plais that I cood get in to injoy

myself and I do it to the best of my ability. I have had som gay times with the officers. We have got a Checker Board at our tent and the Docter has played with me som and I can beat him most evrytime, so he began to call in others and I have stood fast yet. Capt Potter[3] is the hardest one to play with yet that I have tryed. They have got so they com in most evry nite to play. Their is the Colonel[4] & Mager and 2 Captains and the Docter all play-ing against me, and it makes the eavens pass away pleasantly and they like to bother Potter for he has blowed that he cood whip anyone that was in the reg. and it rather takes him down a little, to be beeten. Well sis you must try to make time pass away as pleasantly as you can untill I get back home again and I am in hopes that will not be vary long but then we cannot tell. Well I will close

  By Biding You Good By
  From Your Husband

Guy C. Taylor

NOTES

1. From the start of the Civil War, Chesapeake Bay was one of the most important bodies of water in the United States. The capitals of both the Confederacy and the Union sat next to bay tributaries—Richmond, Virginia, on the James River and Washington, D.C., on the Potomac River. Access to the Chesapeake Bay enabled both sides to receive shipped goods and transport troops, and to strike the enemy deep within their territory.

2. Capt James Spencer, Thirty-Seventh Wisconsin Regiment.

3. Capt Wesley S. Potter, Co. D, Thirty-Sixth Wisconsin Regiment (Aubery, *Thirty-Sixth Wisconsin Volunteer Infantry*, 302).

4. Lt Col Clement E. Warner, Madison, Wisconsin, Thirty-Sixth Wisconsin Regiment (ibid., 293, 335–37).

NO. 39 [NOTE: TAYLOR USED THIS NUMBER ON THE PREVIOUS LETTER.] RECEIVED NO. 36

In Camp Near Petersburg Va
January 27th 1865

My Dear Wife

I received your long wished for letter on the eave of the 25. I sent one to you on the same day, and now it gives me pleasure to sit and write a few words more to let you know that it is all well with me at presant. My health is vary good. I do not know as I ever felt any better then what I do this

winter, (that is in body) and I feal vary contented to stay in the field for I
want to see the end of this war and I do varley believe that we will see the
end of it in a short time from now. You want to know what I did do on the
picket line (well I will try to tell you) you see the pickets are a line of men
that gards the whole armey. They are out in frunt of the armey vary in distance acorden to circumstance from 60 rods to 4 miles. Wheir we are now
it is two miles. They have officers over the pickets each officer has so meny
post, the post are about ten rods apart 6 or 4 men at a post. Then their is
a officer of the day that has a charg over the bregade he goes along the line
3 times a day the leanth of his bregade and then their is a officer of the day
that has charg over the whole divition he goes along the line once a day and
the other officers has to repoart to him when they go along the lines. Then
their is one docter that goes as near the center of the division and stays, so
in case any of the boys are taken sick or hapen to anyone get wounded they
can be taken cair of, and the officers of the day have a ordely to go with them
to take cair of the horses, so dos the docter but the docters ordely has to cary
the medical knapsack, and then they have to run back to camp to get their
own grub and that of all the officers when I was down with the dock, we stop
to a house wheir their was a famley a living, and their was two wimmen
folks their. You say that you do not know but the wimen are as smart hear
as they are in Wis. if so I do not know anything about wimmen and as for
calling them *Ladyes*, that is all out of the qustion. They can talk a purson
blind in 5 minuits and their will be no sence to their talk neather. They are
as igrant as a hog all they know is to eat and Squeal. They is not one in a
dozen that can read a word, and if you ask them the distance to one of their
traiding plais or to any other plais you will get one answer, and that is this,
youans will find it smart bit awais, they do not know one half as much as
the Negro that has to call them Master & Mistress and then they live hear
like so meny savages they will clear up a few acors of land and put up a large
house with two or three large Chimneys outsid of the house and then put
up little houses all around that for the slaves. They have no form or shape
to anything, and the slave has to do the work and the men & wimmen will
lop around and drink their strong drink. I have not got any dout but one
half of the sutheren folks that has gone to Heaven has gorn on a wine cag
or a whiskey bbl but wheather the good Lord will let them drink the cursed
stuff their or not is a dout in my mind. You have made big caltilations on
what you are agoine to do next summer. You wood look smart to go to work
out wont you: if you said that you was goine to hire your board somwheirs

it wood have sounded a little difrance when you go to work out to earn your living I think it will be after this. It may be that that time may com but while I am well and alive, I do not want to hear you talk about working out by the week to earn your living. If it shood hapen so that I cood not get a living for ous why then I do not know what mite be neaded, but then I am well and able to earn our living yet and do not know what I may be for good meny years yet, as for that we must trust to one that is higher then what we are. Well sis the Hospital Stuard and myself went out on a ramble yesterday. We went along the picket line a ways and we was glad to leave it for they was advancing the line and the boys had orders to arress anyone that was walking along the line and we was stop by som of the boys and they told ous what was up and they sed that they did not want to arrest ous but told ous not to let anyone know who they was so to get them into a scrap for not doing what they was orded to do. We was vary glad to get away as easey as that they cood not have don ous any harm if they had stop ous onley it wood have put ous to a good deal of bother to get out again allrite after our fley from the picket we went to a foart[1] that our boys are at work on hear we run another resk of geting snap up but we was allrite. The foart is a large one it is built of timber and earth I will put in a strip of paper with the outlines of it so you can see what shape it is in. You will see a squir block in the center that is a small foart with 6 guns in it that will be kept up as it is now the guns are brass peases 10 pounders you will see this mark /// in the outlines that is guns, the ditch that is marked off is 15 feet wide 10 deap the road wheir it runs into the foart croses the ditch on a bridge then their is 3 heavy log gates, the abates[2] are timbers with one end sat into the ground about 3 feet deap they stand slanting upwards so the points are about as high as a mans head, and their is wires running threw them in evry derrection so to bind them all tite togeather their is two of theas lines. They have not got the guns in the foart yet it is not redy for them their is 2000 men at work on it evryday. It covars 5 acors of ground inside of the foart it is so strong that the whole armey of the south cood not storm the works all the way such a foart can be taken is by a seage and it will be hard work to seage that foart for it is surrounded by a lot of others that wood help them. Well sis I do not think it will pay to take another sheat of paper to write nonsense on so I will close by biding you Good By

From your gabin boy

Guy C. Taylor

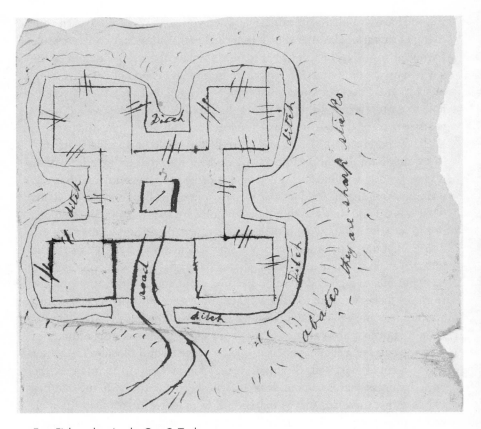

Fort Fisher, drawing by Guy C. Taylor

I hurd from Mrs. Swanton a few days ago she seams to feal pretty well over hur good nuse from Robert and well she mite write often.

Theas abates are sharp sticks stuck in the ground at one end and the other end is about as high as a mans head they are all braised and wiared so it is a orfull job to tair them down this foart covars 5 acors of land that block in the center with 1 in is a small foart you must not worrey if you do not get letters reglar for the boats do not run reglar on acount of storms and the eice in the river by Washington but I will write gust as often wheather I get any or not and you must do the same so good by.

In Camp Near Peapersburg Va
January the 31th 1865

My Dear Wife

I received your welcom letter a short time ago and was vary glad to hear that you are injoying such good health. My health is vary good yet. You say that I have not wrot what I am detail for it was one of my blunders then for I thought that I had writen all about it. Well I am detailed by the Comander of our devison as Hospital Attendent my buisiness is to take charge of the Hospital knapsack and then I have to ack as ordeler for the docter, the ordeley Hart is detailed the saim as I am he takes charge of the field instimants and he acks as Clurk. I am tenting with the Docter now. I have bin with him evry since the Chaplain left ous. You seam to think that we have lost a fine Chaplain. I have not a word to say against him but he has preached 4 times to the reg. and he has bin paid 6 hundred dollars for it by the govament. He was a man that had a vary stiff back he cood not stoop low anough to go into a privates tent as for my part I am vary thankfull that he has left for I had charge of his horse and it was not my plais to do a thing for him unless I had a mind to but I was willing to take charge of it, but he began to order this that and the other, and began to find falt without a caus, and by his leaving it has saved me som work and a reglar fuss with the minister, for if I had known that he was not agoine to stay onley a short time I wood not have took it as cool as I did but I do not want to have any words with anyone but they must mind their own buiss, and let mine alone. I have hurd from home 3 times since I have wrote. The first letter com the same nite that I wrote and I thought that I wood wait untill that had got started away before I wrote again and then I got another one the next nite that was nite before last and then I got that one that Edd and you wrote last nite. I shood have writen to you yesterday but to tell the truath I was about sick, but nothing vary dangerast, you see I eat a mess of beans and they did not exacterly agree with me but I took a good potion of phthisie and I am allrite again today, and I think that I shell be a little carfull another time about eating to meny beans, for it is not vary pleasant to feal as I did yesterday. You say that the Lodge is agoine to send me the Chief. I am vary thank to them for it. I will try and write a letter to the Lodge in a few days. I have got the Journel of the last sestion of the grand Lodge and the Chief that was with it. I have got also the picters of Father & Mother that you sent you say that you wood like to have Charleys picture that was taken first I will send it and that one of yours that was taken in the same case. The case I will not send for it is all mashed up and one of the glases is broke to peases but I have kept the pictures the best that I cood. I can keep potographs the best for I can put them in my pocket book and they will not brake. I do not know of anything new to write about. It is all one thing hear now and that is the cry of pease they all think that the war is most plaid out their is high officers that will bet thousands of dollars that we will not have another Campain but I do not know but it will be so I hope it will but I have my douts you know I am one of little faith anyway but I do think that we will get home by next fall and I hope before. We are getting good nuse evryday and it is astonishing how the rebs are a coming into our line. The 6 Corps reported 17 hundred that had com into their Corps last month and I shood think that their was nealy as meny as that com into our Corps and they are coming in the most down on the rite wheir the 17 Corps lays they com in their from 1 to 100 in a squard. One day their was betwene 2 and 3 hundred com in at one time a whole bregade started so ses the rebs and they was stopt by a divison of their own men our boys sed that they hurd a role of musketry and they did not know what it ment but when this body of rebs com up to our lines they sed it was fireing on their own men that was trying to com across in all that got across out of the body that tryed to com was 300 they say that their was 5 or 6 thousand that started the rest was drove back they do not know how meny was killed in driveing them back but they say they fell in evry derrection and those that had pluck to run the rest of the balls got across to our lines or was shot down when they was a running. I must close so good By

My Dear Wife From Your Husband Guy C. Taylor

In Camp in the field Near Petersburg Va
Febuary the 11th 1865

My Dear Wife

I pick up my pen to try to write you a few lines to let you know that I am well and am in hopes that theas few lines will find you injoying the same good Blessing. I wrote to you yesterday but the reason of my writeing again today is I do not know when I can write again we are under marching orders and we do not know wheir we are goine to. Som thinks that we are goine down to south Caraliney but I do not think that I think that we will go on a raid and if we do we will stop when we are ablidge to. It will take somthing to stop the boys now for they are all exsited with the nuse of pease and they will fite like bulldogs, but then we may run against a snag that will fetch evrything up to a halt and then a retreat but then we do not look for that. We got som good nuse last nite their was 3 of our officers and our post master sent down to 9 Corps yesterday and they saw Alaxander H Steavens of Georgey, Ex Gov. Hunt . . . Virginia, Alaxander Campbell . . . Alabamar, and Lieu. Genral Hatch . . . Louisania. Theas men have com over to see if they cannot settle the thing up and have the war closed. They say that they have not com as commisinors for the southern goverment they have com by the request of the people of the southern states. They got into Genral Grants Carrage and went to sity point their they take a boat for Washington. They com in with a flag of truse and as they com threw the Sap their was a reglar pady[1] standing on the works and as he look down into the sap (or ditch) he got a vew of Steavens he is a vary small slim and Sickley looking man and pat was full of glee and he belch out and seys, "By the Gumping Holey Jases Christ, you have com in gust the rite time be Jases, if yea had stad another month yea wood starved to death." It made fun for the boys and it is a by word all over the armey by this time.[2] Well dear wife you must not get downharted if you do not hear from me again for a long time, for my health is good and I have got a good plais, but then I shell write as soon as I can, and it may be such a thing that we will not moove at all. The docters ordeley Heart, has gust com in and he says that the repoart is up to the bregade that the rebs are a drawing in their pickets in frunt of Petersburg, and it is repoarted that they are a leaving the Sity, if that is so we will soon be after them with sharp sticks. I do think that we

are about to have a peasefull govament again at least it has all the appearance of it to ous hear in the armey and if we can onley gain one or two more
good victoarys it will be a fine thing, for they wood not want anything except
life spaired to them. You see we have got them rite in under our controle
for they cannot fill up their armey and they are a desurting by the hundreds
evryday. It was a great victory for our govament when they Elected the
preasadent last fall. Abe Lincon has shoed ous what a man shood be, he has
stood like a rock in mid Ocian that sets defiance to the ragen billows. He
(Abe) has stood the abuses & insults of the politions and with his strait forward coarse he has set at most all of their deep laid skeems, which is not
vary pleasant to the sneaking trators at the north, but I do not know of any
other way for them to do but to acknolledge that they have acted the part
of a trator, but they have bin over powared or to flee to som other Country,
and if they do flee to som other clime it will not be a vary heavy lost to the
American people. Well Sis I was agoine today to try to get my picture taken,
but it is all nock in head now they take picturs now in the 3 bregade, it is
onley about 100 rods from ous they charge vary high but then I do not cair
for that. In case we do not moove I shell try and get one so to send it in
my next letter. I have sent you Charleys & your picturs that was taken in
madison. Well Sis I do not know but what our moove will all flash out after
all. Their has two divions drawn 6 days ration and we expected to draw
today but it is most nite now and we have not got orders yet to draw any
rations yet and it looks as so we was not agoine to make any great moove,
but then we cannot tell the 2 bregade has gorn out on drill so that dos not
look like marching tonite we may start in the morning and have a good
time of tramping and maybe a fiteing. Well if we must fite let it com now
while the weather is coole. I do not cair about seeing another battle but then
I say let ous stick to our work untill it is finished and then let ous return
home again to injoy the comfets of life again. You sed in one of your last
letters that the Lodge was agoine to send me the Chief. I am vary glad to
hear that they are a takeing som intrest in the caus of Temprance and if I
get the papers or any good Leecturs you may be ashuared that they will
do somone elces som good besides myself. I have had som vary interresting chats with som of the men and I find that men are the same hear as
they are at home they are willing and take delite in talking about morral &
religest Sosietys and I have had sevral tell me they wood give anything if
they cood onley let lickor alone and not drink it. It seams to you I have no
dout as though it is easey anough to keep from useing it but let me tell you

it is not such a easey thing. I have seen the time when I have had the thought com to my mind that I wood take a good drink but then I have bin master of myself so far as for drinking is consurned, but let me tell you when men lay out on the ground threw 3 or fore days rain and not be able to go to sleap onley by laying with their ecutiments all on and their guns laying by their side and then be started up and start on a march and expecting a fite evry miniut, it will try a man and if he thinks their is anything that will keep him up he is vary apt to use it, let the name of it be what it will and then the genrals and smaller officers want to make the boys think somthing of them in time of battle so around com the canteens of whiskey, and the boys think it is not manley to refuse to drink with a capt. or any higher officer that is a great meny of them. Their is som that will not drink but they are vary few in comparison with the armey, but then the time is near at hand when the boys will be back home again wheir they will not want whiskey to drive away the lonesum thought that enters their minds but Sis I guess you will think that I am runing crasy by the way I write lately, well Sis I am not crasy but a little foolish you know that though without my saying anything about it but I must close so I will wish you God spead and Bid you good By

    From your Husband

Guy C. Taylor

NOTES

    1. *Paddy* was a common nickname for an Irishman.

    2. The event that Taylor was referring to was called the Hampton Roads Conference. By 1864, Missouri politician Francis P. Blair Sr. believed the war could be ended by negotiation. Abraham Lincoln agreed to allow Blair to present his idea to Jefferson Davis in Richmond and to meet with a Confederate delegation in Hampton Roads, Virginia, on February 3, 1865. The Southern representatives consisted of Vice President Alexander Stephens from Georgia, John A. Campbell from Alabama, and Robert M. Hunter from Virginia. Davis instructed his representatives to settle for nothing less than independence. Lincoln demanded unconditional surrender, reunion, and emancipation. No agreement was reached, and the war continued (Faust, *Historical Times Illustrated Encyclopedia of the Civil War*, 335–36).

$\sim$

NO. 39 [*NOTE:* TAYLOR USED THIS NUMBER ON TWO PREVIOUS LETTERS.]
RECEIVED NO. 38

In Camp in the Field Near Petersburg VA
Febuary the 3rd 1865

My Dear Wife

It is with pleasure that I take my seat again upon the same bed & in the same tent and on the same ground wheir we was when I last wrote. Little did I think that I shood have another chance to write to you in this camp, for I expected that we wood be a long wais from hear by this time, and I allso thought that a good meny of our noble boys that are now blooming in the best of health wood be laying under the sod ere this, but then we have not made any stur yet of any acount and their is fair prospects now of staying wheir we are now for somtime for it has com one of our lay still storms it is a raining now at a good rate. The nite after I wrote my last we had quite a exsitement we was started up at one oclock at nite, and was ordeard to hunt up the sick ones and send them off to sity Point and the docter and myself was up in no time and at work and I went out and routed up the Stuard & Heart and they was goine with the sick towards the Depot in less then ½ hower we waited for further orders and in a short time the Docter sed that we mite as well go to bed again and try to get a little more sleap. He sed if they wanted anything of ous they mite wait untill we cood get up and dress again, but then we had evrything handey, but to our great surprise we layed still untill morning and we have not had any orders yet to stur allthough we are under marching orders yet, and if the storm dos not prevent ous from mooves, I think that their will be work anough for ous in a few days, for the whole armey is on marching orders and they have sent all of the sick away to give room for the wounded. It is the genral opinion now that their will be a big fite in frunt of Petersburg but then it may not be so no Private or small officers are alowed to know anything about a genral fite untill they get rite into the field of action. All I have got to say is I am in hopes that we will be victoaries if we do have a fite for a defeat at this time wood be a bad egge for ous, for the South begin to think that they are about whip, and if they shood have a victorary now it wood incurage them to go on with the fite, but if we cood gust nock Petersburgs armey to peases it wood be a big thing for ous, allthough we shood loos a good meny hundred men in the fite. Their is a great cry hear about pease. I am in hopes that they may com to turms without any more fiteing, for their has bin anough blod shed now to satify anyone that war is anything but a blessing to a country, but threw the blod of man all Patriot blessing flow, the greates accheavement that has ever bin accomplished has bin by the lost of blod & life, and that is all that upholds a soldier in the field is to think that somday the country is agoine to reap the profets of their labors, and in case they do not live to injoy it their prosperity may. When I inlisted I told you that I shood be back again in the fall of 1865 and I think the same yet but I do not think that I shell much sooner. Most all of the boys think that we will go home this spring but it is my opinion that the nuse of pease will not be spread threwout the land before spring and then it is no small job to pay off the armey and send them back to their own states again, and then it is not any small job eather to take prosesion of the works and guns of the southern armey and that will have to be don before the armey is disbanded but then time will seam to fly after the word of pease coms wheather it is this spring ore 3 years hence. Pease must com somtime anyway and their is agoine to be a armey to be disbanded at that time, and that day is agoine to be a day of rejoysing with a great meny, and while som will rejoyce over the return of their loved ones while others are left to moarn over the fate of theirs, but then they will have one thing to chear them up eaven in the darkest houars of aflictions that is the hope beyond the grave, and then the fruits of their labor on the battlefield is a bryte spark to the wife & children as they see the prosperity of the country increasing and relize that their children & childrens children are to reap the benefit of it, it makes them look forward with briter hopes, and makes them rejoys in their sorafull houers, and times of trubles. Well Sis I am ablidge to close this letter and go at work, but let one say to you do not worrey about me for if it shood be my lot to fall in battle it wood not be more then what has bin the lot of others far wearther then myself but I have not the least fear of such being my fate for I believe that I shell See thoas that I have left again and that a happer day is not far hence, well

I will close By Biding you good By
From your Husband

Guy C. Taylor

PS: I have sent that scarfe have you got it.

☙

In camp in the field
Febuary the 10th 1865

My Dear Wife

I will try to write a few lines to you to let you know that I am yet among the living. When I last wrote to you I sed that we was under marching orders and we have marched in good earnist but then we have not got onley 8 miles from our old camp but then we have had a orfull fite. We started on the morning of the 5th (Sunday) and we comenced driving in the rebs pickets about 3 oc in the afternoon and we went at work and threw up a line of works in about ½ hour and we (the 2 div.) had gust got them don on com the rebs and made sevral attacks and each time they was drove back with a heavy lost. The fite continue untill dark put a stop to it. The rebs com on the ground and got most of their ded & wounded off that nite. We found som ded ones in the morning I do not know how meny but som 30 or 40 and a few wounded that they cood not get off. It was all quiet Sunday nite and Monday untill about 4 oc pm when the 5th Corps had a heavy fite on our left and they was driven back in great disfutsion but the 6 Corps went forward and stop mister rebs before they had time to flank the 2 Corps and when the six Corps got up their as a suppoart to the 5th they gust give it to the rebs write smart and the rebs turn had com to run then as they run they got a ball in their rear, and as nite set in all was still again and Monday nite was another still nite Tuesday was a rainey day and evrything look bad the boys was in the works that they had throwed up, and they did not dair to onpack their KnapSacks for they expected a fite evry minuit but the fite did not begin untill most two oc afternoon and it was on our left again. The 5 Corps had it to do and they don it up in good shape two. They lost a good meny men but they drove the rebs evry time and hill the grownd that they took.[1] That nite it was all still again and it has bin vary still sence our men are at work a fixing the rodes and puting up heavey lines of works. Well Sis we have comenced another campain and I think that it is agoine to be short & blody and the last one that we will have in this war. Well I have received a letter from you that was dated 25 day of January but then the reason I do not hear from you any oftener is owing to the mail and I do not expect that you do get one half of them that I write I do not call this a letter onley a line to let you know that I am yet well and I hope that you are the same. Well good By

My dear wife
From your Husband

Guy C. Taylor

NOTE

1. The fighting February 5–7, 1865, further extended the Union from Fort Cum-
mings to Armstrong's Mill. Union casualties included 171 killed, 1,181 wounded, and 187
missing. Estimated losses for the Confederacy were set at 1,000 (Trudeau, *The Last
Citadel*, 322). The battle is known as Dabney's Mill, or the second battle of Hatcher's Run.

～

NO. 41 RECEIVED NO. 39

In Camp in the Field Va
Febuary the 17th 1865

My Dear Wife

I received your kind letter 3 days ago and I wood have answard it befor,
onley I sent one the same day that I got yours so I thought that I wood wait
a few days. I allso got a paper from you today. You say that you want me to
send you my Picture. I wood if I cood, but gust as I was agoine to get it
taken we got orders to be redy for a march at any minuit so that was the end
of the picture oparation, and since the moove I have not had anytime to go
anywheirs I do not expect that their is any plais now this side of Sity Point
that they take profiles, but then you have got one and that is as good as any
one that I cood get. You well know that you cannot get a deasent picture
unless you have a deasent looking Subjet, and you know how the Subject
looks as well as I do. You sent me the account of Chipmans matters and it
is al rite it agrees with his and I guess all will be strait in the coars of time
with him he has found out ere this that I am not at all afraid to let folks
know what I think of them. We are a having vary disagreeable weather hear
now it is so rainey and mudy but then we have got our tents up again so we
do not have to be expose to the weather. We are agoine to have gust one
of the pleasets Camps that can be Scart up when it is all clean up. They are
at work at it now when it is not a raining but their is a heap of filth to be
got off old logs and evrything that is in a heavy pease of woods, but if the
weather will hold good for 3 or 4 days their will not be a thing left to show
that their was heavy timber their once. Well Sis we have give up all hopes
of geting home this Spring and we have com to the conclusion that we have

got to go threw another campain and it will be a fiteing one most likely. I hope that it will be fite anough to satify the south that it is all useless to try to ruan such a govament as ours. They have bin whip on evry side this last summer and they will be most likely next summer and the Lord onley knows what they are agoine to do to live. I know vary well what I shood try to do if our govament was so short for produise as they are. They wood soon find me and mine somwheir elces beside this plais. I do not see how that famlers of the southen soldiers do live wheir they cannot get a barel of flower for less then 600 dollars of their money and the soldier onley gets 12 per month and no bounty at all. Our boys cannot hardely surpoart a famley at 16 dollars per month and get 5 hundred dollars bounty beside the State ade, and flower not quite 6 hundred dollars per barel eather, but then I do not know but the south is in the rite in this war and maybe that they are fed as som was in olden times, wheir few loaves fed a vast armey and their was a lot left. If they are fed in that way I wood advise them to feed their dogs with the fragments for they are so hungry that they com over to ous for food. Dogs are as plenty hear as cats are around home their. Well Sis I cannot write you any nuse at all tell Edd that I have not forgot him and I will write to him and to the rest as soon as I can but the thing of it is I have had to ack as ordely for the Docter and Colonel both the Colonel ordely has bin Sick for a few days but he is better now so I will not have so much to do in a day or to. Today I went 6 miles to get the Colonel horse shod and it don no good for I went on tom fools earent. We have not got our house all don of yet, inside the shelves are not up and then we have no table yet but then I must close for this time and I hope that I shell have more to write about next time. So Good By

From Your Husband

Guy C. Taylor

Write as soon as you can and all the rest follow suit.

In Camp in the field near Petersburg VA
Febuary 18th 1865

Dear Sister

It had bin somtime since I received your letter, and as today is Sunday and I am not ablidge to work and I will not work onley when I am ablige to (on Sundays) so I did not know of any pleasenter way to pass away time then by writeing and I thought that I wood drop a few lines in Bristoll to let you know that I am yet one of the mooveing things of the earth. We have once more got into Camp and the boys have all got good houses (do not think that they are fraim or stone houses or carpets on the flore) we have left a few hansom pines stand it makes it so much pleasenter. One of the pines that is in our camp wood be a great site to behold, for the yong bagers[1] that never see any pine timber growing. You say that Mrs. Brown is flurting around with so & so. Well all I have to say is evryone to their own fancy you know that it will not do for me to say anything, for my way was & is to suit myself and not others unless they thought the same as I do or did, but then I wood say to evry yong purson to look well ahead for the further I mite talk about such things if it was not for one thing, but as I have bin the caus of one throwing hurself away it will not do for me to make any coments on others for it wood not look well for one to condemn in another what he is quilty of himself, but thank God I am to big a fool to feal the guilt but if you can see anything wrong about this run agates you can see wheir in they are wrong and it will give you a chance to shun all such things. Well, Fan I hope they may injoy themself now heance forath & forever. You say that so & so was wounded and a prisiner I am sorrow to hear that for it is bad nuse to hear that any of our boys have fell into the hands of such hartless trators & murderers as they are in the south I prosume that ¾ of our reg. boys that have bin taken prisiners will fill a grave that is dug by their murders, it is horable to think of but then it is war and I have seen so much of it I now want to see our armeys go threw the trators country and lay at waist evry-thing as they go, not leave as much as a show to let folks think that it ever was settled by white folks. Let them send evry man woman & child to the north and if they will not go put them under the Sod for they are onley a curse to themselfs and to evryone elces, this treating them like men & wimon, and their treating ous worst then dogs is plaid out with me, but then we must be contented with our lot, and I am with mine I think, but then it is hard to see & hear of our boys being used so outragest mean. Their has a lot of the 36 boys bin starved to death in their prisins, but then their is no use in talking, all I can say or do is nothing at all, but their is one thing surtain if a reb officer hapens to run against one of our boys balls and gets wounded if I have to help take cair of him he will think that I have no mursey. I have help take cair of a good meny boys and rebs with others and it may be that I will have to again and I will do the vary best that I can unless a reb officer gets into my hands and then I will have no fealings for the poor wounded (not man, but (Devel) well Fan you will think that this is not much of a letter I know but then let it pass as lines from one that is not the blaim for what he dos not know. Write often

From your Brother in the armey of the Potomac

Guy C. Taylor

NOTE

1. *Badgers* was the nickname given to early European settlers of Wisconsin. They mined lead and often lived in primitive shelters dug into banks or hillsides.

NO. 41 [*NOTE:* TAYLOR USED THIS NUMBER ON A PREVIOUS LETTER.] IT HAS BIN 6 DAYS SINCE I GOT YOUR LAST LETTER BUT I THINK THAT TOMORROW WILL BRING ONE.

In Camp in the Field VA
Febuary 18th 1865 [Note: Taylor used this date on the previous letter.]

My Dear Wife

As the Son sheds foarth its lite and warms the fais of the earth, and the gentle wind is murmering in the tree tops that shades our pleasent camp, I am setting in my tent trying to pen a few scatered thoughts that may com to my mind. It was gust two weeks ago this vary Sunday morning that we broke Camp and it has bin long anough time to let men know, that they do not know how much a man can indure untill he is tryed. Today is Sunday to me and it is the first Sunday that I have seen for three weeks, and the boys in the ranks have not seen one for as meny months but then it dos not make any diffance as I know of wheather it seams like Sunday to ous or not, for that is onley a custum for a man shood be alike evryday. If he is onley a man on Sundays he is not a man on any day. I do not know wheather you have hurd of the Death of Mr. Brazee[1] or not. He died in the prison down south. It will be a sad infirmation to his wife, and what will ad another pain to hur sorrow is that Alen Brazee[2] is sick as I help him into the ambulance I cood not help but think of his folks at home. Their is a young widow & a young dauter that has neather Father or Mother and hur onley brother is sick in Hospitol and not onley that but the one that she has set hur affection and all of hur hopes on is now in the prison at Richmon, but then their is thousends of such cases, and we must expect that som houses will be the plais of moarners and as we are in great danger, we shood try and get the controle of ourself the *best* that we can and try to content ourself let what will com, for ous hear in the armey it will not do for ous to think that we are agoine to be sick or wounded or that our folks are agoine to be sick, if we wood let such things as that run in our minds we wood all be sick and ded before our 3 years are up. It is hope that keeps the Soldier up. He must look at the brite side of the picture and let the dark side go for what it will bring and folks at home wants to do the same. Let evryone injoy life as long as they can and let truble alone for it will com soon anough at any rate. The talk is now that the paymaster will be hear this week but I am in hopes that he will not com for we will muster again in a few days and if he waits untill the middle of next month we can get two months more pay and get the installment of bounty, and if we get our pay now it will not be much and I had rather that my pay wood com more togeather, but then they can pay ous when they have a mind to. I am owing about 25 dollars and then I shell save 5 or 6 for myself and send the rest home. I have bot so much of my own cloths that I have not run over the govament isue. They give ous 42 dollars a year I have drawn $40.48 cts most all of the boys have drawn from 60 to 75 dollars, and a good meny have run in debt 30 to 50 dollars I think that I have spent money fast but then I am nowheirs with the most of them. I have bin reconing up what it cost me to write letters it has cost me about 16 dollars for this year and I do not begrets it eather. I wood not stop writing for $50 per year. The docter will try to go home next month and if he dos and we get paid off I shell send the money by him I am in hopes that he will go for it will seam as so I knew what was goine on at home and then he is a great hand to talk and that is what I like, for I am a good deal like a crow more sequart then anything elces. Well Sis I hurd last nite that their was a picture shop goine up in the 3rd Bregade, if I can get my *prety* little profile taken I will and I will send it to you. The weather hear is vary warm for this season of the year it is like the pleasent weather in May in Wis. It is most likely that we will stop wheir we now are untill the ground get settled so we can moove artilary. It is now so you dig down 3 feet and you can get plenty of watter on the highest ground so we do not have to go dry for want of watter and it is not bad watter neather now but in the sommer the watter is orfull hear it taist gust like swamp watter wheir it is warm anough to wash in without any fire and then somtimes men get so dry that they will drink the watter that is in little holes that has bin dug out no one knowes what for wheir their is a scum ¼ a inch thick but then it is all for the good of the Country But I must stop my nonsence for it is nothing elces so good By

From your Husband Guy C. Taylor

NOTES
1. Pvt Martin Brazee, age 41, farmer, Sun Prairie, Wisconsin, was captured August 25, 1864, at Ream's Station. He died in Salisbury Prison, North Carolina, November 25, 1864 (*Roster, 36th Wisconsin Infantry Regiment of Volunteers and Draftees*, 126).
2. Cpl Allen Brazee, age 16, farmer, Sun Prairie, Wisconsin, mustered out July 12, 1865 (ibid.).

NO. 42 RECEIVED 40

In Camp on Comstock Farm
Febuary 21th 1865

My Dear Wife

After falling in with the reg. and giving three Hearty Chears in Honer of Shurmans victores[1] in South Caralina, I take my seat by the Medical Desk with pen in hand to write you a few lines to let you know that I am well. As I was out with the reg. this eavening I cast my eyes up towards the Heavens, and look threw the pines tops, and saw the same brite Glittering Star (the North star) that I have often gase upon when you have bin by my side, and I wonderd in my mind if I ever wood see that time again, and when if I ever do (God onley knowes) I hope that I may soon see that time again. As I sit a writeing the Bregade Band is filling the air with Music, and as we lison to the music we can hear the boys giving three harty Chears at the good nuse they have gust hurd, and we lend a listening ear to their voises for it is far pleasenter music to our ears then that of the Drums & Horns, for it ses victory in evry sound and we know that threw victory we will have pease . . . and what music cood sound so sweet as the wild cry of pease.

(Feb. 22ed morning)

Warm and pleasent. Well and harty. I gust red a letter that was writen in Bristol and it gave me good nuse, and I wood write one that wood give good nuse if I onley knew how to write such a one, but all I can write is that I am well, for siting down and composing a letter is far beyend my power, but then you know that as well as I do, so their is no room to put in a excuse, but then I am not intialy to blaim for if I have not never had but one tallent, their cannot be much expected from that one, but their I am to blaim. I have followard the example of a surtain purson of olden times. I have bared that talent for fear of looseing it, and the worst of it is I do not know wheir it is barred in. Well Sis I see that you want me to write to you for you send me paper stamps and invelops, well I wood like them first rate if they was onley scratch over with a pen such paper I take a fancy to but as for blank paper it is as plenty hear now as grayback lise was last summer and evryone has som to spair. Well Sis I met with a orfull axident last nite, you see I had got a letter about half written and in com the Docter and I went to moove my chair and I hit the leg of the desk borad and drop it went, and down went paper ink candle and all that was on the stand, and as good luck wood have it the ink upset rite in the center of my letter, so I had to write it again (warnt that orfull) but I had 1½ quire of paper and that did not get a bit of ink on it (but then the writeing tis horable to think on).

Afternoon. Paymaster has com is the cry and good meny of the boys ack as so they never see any money before, and it will go when they get it like due before the summer son. Their will be good meny thousand dollars paid to the boys tomorrow and the sutler will take good meny thousand dollars out of the reg. We will not get but fore months pay the paymaster has waited gust as long as he cood and pay ous onley 4 months pay. If he had onley waited 20 days more he cood paid ous 6 months pay gust as well but he cood not have took the 2 months pay to speculate on then, you take the intrest of the money that pays our divion for 2 months, and it makes a little *pile*, if he cannot let it lay onley 4 months it is a purfet swindle in the paymaster but then who cairs, nobody, for a comon soldier is nobody in the eyes of theas Big Bugs. The Docter will try to go home in a week or two and I will send the money home with him if he dos go and if he cannot get a leave of absents I will send it by the same rout that I sent the other but I shell not send it yet a whole but you may look for it in the coarse of fore weeks from the time you get this but I think that the Docter will get so to go home I hope so at any rate. If the Docter dos go home I will send a few trinicks by him if he can take them but I do not want you to send me anything unless I send word for it for if you do their will be ten chances to one that I will have to throw them away what tents & blankets I have got wood be worth a good meny dollars at home but the next time we make a moove I will have to throw them away for I cannot cary them and they

will be no use to me in warm weather. You ask the reason that I sent home
your picture with Charles the reason was that the case was all broke up
and I knew that I shood get the picture distroid. I shell send home all the
picturs that I have got except yours & Charles for I will get them spoilt in
the somer but I do not want you to let them go to anyone elces but gust lay
them away for saft keeping. I think that I can get mine taken in a few days
I will try any way. I sent a buget to you and if you get it pleas let me know
how much it cost and if it dos not cost two much I will try it again, anyone
cood pick up more then a thousand dollars worth of clothing in our marching three miles they thought that they was goine into a fite so they threw
away evrything that they cood spair but as it hapen they made a poor bargin
for it did not make a good rode for all they carpeted it with clothing. It may
be you wood like to know what I am up to now days. Yesterday I got onto a
horse and rode down to the Hospitol it is about 3½ miles from hear and
work vary hard. You say that next fall you expect to see me at home I think
so two and it may be a little before fall Shurman is whiping them at whole
sale & retail I do not know as you can read this and if you can I know you
cannot get much sence out of it but then gust think who it com from and
then you will not wonder at it. You must be a good gal and not get to sausey,
and keep your hands clean if you have to mix bread evry day to do it but I
must close so Good By From your Huzzy Guy C. Taylor

You say that you fell on the eice I thought that you had better understanding feet then that but be carful next time.

NOTE

1. The Army of the Potomac celebrated Gen Sherman's victories of the capture of
Columbia, South Carolina, February 16–17, and the surrender of Charleston, South Carolina, February 17–18, 1865.

NO. 42 [NOTE: TAYLOR USED THIS NUMBER ON THE PREVIOUS LETTER.]
REC. 40

In Camp in the Field
Febuary the 23th 1865

My Dear Wife

I have gust red your No. 40 letter and glad was I to hear that you are all
well. Their is not much stur hear gust now we was all pack up hear 3 nites

ago and expected that another fite was a coming off but we have not stured yet, and we do not expect to for awhile yet. What caused the stur was the massing of the rebels troops in frunt of the 6 Corps and we had to be redy to run to their rescue in case they was attacked but to our grate surprise the nuse came to ous that a reg. of the rebs charge on their own pickets and com up to our picket line and raised a white flag and they let them threw and they com up to our line of works and threw down their arms and they are now at sity point. They say that the rebs orded their men to charge on our works and the men wood not stur, and well for them they did not for they never cood get up to our works. The reg. that com in Numbered six Hundred with all of their officers from Colonel down. Dave Conors of sun prairie got hear last nite and he says that he had a talk with one of the Captains at the point and he told him that the meat that their boys got for their Breakfast was as much as they wood get for 3 days in their armey they say that they cannot get it for any prise the boys that comes over in our reg. ack as so they was half starved. When they com in somone of our boys will run along the line and get a little from sevral boys and then go to work and cook the Johney reb a good meal and som stout hardy men have eaven set down and cryed before they cood eat. To think that we had such a plenty and they was allmost dien with hungry, and they say that wimon and Children in meny plaises have to go around and beg for their living, but they know the turms, and when they get spunk anough to turn against their own officers and put them down they can then see better times. You say that you do not get letters as often as you did well I write gust two a week unless it is as it was the first of this month. You say that your last was writen on the 3ed of this month, you see the 3ed we was in camp that was on Thirsday and Saterday nite I was up at 12 oc and Sunday morning we started at 7 oc and I did not get a chance to write for my paper was all packed so I cood not write and then it is not any time for writeing upon the field of battle when you do not know what minuit you may have to start or get started in the way that is not so pleasent, but as soon as a battle is over I will write if their is any such thing as writeing if it is not more then a dozen words. You seam to think that I do not get all of your letters because I ask som qustions that you have writen about but the thing of it is I ask the qustions before I get your letters, somtimes I will write about somthing and in the same day or the next, I will get a letter stating gust what I had writen about, I think that I get all of your letters but they com evry way somtimes I will get 3 and 4 a week and then somtimes it will be most 2 weeks before I will get any and

I think it is som so with the letters that I send. You say that you thought that I was not vary well when I wrote on the 3ed but I was, well as I ever was I will not say that my mind was at ease for I expected that we was on the point of goine into battle and if I know myself it is somthing that will make anyone a little uneasy. It is a good deal worse fealing then it is after the fite begins for then their is somthing that seams to drive away that kind of dread, for we are into it and all we want is then to com out allrite, and then their is no time to sit down and think about anything. It is all stur and nois and the nois is gust what we like to hear when it is made on our side, but I have bout made up my mind that the fiteing is about over with. Evrything begins to show that the south is whiped and the derserters say that their men are goine home in large numbers and it looks so two by the order that Gen. Lee has isued in regard to their armeys, but he may threten to hang and shoot all he has a mind to it will not incourage his armey they have got whip and they know it to and they are bound to return to their own state but then I must stop this scribiling for you cannot read this and their is no youse and wairing out the pen in doing no good.

So Good By From Your Husband

Guy C. Taylor

Write often.

NO. 43

In the Field
Febuary 28th 1865

My Dear Wife

I received a letter from you yesterday it was No. 41 and I was glad to know that you was in good health at that time. You say Moses is sick I am sorrow to hear that, for sickness is not a desiarable thing. My health is vary good and it has bin good all winter. I do not know when their has bin a winter that I have kept so free from colds as this winter and I have bin out in the rain a good deal to. When we made the moove on the first of this month, the first nite I took a hard cold and the next nite I laid out on two peases of a log, without any blanket and it about couared my cold, that is the way that we docter down hear. Well Sis it is a raining like all blixey now and in about one hour from now we have got to go out and be musterd for pay. We got our pay a few days ago and they kept back ten dollars from my pay, and they sed it was on the allotment that we made at Madison they had gust got the paper work straten out so in case that is so you will draw the money hearafter and you will get this ten dollars and I want you to let me know wheather you get this ten dollars or not for if you do not I will see to it the next payday, their is som dout in my mind about that alotment for most all of the boys sined the allotment but the paymaster had no acount of onley a few of the names, and som he stop, 10 others 12 to 20 dollars appease, he stop 10 dollars on mine it is a mix up mess anyway and I do not think that the paymaster is any to honest anyway, he has had a fuss with a good meny about their pay one of our Company boys had 4 months pay due and 40 dollars bounty and he (paymaster) declaired that he had drawn his bounty and the Captain sed he had not and told the paymaster that he had got to pay it all or not any and he wood see that at the next pay day that his men wood get their pay that was due them the paymaster did not cair about leting run in that way so he handed over the money. A purson can get their gust due if they onley look out for it but then he may have to let it run along for a good while for if their is any dissafaction, it will have to run along untill the next pay day. I do not think now that I will sine the pay role againe untill I sine it for the last time, unless you have to have money for somthing, but then I do not think that it will be meny months before I can settle up with the govament for good, that is in the line of warfair, for it is my opinion that the war is fast playing out. I will send you som money by the Docter if he goes home and most likely before I get a answer from this letter he will be on the road for Sun Prairie. Their is nothing new hear onley a fiss fite in the 19 Mass. Reg., and the fiters all got punished and maybe you wood like to know how they was punished, well they put up two post and put a pole across from one to the other it was about 12 feet high, and then they had to get up on the pole and sit stradle of it, and their feet was tied togeather under the pole and their hands was tied togeather in frunt of them their was 5 of them and they was kept up their all day with-out anything to eat. It made a genral show for all of the camp.[1] More then a thousand eyes saw them, and made remarks about them, and the officers that put them up their, I wood not like to be in their Colonels plais if one of them boys ever gets a good chance at him in time of battle. He may be lay as low as the Colonel of the 36 Wis. did, allthough he was shot by a reb (maybe) sharpshooter anyway he was killed. Their is not meny that moarns over his lost hear in the armey he is known all threw this armey, and no one thinks that he got more then his gust due. You say you do not know for surtain what department that I am in, it is the 1th Bregade 2ed Divion 2ed armey Corps. I've got a letter from George this morning and they all are well up their Add seys it is rather losom now Storm Bates has gorn to the war they seam to like it up their vary well I am in hopes that they may do better their then what they did in Bristol. It is most time now for the armey to be on the moove so you must not get the blues in case you do not get two letters a week for when we are on the tramp I do not get much chance to write for I do not cary any paper or ink I put it all in the desk I go gust as lite as I can I find it is easer for me to travel without a lode then it is with one, so I will let the mules draw it for me in the wagon. Well I will Close for this time by Biding you good by

From your Husband Guy C. Taylor

Write often so will I

NOTE

1. The military maintained order by discipline with shame and pain. The most common offenses were straggling, drunkenness, fighting, dereliction of duty, theft, cowardice, bounty jumping, and insubordination. Punishments included buck and gag, guard duty, carrying a heavy log instead of a rifle, being tied by the thumbs, riding the wooden mule, extra duty, fines, time in the guardhouse, and reduction in rank. Cowardice, desertion, theft, sleeping on guard duty, spying, murder, and bounty jumping brought the most severe punishments. Execution by a firing squad or by hanging could be applied to all of these, but frequently cowards, thieves, and some deserters were branded and drummed out of camp in disgrace. Artillery and cavalry units often tied the soldier spread eagle to a gun carriage wheel (Faust, *Historical Times Illustrated Encyclopedia of the Civil War*, 220–21).

In Camp in the Field
March 4th 1865

My Dear Wife

You may think that it is a long time since I have written. I shood have wrote sooner but as I had not hurd from you for somtime I thought that I wood wait untill after the mail got in and see if it wood not bring me one from you. The mail got in a short time ago and it brot me two letters from you one that was written on the 18 teanth the other on the 23ed, and as I have got threw reading them and one from Amanda, I thought that I wood try to send one out tonite. Their is nothing to write about evrything is still except what little exsitement is got out by the rebs, coming into our lines. We get now the acount of thoes that goes threw Washington per day it will run from 100 to 300 per day. That soon will get a armey discurage for they dair not trust their pickets they do not know what nite the pickets may desurt and let a armey rite on to them while they are in their tents asleap, then another thing will be a bad egg for them I think that is this arming of the Negroes[1] they are about half and half so, it is a good chance for them to quarel about it, and it seams that they are doing so to when I hear their leading papers talk about not surmiting to the vois of the senet. It satifies me that they are in a hard row of stumps. If Shurmon makes one or two more good mooves I think that their will be som more men on the rode towards Washington to see what can be done. The south will find out that Coten is not King of America . . . You say that you want me to get my picture taken about the sies of that one of Mars & mine. You have spoke to late for it is taken, but it is not of that size, and I do not think that you can tell who it is eather, for it is a misrable one but then I cood not do any better, at that time, it was a raining like fury and I was great wet, when I was geting it taken. The rain com in threw, wheir the sky lite was, mud 6 inches deap in the tent, but then I was afraid to wait untill a fair day com for fear that I cood not get one at all, for we are now all a time under marching orders so we do not know when we will have to start, but then it is most likely that we will stay wheir we now are for somtime yet for it is raining evryday their has not bin a fair day for most two weeks and I prosume that it will be rany for sevral weeks to com it cleared off about one hour ago and the sun is now shining out warm and the wind is high so it will dry up the mud a little but then it may rain hard again tomorrow. That is the way it goes now but then it will soon com May and that is the month to go to work in and, we are hear redy to go at it. The armey has not got to march two or three hundred miles to get to a fiteing plais but they can start and in one hour find their game, and the men can march by the music by musketry in room of that of fife & Drum, but then I am in hopes that that kind of music is about plaid out, but then it is hard telling what may turn up yet. We may all get swep off yet, but then our boys are redy to try them at any time that they will get out of their works we do not want to frunt their brestworks more then it is nesessary. We have got our pay and I will send 60 dollars to you by the Docter and som other things their will be two letters that he will take I want you to

put them away and let no one know that you have got them. You say that
you want me to write you a good long letter and send it by the Docter well
I will write a few lines if I can but then it will not be anything new for their
is not anything to write about hear. Well Sis as it is geting late and I want
this to go out tonite I will have to close so good By from yours

Guy C. Taylor

NOTE
　　1. Late in the war, the Southern government became so desperate for soldiers that it
enlisted African American troops in exchange for the promise of freedom.

NO. I DO NOT KNOW I GUESS 44

　　I expect a letter from you evryday the last one that I got was last Wendes-
day and today is Satarday

In Camp
March 11th 1865

Dear Wife

　　I once more pick up my pen to write you a few lines to let you know that
I am yet injoying the best of health and am in hopes that you are injoying
the same good Blessing. This morning the sun rose up fair to our vew. It is
the first sunrise that we have seen for a long time. It has rained 14 days
out of the last 16 days but it looks now as so we was agoine to have a spell
of fair weather. Their is no great stur down hear for the mud is so deap
that it is imposible for anyone to stur a great deal at all. They have got the
railroad built up threw to ous again it dos not take Grant long to make a
railroad. If it was not for that road we wood have to fall back again to get
surplyes but Grant is at our helm in room of little Mc and Grant dos not
know what runing back means, at least he has no notion of letting the rebs
get up to Washington again. He seams to take a likeing to the sity of Richmon & Petersburg and I think it will not be vary long before he will march
his armey into thoes sitys with the stars and stryps a floting over his mens
heads. It will not be but a short time now before we will know how it will
be, this spring campain will let ous know wheather we will go their or not
and it is onley a few short weeks before we will be at the work again the last
of April or the first of may will tell the story and that is not but a little while

to wait but then we may not be sucsesfull but we all look for one thing that is for a heavy fite and a great victory we do not have any ide of our being whip this spring and if you cood look along theas lines of work for 10 or 12 miles you wood say that the whole wirld combind cood not whip ous. It is one mass of tents along the lines and you will find from 4 to 8 men in evry tent. Grants armey hear is as ny as I can get at it, consist of the 2nd 5th 6th and 9th Corps, 2nd 20,000 5th 60,000 6th 40,000 and 9th 50,000 this is the amount of infanty 170,000 then their is about (calavy) 20,000 it makes the totle amount of men 190,000 hear present for duty, and they are still a coming in at a fearful rate and by the time that the campain opens we will not number less then two hundred and 20 thousend men so you can guess wheather their is any streanth hear or not, and besides this we have got nealy six hundred peases of artilary and men to man them, the whole foarse from the James River up to ous will be about 250 thousend men, a small armey for one plais and, you may well know that it takes a good meny hard tacks to keep that amount of men from being hungry but they all have anough and som to spair but then I will close, the docter will go home in a few days and you had better go or send down as soon as you hear that he gets home for I will want to hear wheather you get the money allrite or not. I will send the picturs that I have got and som other things but I cannot send anything that is of any acount for I have not got anything that I can send. Well good By Sis for this time be a good gal to Sarah J. Taylor

Guy C. Taylor

NO. 45 REC. 44

In Camp south of Petersburg Va
March 13th 1865

My Dear Wife

I received your kind letter this morning and was glad to know that you are all injoying such good health. You say that John Slingaland says that I am a owing him. That is so and I have saved out the money to pay him with, I borrowed 4 dollars off him when I was sent to sity point sick, and I was vary thankfull to get the money, but when John got to Anapalis[1] I sent him 2 dollars but I have hurd that he did not get my letters and if he did not I owe him 4 dollars. I am willing to loose the two dollars that I sent that is if he has not got it for that 4 dollars was worth more to me at that time then 24 wood be at this present time but I do not want you to pay him out of your state money I am agoine to send a fifty dollar note and a ten dollar one and I want you to pay John 4 dollars out of that ten and then do what you have a mind to with the other money but now I want you to be shure to pay him out of the ten that I send to you, and you must let me know it as soon as you can. I have writen to John and he will let you know wheather he got the 2 dollars that I sent him or not. Well Sis I will try and write a few lines and send with the money by the Docter, seeing that you want me to so bad, I will try to pleas you once as well as I can but then I know that I cannot do it but if I do not write anything that is any sense in you must not scold to hard for you know that I am no writer and you must think it is allrite if it is evry so bad. Well Sis I do not know what to write about if you cood understand what I cood write I wood have somthing to write about but you cannot give any ide of the works and lines and guns and such things that is around hear. I say you cannot give any ide of things you (must not think that I think you are short sited) but to tell the truth sis no one can tell the meaning and the plais of things unless they have seen the things and lines, all their is about it a purson knows nothing about things that is hear, nor can any one dissribe them to another untill they themself have seen such. You may think that I am crasey the way that I write but if you knew how meny times I have tryed to write today you wood not wonder that I cannot write their is to much horse traiding or trying to traid for anyone to get a chance to sit down 5 minuits to a time to write and now it is most nite and I will try to finish my letter if they did not finish the horse traid tomorrow morning I will take the sed horse and go to the blacksmiths shop with him and get him shod. You may call this whatever you have a mind to but dont call it a letter for it is not one. Well I will close so to send it out tonite, now when the docter gets home you pay John out of the ten dollar Bill that he will take home well good by

From your Husband

Guy C. Taylor

NOTE

1. Pvt John G. Slingerland was sick in a northern hospital to May of 1865 and was absent at the muster of the regiment on July 12, 1865 (*Roster, 36th Wisconsin Infantry Regiment of Volunteers and Draftees*, 141).

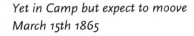

Yet in Camp but expect to moove
March 15th 1865

My Dear Wife

I pick up my pen to let you know that I am yet well and harty. I received a letter from you yesterday and from Lydia and one from the Crick and glad was I to hear that you are all geting along so well, as for nuse their is nothing but that evrything is on the stur we expect to moove evry hour now the hospitol is all cleared out and the sick that are in the regaments have bin examed and are redy to go at a moment warning, and the Sutlars have all got pack up to take the cars they will not be any more sutlars in the armey untill next fall and I think their will no armey by that time. Well Sis I now think it is doutfull about the docters geting home this spring. He has started his papers and it time that they shood be back but they are not and we are on the brink of a moove so he will not get his papers untill the moove is settled if he dos then. I am sorrow for I wanted to sent my money by him for I do not want to go into a fite with so much money with me for fear what may hapen. I have bot a lot of paper, invellops, & stamps so I am redy for a moove. You see Sis this moove is not like the last one we had, this is the opening of a spring Campain, and we will not fix up another camp this season if ever, you may look for sturing times hear for a month or two and then look for ous to com home. Well Sis I will put 2 dollars into this letter it is som that I have saved for my use but I do not want it, for if I want any money I will let you know it and you can send me a little. Well sis I do not know as you can read this tell Lydia that I will write to hur as soon as I can but the Lord onley knows when I shell get a chance to write again and it may be that we will stay hear for 2 or 3 weeks yet. It looks as so it wood rain and if it dos it will stop the moove for the land is so soft now that it will bother a good deal about mooveing artilary. Well Sis I cannot write any more now so good By to all

Be of good Chear for all is well that endes well
From your husband

Guy C. Taylor

I will send you a book and the money I will keep awhile and see wheather the Docter goes or not.

March 15
Still in camp afternoon

Dear wife

I will write a few lines more to say that it will most likely be a long time before I can write to you again for it is most likely that we will go to North Caralina. We are to take 12 days rations with ous 4 to be carred by the men and 8 to be in wagons. So you can see that is no small moove and it may be that I shell not get another chance to write for 3 or 4 weeks for no one knows wheir we will stop, all I wish for is, I wish that you had what money that I have got. I wood send it in this letter but I am a little afraid to for their is so much mail goine out today and so meny sending money, but I will resk 10 dollars in it anyway and the fifty I will send as soon as I think it will be safe to. Well Sis now, you must not get the blews if you do not hear from me, for along time for I am in a good plais and a easy one, I am cooking now for the Docter and shell untill we get settled again, so I do not have to cary eaven my grub and we have good living now to for the Docter will live & I fair the same as he dos I do not know but what the dock and I will get mared yet then you wood loose your (Dunce) or whatever you call him. Well we are in old VA now one week from now wheir will we be, today in camp, wheir will the morrow find ous who can tell onley one and he is one that no human eye can see, this will make 3 letters that I sent to you today or 2 letters and one invelop of picturs and one book and 12 dollars in money. O, Sis if you cood gust look into our (the Docters tent) you wood see a prety site papers tracks little books of all kinds clothing and finley evrything that you can think of throwed hilter skilter, all over the tent and it is the same thing all over evry tent you look into you see gust such site. You speak about sending home things I wood if I cood but it is no easy matter to send things when you can get them most likely I cood pick up a thousand dollars worth of clothing in 3 days but what can I do with it, it is all that I can do to take my own, and when we get so we can send things home then you cannot pick up anything at all so you can see that it is no easy thing to get things threw. Well I will close By Biding You Good By

From your what you call him

Guy C. Taylor

Be of good chear for I am, let ous go wheir we will

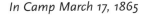

In Camp March 17, 1865

My dear Wife

I received a letter from you last nite, and sory was I to hear Charley was not well and that he had a sore mouth you will have to be carfull . I wrote to you day before yesterday two letters sent one book and one invelop with picturs in and their was 2 dollars in one letter 10 dollars in the other one this I send to you to use for yourself, the 50 dollars I will send after a little, but I cannot tell when but you may look for it when you can see one corner of it in a letter. The docter cannot go home so I will send what I can home and what I cannot send I can keep or throw away. My likeness I will cut it down so to put it in a letter. I wrote to you that I wood send you something that I wood not tell what is was but as it is all day with my sending anything I will let you know what it is. It is a medil the pin is a silver head of Gen. Hooker, the round medil on one side is my name Co. & Reg. and the plais of residents on the other side is the fites that I have bin in it is nothing of any value but then if it was at home it mite be of som acount, in case that I shood not ever get home but then I am in hopes that I shell see Bristol again, but then it is not for me to say wheather I shell or not, all that I have to do is to do my duty and let the issue rest with one that is far above the things of this world. Well sis I am sitting on the same old seat that I was when I wrote to you before, but little did I think that we wood be hear now when I last wrote, but then a soldier cannot tell anything about what order he gets, but then we are all redy for a start at any time and it is most likely that we will soon be on the moove. The docter says (let them rip) that he and I can standet as long as any of them and I think that is so to. I know if my health is good I can stand all the marching that they can put ous to for I will not have 5 lbs, to cary while the others are loaded down. You say that you think that the lodge has gorn up. Well let it go up but the most that I am afraid of, is that som of the leadeing members will not go up the same way, when their final setlement coms for it looks to me that the men & wimmin are geting so the most that they think of is partes if the men have got so they want to be to partes all of their time they had better com down hear this is the greatist plais for partes that I ever see and such large partes to, and then they have fine music and haves balls, plays, and the greatist kind of dancen our hall is large anough to comodate all the men of

Wisconsin, and then be room, and Father Abe says "com all of yea that is heavy laden for my knapsack is easy and my guns are lite." I may and I may not write another letter from this camp but that be as it may, it is all the same to me wheather I am in camp or on the march. The old saying is, "a contented mind is a continual feast." I am bound to make my mind contented wheather it is a feast or not but I must close by biding you good By

From your husband

Guy C. Taylor

You wanted to know how meny corspondents that I had 2 in Vermont, 2 at the Crick, Wis. 2 in Leads, 1 in Speaventown (illegible) and you know how meny in Bristol

∾

In Camp in the field S.W. of Petersburg
March 19th 1865

My Dear Wife

I have gust received a letter from you and glad was I to hear that our little Boy is geting well again. We are yet in our pleasent Camp but no knowing how long we shell remain hear for evrything is on the stur. The nuse com to ous last nite that Shuarden had cross the James River at Burmuda Hundred,[1] if that is so it is most likely that we will have sturing times in a few days and I shood not be atall surprised if we was in prosesion of the Sity of Petersburg in less then 2 weeks, but then it may be that we will not stur in that leanth of time, but evrything looks that way. The men are coming into the armey vary fast we will have to make a strike prety soon to get more room for camps. Without any gasting their is a large armey hear and it is groine stronger evry day if we shood lay still for 6 weeks and the armey keep filing up as fast as it is at the present time we will number not far from three hundred thousand men and they are in the best of fiting order. They all think that they can gust eat up the rebels if they can get them out of their strong works and it is the genral opinion that we will make another flank moove and swing around to the rear of their lines if we have means to get our surplyes along I think that we cood sweap evrything that wood com before ous, but that is the great truble hear we cannot get teams to take our provisons for to run a surply train the roads wood have to be all corderoared.[2] The weather is vary fine hear now it is like warm weather may

or june in Wisconsin, flowers that are around the buildings are in full
bloom. The grass has not started yet and that is not the worst of it neather,
their is not grass hear anytime of the year onley wheir it has bin seaded
down and it is vary seldom that you find a pease of medow land on the
low wet land their is a kind of wild grass, and on the dry land their is a kind
of weed or grass I do not know what they do call it grass or weeds but it
dos not start to gro not untill May then it groes vary slow. Oh aint this a
splended Country though, wheir you can get watter by diging from 4 to 10
feet deap and have watter that is warm anough to boil cloaths in without
any fire, and then the white prety sand it is so nice for scouring the flowars
with, then the Beautifull pine treas wheir you can sheal yourself from the
heat of the summer sun in under their green tops and then when you go
to your hous again you can find that your cloaths are all covard with that
splended stuff that is called pine pitch. Oh Vergina, you, you that was once
roaling in wealth is now reduced to povity, by your own conduct, you that
had wealth in human fleash, you that bound both mind and Body in chanes,
has brot a curs upon your own heads, for the Lord has spoke in thunder
tone, let my Children go free and you have not hurd to the voises, and you
are the ones that must suffer the Condemnnation, of your sins. Well Sis
you say that you have not hurd anything about that money that was aloted
to you I am of the opinion that you will not for I think that it is a game in
the paymaster but he may try his best he dos not get much out of this child
unless I am greatly merstaken, but then it may all be strate yet. You wood
not hear anything from it anyway untill the returns got to Madison that we
was paid off and it wood not have had time to have got their when you got
my letter about it, but by the time you get this letter you ort to hear from it.
If you do get it you must let me know it as soon as you can for in case you
do not get it I will have it put on my next pay roal so when I do sine them
it will be all strait, allthough I do not expect that I cood not draw it in the
field hear that is the vary reason that I do not mean to sine the pay roal
again in the field they have took good meny dollars out of the men hear for
one thing and another that the boys mite get if they wood gust set themself
at work and trais it out. Their is one boy in our Co. that has bin charge 24
dollars for transpertation and he never went anywheirs you see he was at
the hospitol and he applied for a furlow and they went to work and got out
his papers of tranpertation and charge it to him and he did not go home but
was sent rite to the frunt, and he is agoine to let it go and loose it. I think
that I shood a heap, if it was my case I wood keep a purfet stream of letters

runing to Washington untill it was straten and it wood not take meny to straiten it, for the paymaster Genral knows that he has got to hear to the call of the men and hunt up such things or he will be in hot watters, as for the picture that I have got I will send in a letter, and for the money I will send that in a letter to somtime but not yet awhile, so you nead not look for it untill it coms. I sent 10 dollars in one letter 2 dollars in another you must let me know wheather you get that or not for if that is lost I do not know as I shell trust the rest in a letter or not, but I will close for this time. I do not know when I can write again may in two or 3 days maybe in 4 or 5 weeks but all is well that ends well so good By

　　From your Husband

Guy C. Taylor

　　I shell write to Lydia tomorrow if we stay hear so you can hear from me one day later.

NOTES

　　1. Bermuda Hundred, Virginia, was a large neck of land between the James and Appomattox rivers. It is located fifteen miles south of Richmond and seven miles north of Petersburg. During the Civil War, the Richmond and Petersburg Railroad ran across its western base.

　　2. Roads were lined with wooden poles to drive over in order to solve the problem of sinking into the mud.

NO. 46 RECEIVED NO. 45

In Camp Near Hatchers Run
March 23ed 1865

My Dear Wife

　　I once more take up my pen in hand to write you a few lines to let you know that I am injoying good health, and am in hopes that you will be injoying the same blessing. When this reachis you we are yet laying still in our old camp, and we have bin redy and waiting so long to moove that it has got to be a old story and the excitement has intialy subsided, and the boys are on their high heal boots again redy for any kind of fun that may present itsself, but they keep evrything redy for a start at evry call. The weather is vary fine. The worst falt anyone can find about the weather is the wind. The wind is orfull hear their has not bin much damage don yet by it, all the damage that has bin don to our reg. is that 3 of our tents has bin crushed to peases by the fall of the treas, but in som other reg. their has bin som men hurt and som killed. I thought that the prairie winds was hard winds but they are no compairson to the winds hear . . . it is the opinion among most of the men that we will not have to fite meny more battles if we do any more, but I think that we will have two fite 2 or 3 heavy battles yet, but then the war is on the vary vurg of its end, and it will not be meny Months hence before the air will be rant with the chears over the gloeas nuse of pease . . . well Sis it has got to be a settled thing now about the docters goine home. He will not be at home this Spring so I will send you the money threw the mail or threw the express but I want to hear wheather you have got what I have sent yet or not, for if that is lost I will not send anymore by mail but by express but it is a good wais to go to the express office hear but then I shell go before I will run resk of loosing more in case that is lost. I have not got a letter from you for sevral days but I shell expect one tonite or in the morning. The mail coms in at nite but it is so late somtimes that it is not disscribeted untill morning I got a letter from Mart, this morning and was vary glad to hear Father was againing in health. I allso got one from George they are vary well, he is trubled with his throat, but is not vary bad. Well Sis I cannot write you any nuse, onley that yesterday their was 83 rebs com into our divion yesterday as I have nothing to write about I will close by Biding you Good By

From yours Guy C. Taylor

CHAPTER 7

Lee's Retreat

March 27 to May 14, 1865

In this segment of letters, Taylor captured the emotions of the Union soldiers as they anticipated the last great offensive of the war. He also described their reactions as they dealt with the possibility of losing their lives in order to save their nation.

In his April 4 letter to Sarah, Taylor announced, "We broke the rebs lines in frunt of ous at ½ pass 9 am April the 2ed." After nearly a year of conducting trench warfare in front of Richmond and Petersburg, Union forces were ending the stalemate, and the final stage of the struggle between the Army of the Potomac and the Army of Northern Virginia was at hand. In his letters, Taylor described the retreat of General Lee and his proud Army of Northern Virginia and recounted how he and the other men in the Thirty-Sixth Wisconsin were actively involved in the military events that culminated in Lee's historic surrender at Appomattox Courthouse. During the chase, some of Taylor's letters took the form of mere notes hurriedly written, an indication of an army being on the move. Other letters were longer. They revealed the horror of war as Taylor witnessed dead and dying Rebel soldiers left behind as others raced to escape the relentless pursuit of Grant's Army of the Potomac.

After the surrender, Taylor's letters documented the march back to Richmond and his subsequent journey to Washington. In addition, they revealed to Sarah the various dangers he had been in during his service since he no longer needed to shield her from the truth of his previous encounters. His letters also demonstrated the soldiers' gradual transition from wartime to peacetime as the men's focus began to shift from fighting battles to longing for home and seeing loved ones again.

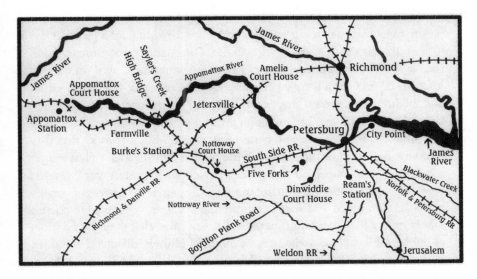

Petersburg to Appomattox, April 2 to April 9, 1865 (map by Patsy Alderson)

Near Hatchers run
March 27th 1865

Dear Wife

I received your welcom letter yesterday morning and was vary glad to hear once more from home for it had bin somtime since I had hurd from you, but I was well provided with nuse from home yesterday I got two letters from you and one from Mother Thompson, and one from Amanda so you can guess wheather I injoyed the day or not, (after a battle) ear you get this you will hear threw the press the work that has bin don hear in a short time, but you will not hear the perticulars about our reg. in the papers, (it is worth note) to the great surprise of the 36 their was a fite and the 36 Wis. Vol. was not in it at all. All that they don was to string along the line of works so in case the line of battle that went out in frunt shood be broke and have to fall back their wood be men all along the line to have them raly on the works, but the line of battle went rite onward and took two lines of the pickets works of the Johneys, and the fire was so hot that our men had to make use of the Johneys pits to cover them from the fire, and we have now made a line of works their for our pickets. Everthing was still yesterday our

men was makeing works and bararying the ded . . . I was all along on the
picket line wheir the fiteing was don and it was anything but a pleasent site
to see but then we are youst to such things. Our men are not more then ten
rods from the rebs, but they do not fire on one another at all if they shood
it wood slay men at a great rate but we do not cair about fireing on picket
and the Johnyes knows if they begin it we will keep it agoine and they well
know that they will get the worst of it for they will have onley our pickets to
fire on and our pickets are so close to their main line of works that they
wood not dair to show their heads, if they shood they mite as well have a pit
dug for them for one of our sharpshooters balls wood find its way threw his
head. The lost on our side I do not think is vary heavy, their was good meny
killed and wounded and som taken prisiners the rebs lost is about 4000
that is in our hands, the number killed & wounded that they got off must
of bin sevral hundred, we had som 5 hundred of their killed and wounded
fall into our hands so they met with a heavy lost. I think that their killed &
wounded will amount to as much as our whole lost the rebs played smart
the nite before the fite they made a dash at our lines and run in and took
one of our foarts[1] and good meny men but they payed dear for their bravery
for one divion of our men fell in the rear of them and their was not scarsely
a man got back. They got into a trap that was not bated with vary sweet
meat, they was like the eagle that thought that he had cetch the hair, but
soon found out it was a wildcat, and got himself into a bad scrape. Their
was heavy fireing last nite on our rite we do not know yet what it was but
the pickets keep up a fire today so I think that we was all hunk last nite and
the rebs keep up the fire today so we cannot com upon them without their
knowing it for we wood not go rite up still in the mids of flying balls, but
they are geting badly whailed out and they seem to know it to. Well Sis the
Colonel[2] wants me to go away for him and I will finish this when I get back
again. Well Sis, I went on the earent that the Colonel wanted me to and it
was a toms fool earent he wanted me to go and get his horse shod and I
went to the shop and I cood not get him shod so I will go again this afternoon. Well Sis, you wood laugh yourself half to death if you cood had onley
seen our boys yesterday they got evrything redy to march and formed in line
at the works and stack arms and then they went to playing ball and pitching
quates and all kind of plays you cood think of while the rebels shells was
bursting out in frunt of them and the peases whirling and flying in evry
derrection and now and then a pease wood strik pretty near by them and
they wood stop their play and their wood be a grand rush to see who wood

get the pease of shell, and when they see a squad of prisiners a coming in they wood howl like so meny wild men the men are allredy for a fite they do not seam to fear death at all and the more killed and wounded men they see the noiser they are and the more fearst they are to go and fite. They seam to think that they are shure to whip, and they want to see the rebs com in under gard and they do not feal vary bad to see them laying ded on the ground. Well Sis the Spring campain is comensed and it is no knowing what day their will be fiteing we are yet in our camp and may be for a long time yet. You must not be worred any about me if you do not get letters reglar. Well I will close so good By

From yours

Guy C. Taylor

Write and let me know wheather you got the money or not and wheather you have hurd from the allotment or not.

   1. The fort that Taylor was referring to was Fort Stedman, which was one of the Union forts on the Petersburg front line. Early on March 25, 1865, Gen Lee ordered an attack on Fort Stedman in a bold gamble to force Gen Grant to retract his lines. Maj Gen John B. Gordon's Confederates seized Fort Stedman east of the city, but the Federal counterattack took the works back from the Southerners, whose estimated losses range from 2,681 to 4,000. Union losses were approximately 2,100 (Trudeau, *The Last Citadel*, 353–54).
   2. Lt Col Clement E. Warner, town of Windsor, Dane County, Wisconsin (Aubery, *Thirty-Sixth Wisconsin Volunteer Infantry*, 293, 335–37).

March 28th 1865

My Dear Wife

   As we are expecting to make another moove tomorrow morning at 6 oc I thought that I wood write you a few lines to let you know that I am well and redy for a start. Sheriden is hear with his 25 thousand horsemen all armed with the carbine or 7 shooters rifles. We will most probiley go to the left, how far no one knows but it is my opinion that we will go so far so we will bid farwell to this part of the state I am in hopes so at any rate we have got to have sturing times yet and let it com, and it is rite hear now evrything has bin on the stur for the last 2 weeks, and we have had a sharp fite since

Petersburg, Virginia, bomb-proof at Fort Stedman, 1865 (courtesy Library of Congress
Prints and Photographs Division; Timothy H. O'Sullivan, photographer)

we have bin pack up but our reg. was in luck once, they was not in the fite
at all. Well sis it may be somtime before you will hear from me again but
you must not get the blews any for you know that I am in a good plais,
allthough I mite get hit or taken prisioner, but then any one hast to trust to
providents for that. I have bin offard large amount of money for my plais
but money is not my God, allthough I like money pretty well, but not as well
as the poart did when he wrote a few lines about wifes as he says, "God
Bless the wifes that fills our hives, with little beas & Huney they eas lifes
Shocks and mend our socks, but dont they spend the money." Now as for
me I wood not give two sences for a wife that cood not spend money. I
know that I can spend money and I want a women that can be my match.

Well Sis, I think that we will have a long march, but I have no doubt but what we will have a joly time of it we may see prety hard fiteing and may not see any at any rate we are agoine to have a large foarse with ous they say that the fif Corps are goine with ous most likely we will have a armey of 30 thousand infranty 25 thousand of Caverly. Well I have not much time to let run away and I have not no nuse to tell about the armeys so I will close By saying once more do not get downharted nor get the Blues if you do not hear from me again for 3 or 4 weeks. Well Good By

From Your Husband

Guy C. Taylor

In the Field
Apr 1th 1865

My Dear Wife

I will try to scribble you a few lines to let you know that I am well yet and fealing first rate. We have bin on the tramp now for 2 days and this is on the morning of the 3ed day, and we are laying behind som works that has bin throwed up and in our frunt is our skurmish line they are shooting at a fearful rate and our artilary that is rite to our side makes the earth jar evry little while. We have drove the rebs out of two lines of works since we started but they are now in their main line of works but they will have to get from that I am a thinking. We have not had onley one man wounded in our reg. He was shot in the little finger it took his finger off at the first joint, but we do not know how soon our men may lay wounded on the grown but the boys are redy for the fite for they have all laid out two days allready and it has rained all the time untill last nite it cleared off and it is a fine pleasent morning the pine woods fairley ring with lafter from our meary boys, the cracking of the musketry out on our skurmish line dos not give them the least mite of larm, nor dos the bellows of our brass canons. We are now pressing twoards the south side railroad and the rebs are deturmin to stop ous if they can but old Grant, (I think) caryes to meny guns for Lee this time, but then dont know but time will tell. Their is a genral stur with the officers now and looks as so we mite be on the moove again in a few minuits, but then we may go 10 rods and we may go 5 miles we are not still 6 hours at atime any of the while. It is doutfull if we go into camp again for

2 or 3 weeks this is the movement of the grand spring Campain, and it will be a grand thing eather for the rebs or for ous, but we have all hopes yet of success. We are a having a gay time of it you may bet for jokes are free in war times espesualy at the frunt and the men are redy to crack jokes and as today is the Aprils fools day it is a little more amusin then genral and if the rebs dos not get pretty well april fooled they may think themself pretty well off. One of our sharpshooters fool one of the rebs pickets yesterday the picket was watching to have a chance to shoot and our sharpshooter raised up his cap with his hand and the reb let drive at it and he had not any more then shot when the man that he shot at shot at him, and he did not waist his shot neather for the ball went plumb threw his head and then he was not satifide with shooting him but went up to his pit and took $140.00 dollars of confedrate money out of his pocket and got wheir he cood take charge of one of the rebs canon as fast as the rebs wood com up to load the pease he wood send him back with a whole threw him. Their was alot of our sharpshooters went out and they kepp 4 of the rebs big guns still they cood not get up to man them at all it was fun for our boys to lay in the slashed timber and pick off the men as they showed themself. The same game is goine on today this morning the rebs opened their guns once and then it was stop rite short they do not cair about our sharpshooters balls goine threw their bodyes and they are shure to get them if they show themself. I got a letter from you nite before last and I was glad to hear that you was all well. Well Sis I will close By Biding you good by for this time when I write again I am in hopes this moove will be to an end and the end will be a gloeas one. So Good By Guy C. Taylor

I have sent you 69 dollars that I have not hurd from yet.

Near Hatchers run
Apr the 2ed 1865

My Dear Wife

I am yet on the field of strife and Blod and am injoying myself first rate. I am curle up on a pease of a blanket that somone had throwed away and am trying to write to you the fite was goine on all last nite and today it is one tremendes roar. They say that we are agoine to the sity this time but then we cannot yet tell but evrything looks well yet. It is repoarted that

Shurden has sent in 4 thousand prisiners and the 6 Corps took 2 miles of the rebs works last nite but we do not yet know this to be a fack but we do know that their was a heavy fite in frunt of the 6 Corps and we cood hear the canons of Shurdens[1] so it looks to ous so it was so. Their is not a great deal of fireing gust at this minuit but we can hear it off to our rite it is a purfet roar. One way or the other you see that is Grants plan to strike one plais and be redy at another plais and as soon as one dash is made and shakes up to open in another plais their is fireing along the lines for 25 miles or more, first one plais then another[2] it is now about 9 oc in the morning and it is a good while to fite from now untill nite and we have got men and amanition anough. As soon as the men are releaved they lay rite down and go to sleap and no matter how loud the guns boom it is all the same to a Soldier it makes him sleap better if anything. Well I will close so good By

Guy C. Taylor

NOTES

1. Union infantry and cavalry routed a Confederate force at Five Forks on April 1, 1865.

2. On April 2, 1865, Gen Grant unleashed a massive assault all along the Petersburg trenches. Gen Lee's thinly held works dissolved under the onslaught, and the siege of Petersburg came to an end. Some of the most vicious fighting occurred in front of Gen Wright's Sixth Corps and, later in the day, at Fort Gregg, Fort Mahone, and Southerland Station. Breaking the Confederate lines cost the Union an estimated 350 killed, 2,850 wounded, and 500 captured or missing (Aubery, *Thirty-Sixth Wisconsin Volunteer Infantry*, 274).

Apr 4th 1865

We broke the rebs lines in frunt of ous at ½ pass 9 am April the 2ed. We took two foarts and then swung around to the rite and left and it put the whole line to flite. We took a heep of prisioners but I do not know what number but you will know by the papers. Today we are somwheirs in Va. but wheir I cannot tell you. The most that I can tell wheir we are is that we are som 20 miles west of Petersburg and are goine for the rebs and for the Danvill railroad.[1] Shurden is at work at the blod howns at a fearfull rate. He keeps sending back prisioners evry little while and the repoart is today that he has got sevral thousend. He sent in yesterday nealy 2 thousend and it is

allso stated that the rebs are fortifeing about 4 miles in frunt of ous but I
do not think that for it wood be a foolish thing in him to try to make a stand
anywheirs this side of the railroad but then I hope he will make a stand for
if he dos we will give him another thrashing and get most of his whole
armey we have now got about ¼ of it and most of his artilary in frunt of
Petersburg. Well Sis we have pushed rite on after the rebs armey and they
had to leave evrything. They eaven left their big tents after they had got
them all roaled up redy for putting into the wagons, and they left a good
meny wagons all loaded, their govament papers was found by the bushells,
and they was throwed around by our boys at a fearfull rate the roads was
lined with papers for miles. The way the boys went in for baken, tobaco &
molases was a caursin and the Chickens and Sheep had to suffer and you
may be ashuard that I am not the last one to go in for such kind of living

Farmville, Virginia (vicinity), high bridge over the Appomattox River, April 1865
(courtesy Library of Congress Prints and Photographs Division; Timothy O'Sullivan,
photographer)

but I am sorry to say as a party of ous was out after sheep that one of the boys was vary carless how he shot and one man got wounded but not vary bad but it will lay him up for 3 or 4 months. I made a good hall in the sheep buisiness today I got one good large fat sheep we keep ½ of it and let the others have the remainder our reg. got 8 good Sheep today. I have not got any Chickens sence yesterday then I got anough so we had a good feast of them. I shell not try to get any more untill we get short again for meat then I will go in for them again. Well I will close so good By

Guy C. Taylor

Writeing on the ground but don't know when I can send it out

NOTE

1. The Richmond and Danville Railroad was the last operational railroad in use by the Confederates. After his retreat from Petersburg and Richmond, Lee hoped to connect with Gen Joseph E. Johnston's army in North Carolina. The plan was foiled when Federal cavalry cut the Richmond and Danville line at Jetersville, Virginia.

⁕

at the High Bridge
Apr. 12th 1865

My Dear Wife

It has bin a long time since I have writen to you but it was not becaus I did not want to, but since I last wrote to you we have had a great change in the moovement of this armey. We have bin on the march for 11 days and have drove the enemy into nothingness or made Lee surrender[1] himself and his whole armey. We have gust stop marching for the nite. It is the 2ed day that we have bin on the backward track. We have had a hard march threw a unknone Country and drove the enemy the distent of 130 miles. This high Bridge[2] is the railroad Bridge on the southside road it is now sed that we are agoine to stay hear for a few days. We can get rations from Petersburg by railroad hear. The rebs tryed to stop ous a crossing the river by seting fire to the railroad bridge and allso to the wagon road bridge but we press them two hard and we put out the fire on the wagon bridge before it don any hurt at all but it burnt som 4 hundred feet of the high Bridge. The bridge is 23 hundred feet long and it is about 100 feet high. We have not lost but a few men for such a rase as we have had and we have fot evryday untill Lee surrended and since that their has not bin a gun fiard hear and I think that the last Battle has bin fot and it is my opinion now that the last of July next[3] . . . Well Sis I will not write any more tonite but I will write som more tomorrow if I can. You must not worrey any about me for I am as tugh as a buck and am in my glory when I can run at larg and when evrything looks faverable. Well Sis good By for tonite

Guy C. Taylor

NOTES

1. On April 9, 1865, Robert E. Lee surrendered his army to Ulysses S. Grant in the home of Wilmer McLean at Appomattox Courthouse, Virginia. The official surrender of Lee's army occurred April 12, 1865. As Southern troops marched past silent lines of Federal soldiers, a Union general noted an unusual stillness and breath holding, as if the procession were an actual passing of the dead. During the Appomattox Campaign, casualties for the Confederacy were approximately 58,000, of which 28,251 surrendered at Appomattox. Estimated Union casualties were 11,000 (*Encyclopedia Virginia*, s.v. "The Appomattox Campaign," http://encyclopediavirginia.org/Appomattox_Campaign; accessed October 4, 2011). The Thirty-Sixth Wisconsin casualties from March 29 to April 9, 1865, were 3 men wounded (Aubery, *Thirty-Sixth Wisconsin Volunteer Infantry*, 223).

2. The High Bridge spanned the Appomattox River at a point where it was necessary to build upon sixty-foot piers. A town named for the structure was the site of an April 1865 engagement that cost Federals about 800 casualties.

3. Taylor did not finish his sentence but was probably predicting he would be home by the last of July.

∾

In Camp 2 miles from Burksvill Station
Apr. 14th 1865

My Dear Wife

Burksvill Station is the Junction of the SouthSide railroad and the Danvill road. We got hear last nite and a glad lot of boys we was to, two get wheir we cood draw rations and som cloathing, for the men was hungry tiard & foot sore, but this morning they all seam to be all in town and you may guess wheather we was glad to get any mail or not for last nite was the first time that we got any since the 1st day of Apr. 13 days seam to be a long time without any mail, but glad was I when I open yours of the 5th and found out that you was all well my health has bin vary good. Evry since we started their has not bin but a vary few but what has kept along with ous, and it is a straing thing that we cood march so meny days and have more or less

Appomattox Courthouse, Virginia, McLean house, April 1865 (courtesy Library of Congress Prints and Photographs Division; Timothy H. O'Sullivan, photographer)

fiteing evryday and not loos any more men. Our reg. had not lost onley one man and he was wounded in the Sholder and it is not vary bad wound neather. He will be allrite again in a month or two. We pass threw farms- ville day befor yesterday on our way hear it is quite a town. I shood think that it was a plais of 2,500 inhabents before the war but now their is not onley a few white folks in the town but the streats was lined on both sides with the *Colerd individuals,* and they seam to be full of glee . . . I noticed one old culard women as we was on our march and as the genral and his staff wrode by ous with the cullars a flapping in the air . . . she look first at one flag then at the other and claped hur hands and cryes out, "My God, I nevre see such site since I was born," it must be a spended site to thoes that are not use to seeing it, for let a staff ride by a colemn of men with sevral bryte shining flags a flapping in the breaths and then look along the line of blue and see their flags floting over each reg. it will tuch the immagination of any purson, I do not cair how much he has seen of military display, and what makes it the most attrative is to know that they are on the march to give battle to the enemy . . . Well Sis Old Lee has had to give up that he has bin whiped, and he was glad to cry for turms old Grant was huvering around him like beas around a hive and he sent word to Lee to surrender or he wood let into him with a hundred thousand muskets, and Lee well knew the Streanth of our artilary for 30 pease open on his armey the nite befor and that was on one wing of the armey but it was anough with what muskets that 6 Corps had to lay 16 hundred of the gray Coats ded upon the ground. I have seen men shot but never did I see men strung along the roads as they have bin this time but then the majoyety of them was rebs. The first man that I help take cair of was a reb he was a smart young man to he was wounded threw the thy (not dangers) I was with him for about 2 hours it was in the eavening after we stop and as I help do up his wound and got him som vuitils he wanted me to stop awhile with him and I wanted to for he was a man that anyone wood be interrested in, he knows the whole run of the war operrations. The rebs, are a swarming along the roads on their way home they are glad to get the chance to go home once more as a genral thing their is som of them that will go into the armey again if they can get a chance to but they do not say much their was one man that sed that he wood not pay any regard to the oath[1] if he cood get a chance again to get into the armey and a officer that was clost by hurd him and rode up to him and told him if he did not want his brains blowed out he must not never utter thoes words again and he was mity still after that while he was with ous. Most of the folks hear thinks that we will be at home inside of two months but I do not think that but I do think that July will see ous at home, and we will wait with patiants untill then. We are hear now but how long we will stay I do not know nor do I know wheir we will go to when we do go, but their is one thing surtain that we cannot go into any fite rite away for their is no one to fite in old *VA*. Well Sis I will close for this time but will not say when I will write again for I do not know and I will not say that I will do anything that I do not know wheather I can or not. Well Sis Good By

From your Husband

Guy C. Taylor

NOTE

1. Taylor was referring to an oath of allegiance to the Union that the Confederate soldiers were forced to take as a condition of surrender.

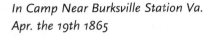

In Camp Near Burksville Station Va.
Apr. the 19th 1865

My Dear Wife

I once more take my pen in hand to write you a few lines to let you know that I am well and hope that this will find you all injoying the same. I got a letter from you yesterday and was glad to hear that you was all well and allso to hear that you got the money allrite I was a little afraid of the 50 for their was a genral rush with the mail at that time. We had got orders to moove and evryone was sending out one or more letters. I have no doubt but what their was 10 wagon loads of mail at sity point that nite that we broke camp, but then the money is allrite so I do not cair anything about the other mail but then I wood like to have this reg. put into the mail or into som other boat and sent home with their letters for I have bin in Va. as long as I cair about but then I expect to have to Stay untill the State get their state laws a runing again, but that will not be vary long. Well Sis I am on the go one half of the time a runing around geting one thing and another for the Officers, but not a forageing[1] for that has played out. As soon as Lee give up his armey we had know rite to take any private property without paying for it but their is som that will take evrything that they can I have bin about 3 miles out from camp today and found a grist mill and bout ½ of a bushel of meal and then went to a house and got my meal sifted and had a good long chat with an old man and his wife & Grand Dauter a young miss of 16, I guess and when I com away they gave me a pelite invitation to com again, and as I went out I see a lot of chickens a runing around and the old Lady sed I mite have one of the chickens and sent out the little black boy to cetch one for me. I handed the old lady 50 cents for hur hen and she was vary much pleased with our kind of money and as I stood talking with them up com 4 soldiers and one of them went to kill som of the hens and I told him that if wanted the hens he must by them he stuck up his nose som but I droad out a revolver out of my pocket and told him I knew my duty and he had better be carfull how he went to insult a safegard[2] so they thought that I was a safegard so they com up and paid their 50 cents apease for the hens and the darkey cetch 4 for them and the old folks got their reglar 2 dollars from them boys. The old lady thought that I don them a great favor they had onley to more hens left and they have got slole chickens

so they will not be disturb. I think that I shell go and see the old folks again
if we stay hear meny days you know that I do not want to see the prety miss
of 16 or little more, well without any jokeing they are vary intelgent folks
but the girl is a Sickley girl she is vary prolite appearing yong women but
hur being sickley it makes hur look downcast. Hur grandfather ses she has
allways bin sickley but I do like to talk with the old man he gets so interrested in talking then the old lady is not much behind time. Well Sis I
expect that you have all had full acount of the death of our Presedent[3] is
it not horred but it shows that trators will do anything no matter how low
and mean, but they will pay dear for their work or I am greatly merstaken,
but if they get that Booth[4] he will be vary apt to streath hemp it wood do me
good to See him hang dingling in the air. Well Sis I do not know of any
nuse to write onley we are agoine to have som corn panicakes for Supper
so I will close By Biding you Good By

From your Husey

Guy C. Taylor

NOTES

1. *Foraging* was the word for plundering the countryside and stripping civilians of
food, clothing, and valuables. The practice served to deprive the Confederate army of supplies while supplementing the Union soldiers.

2. Union guards were placed over civilian properties, provided the civilians were
loyal to the Union.

3. President Lincoln was shot the evening of April 14, 1865, and died the morning of
April 15, 1865.

4. John Wilkes Booth was the assassin of President Lincoln.

In Camp Near Burks Station Va.
April the 20th 1865

Dear Sister

I expect that you think that I am a scornfull retch for not writeing to you
before now. Well you may scold all you have a mind to and I will take it all
in good humer. Well Fan we have had a wild goos chase since the 2ed day
of April, and we had good luck and such squacking never was hurd before
in old Va . . . and I guess by what I have hurd that the folks up north has all
run crasey about our wild goos chase. Well Fan we are now in camp near

Burks station 60 miles from Petersburg they are all at work fixing up the Camp they think that this is their last Camp to fix up but then we cannot tell yet but most likely we will not have to fire another gun hear in Va. The cars are now runing reglar from hear to Petersburg so we can get ration now rite along we are a having vary good time now but we are more anxious to go home now then ever. While their was work to do we was redy to do it but now we do not have anything to do. We are crasy to leave this sand hole. The whole of Va. is sand as far as I know anything about it, that is with the exception of rocks. Well Fan their is som of the pretyest yelow boys down hear that you ever see and they are as smart as anybody . . . and then they can cook first rate to, their hands look so shiney and clean when they get them into a batch of dough then they have got such thin lips they must be great on kissing, but their hair curls so tight to their heads that they cannot see. Now Fan if you want me to gust speak to one of the Colard individuals, gust say so and you may be shure of soon seeing a dark cloud coming up before your dore. Oh Fan how much music their is in their laugh. Yah. Yah. Yah. Well Fan I do not know of anything to write so I will close by biding you good By write soon and tell all the nuse

From Yours Guy C. Taylor

Tell Hen I will write to hur next time so to keep hur good natured

∾

April the 23ed 1865
Near Burks Ville Station Va.

My Dear Wife

I once more take my pen to let you know that I am well and am in hopes that theas few lines will find you the same. We are now in camp and it is most likely that we will stay hear for sevral days, but then we cannot tell. The 9th Corps has gorn to Washington and the 5th Corps are now on their way to Petersburg so it leave the 6th & 2ed Corps hear. As the 24th, went to Ritchmon sevral days ago, I think that it will be so we can live a little better now when their was 5 Corps laying around hear they cood not fetch up anything onley Suger Coffee & hardtack, as the railroad was vary poor and then 100 thousand men makes way with a pile of stuff besides what the horses have to have their is now onley, or about 40 thousand hear now. We drawed

potatoes last nite for the first time for three weeks but then we will be vary
apt to get our reglar rations now. Well Sis we was a hungry set of boys once
now I can tell you som of the men got so hungry that they wood take a ear
of corn and eat it the same as a hog wood. I do not know what they wood
have don if we cood not found any corn, som of the time we cood get most
anything that we wanted. As for our famley we had plenty to eat as we got
to mules to pack our grub on, and the Stuard caried the medical knapsack
so I cood go and com as I pleased so I look out well for grub you may bet,
I wood get outside of the gards and then go ahead of the bregade and go to
a house before they cood get a gard their and I most genraly got a back load
but it took me ½ of the day for it wood not do for me to com in threw the
gards with my stuff, so I wood keep outside untill they stop to get their
dinner or Supper and then I wood com in so we had a great plenty to eat
and then I gave our Company about 2 hundred powns of flower and meal
besides a lot of Baken. The docter wood not let me do anything he wood
make the darkeys do all the work he sed it was anough for me to do to for-
rege, and it was gust what I liked to do. I never took anything with leave
onley once and then the man went a cursind our armey and I hurd him for
a few minuits and I told him that he mite think himself well off if he had a
building left to shelter his head in that nite and as I was a talking up com
one of our boys name Brown. I told him what we had bin talking about now
Sis I tell you he broke open that storeg hous and I drawed out my revolver
that I was a caring at that time and told the man to keep cool or he wood
get the contents of the pistol we got as much Baken as we cood lug and left
the man to gard his own house but he was not a vary good gard for we went
into a pease of thick pine grove and waited for the troops to pass and while
we sat in the pines we see the smoak arrise from his hous and we allso see
him being garded along by a soldier with fixed bayonet. We got into our
reglar plaises allrite gust at dark and we had a good laugh off the Baken.
Our Colonel & Mager[1] wood give me a reglar lecture evryday they threten
to Court marshell me and evrything elces, but a good pease of Baken or a
few good panicakets cook by our darkey Jack wood make them allrite of
coarse I understood their talk but the rest did not they seam to think that I
was a runing a great resk, and when I took anything to the Company the
boys wood take the stuff and I wood leave and then one of the boys wood
com around with my bag, so no one cood expose me if they felt so dispose
but we have got threw with all such work and if we go on a march we wood
not be aloud to go into any house now but then we was driving the enemy

before ous and we ment to take evrything so in case we shood be oblige to fall back they wood not find anything to live on, but as soon as Lee give up his armey I told the Docters that I wood not take anything without paying for it. After a class of people give themSelf up to the power of another one it is cowaredly in them to take the advantege of their power after they cry for turms but while at war as you mite say go in for their Stuff that will do you any good and them harm But I must stop Scribbling for this time. I will send you som money in this letter and I wish you wood send me a few stamps So Good By From Yours

Guy C. Taylor

NOTE

1. Maj William H. Hamilton, Spring Green, Wisconsin (Aubery, *Thirty-Sixth Wisconsin Volunteer Infantry*, 293).

ᖰ

In Camp Near Burks Station
April 26th 1865

My Dear Wife

It has bin somtime since I have had a letter from you . . . but then you may get my letters if I do not get yours. At any rate I shell write the same as ever. I got a letter from you 8 days ago and you wrote in that you had got the one that I wrote on the 1st day of this month I wrote to you the first but I did not get a chance to send it not untill the 4 and I did not think then that it wood get to Sity point we was at that time runing after Lee. Oh Sis you cannot give any ide of the time that we had som was on their tip toes while others was layed low by the wepons of the war, but the men felt first rate as a armey they felt better when they was on the march then they did for a few days after we got into Camp again for the men (all most evryone) had the diarie the docters layed it to eating fresh beaf and to the Sent of ded horses. Let anyone com from any other plais except from a battlefield wood have bin sick gust by looking at the ded carcasus that layed around along the road for 40 miles you cood not find a plais wheir you cood look all around you and not see a ded horse and somtimes you wood see 8 or 10 and they was scattered all over the fields the Cavaly had a sharp fite and lasted for 10 days. Well Sis you cannot eaven think how things are wheir their is a fite and I am vary glad that you cannot know but then no it wood make no diffrance for the fiteing is all over with that is for this Corps the Southern armey[1] may have to do som more yet but then I think not. War is a horable thing but then fiteing has to be don, and wheir fiteing is, their is shure to be sombody hurt. I will tell you what I see one morning on this last march. I Saw 8 men laid side by side redy to be covard up, and I cood see others laying all around me that wood soon be laid in another pit, well it is hard to see our fellow man laying in such shape but it is not so hard a site to look at as it is to see the men that is wounded. I have vary often seen men when it barely pleased me (as you may say) to see them draw their last breath for I well knew that they must die, and they was in such agony, but then war is war and the boys on both side try to make their balls count, but I am in hopes that this war has made the American people more wise, then what they was 4 years ago. I do not think that a part of this govament will want to try to divide the govament again for somtime to com. Well Sis I will send you a pease of eigen glass that I pick up near the blew ridge. It is vary plenty in that Section of Country. I suppose that you have hurd all about Shurman pease opperrations.[2] We cood not beleive that Shurman had made a fool of himself for somtime but then we had to beleive it after all but old Grant has gorn down that way now and Shuraden, Joe Johnson[3] & his friend Jeff will have to cut sticks if they save their lives but then they are two Smart men and they will try their skill once in their life, but poor Shurman has wilted like a cabage plant that has bin bitten by the frost and he will want good cair to com up again. Well Sis you must tell all the nuse and I will tell the same to you when their is any to tell. Well I will close and write a few lines to Hen

So Good By From Your Howzzy G. C. Taylor

NOTES
1. The Union Army of the Tennessee.
2. Gen Sherman conditionally agreed to generous terms for the surrender of Joe Johnston's command. The U.S. government refused to approve the terms of surrender.
3. Confederate Gen Joseph E. Johnston was in command of the Southern Army of Tennessee.

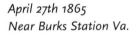

April 27th 1865
Near Burks Station Va.

My Dear Wife

I received your kind letter yesterday and was glad to hear that you was at that time injoying such good health, and I am in hopes that you will be injoying the same when theas few lines reaches you. You say that, that picture looks like me onley I am so fat. I am a good deal fatter now then I was when that was taken, and I feal bout as a whiskey blote looks, as logy and lazy as can be. I think it wood do me good to get out of the armey and go to work at somthing that is a little harder to do, for if I shood have to stay hear untill my time is up I shood get to lazy to breath and I shood die for want of breath all don by being lazy. Well Sis you say that you have got my April fool letter, and you say that you want me to let you know how I like my new home. I like it first rate for all I have to do now is to eat and to sleap, and who can find falt with such work as that, but they say that we have got to go somwheirs in a day or two. The train of wagons starts tomorrow at 7 A.M. most likely we will go to Sity Point or to Petersburg and good meny think that we will soon take boats for Washington, from their to our own states but I cannot see the point gust yet but I do think that we will be to our own state before the last of July next. You say it is repoarted that their is to be no more comision for recruiting, of coars you found out that to be a fack before now. Genral Grant never went to Richmon at all he was so ancious to get to Washington so to stop all recruiting and all other military expences that cood be disposed with. You of coarse have seen the full purticalers of his goine to Washington I raly Beleive that Genral Grant has and will do all that lais in his power to do, to Stop the expenses of the govament, and he will send the armey home as soon as it will be Safe to disband them. Well sis I have sent a roal of papers they are armey papers if you get them I wish that you wood presurve them I have allso sent a book & a shurt I have not paid any postage on them for I am about out of stamps and we cannot get them now and what few I have got I must keep for letters. Well Sis you say that you was disapointed by not geting a letter. I well know you was for good meny days their was 12 days that we got no mail nor sent out any but then that is nothing for what som armeys have to pass threw they go somtime 3 months without any. When anyone is waiting for mail as long as that they know how to appreciate Soldiern wheir their mail runs reglar. Well I do not know of any nuse to write so I will close by Biding you Good By

From yours Guy C. Taylor

～

Headquarters 36 Wis. Vol.
Near Burks Station
May 2ed 1865

My Dear Wife

    As we cood not get redy to start this morning, and will not start untill tomorrow morning it gives me a chance to write you a few lines to let you know that I am injoying the best of health, and I am in hopes that you will be injoying as good when theas lines reachis you. We now expect to go rite to Alaxander 8 miles from Washington and it is the genral opinion that we will be in Madison within 4 weeks from now. We cannot get their any to quick to suit me. You ask me if I had hurd of the death of Chapens.[1] I hurd of it 4 or 5 days after his death. Our boys has gorn like the due before the hot sun, but then we cannot expect but what men will, wilt, when they go threw as much fiteing as this reg. has bin threw the Streanth of our reg. this morning is 409 men. This is what is left after one year surfese out of 964 men, which makes a lost of 555 men they are not all killed nor wounded their is a good meny that is sick but their will be as meny as 400 that will be ded or worst then ded. The genral story is that a man Stands 4 chances to one to get home allrite after surving 3 years but if I know any-thing about warfair I say that a man dos not stand anymore then a equil chance in one year surving. Their is as meny as 600 men in our reg. that will never be more then ½ as good as they was before they com into the armey. They will pick up so they can do a good deal of labor but then they will have to work in misary the rest of their days. Well Sis they say that we start for Alaxander at 2 oc this afternoon. It is now 11 oc so you may know that their is no time to be lost for it takes som time to pack up for a moove, but let ous go the sooner the better we do not yet know how we are agoine but a foot most likely. It will take ous somwheirs between 15 and 20 days to march their and it may be so we cannot get any mail out while we are on

the march, but then you must not be discurage if you do not hear from me
for som time but you must think that we are homeword Bound for such
seams to be the cais and we are ancious to be on the tramp but I must close
for this time so good By

From Your Husband

Guy C. Taylor

May 3ed, 9 miles north of the Junction on the rode to Richmon.

Allrite and hope you the same. 3 oc gust eat my dinner 1 mile north
of Amenlia Coart Hous[2] allrite and full of mischeif gust stoped for the Nite
allrite yet—28 miles from Richmon well good By for this will go out
tonite

NOTES

1. Pvt Marvin J. Chapin, age 26, farmer, Leeds, Columbia County, Wisconsin. He
was captured August 25, 1864, at Ream's Station; paroled March 15, 1865; and sent home
on leave, where he died March 31, 1865 (*Roster, 36th Wisconsin Infantry Regiment of Volunteers and Draftees*, 127).
2. Amelia Courthouse, Virginia.

In the Vercinity of Richmon
May 5th 1865

My Dear Wife

I will try to pencil you a few words to let you know that I am well and allrite we got hear today at 11 oc and we will stop hear untill tomorrow morning when we will take up the line of March again. We have got to march
threw to Washington it will be a march of 220 miles. You may well recon
we will be a set of glad Boys when we get threw to Washington but the boys
are redy for the tramp for they well know that they are on their way home
but then we do not know when we shell get home but we all think that we
will be at home to selabrate the 4th of July. It is most likely that we will stop
onley a few days at Washington. I hope that we will be at Madison in June.
Well Sis I have not got a letter from you for sevral days and I do not think
that I shell get anymore untill we get to Washington and that will be 10 days
surtain if not 15, and I do not think that I shell be able to send another untill

we get their so you must not worrey for we are on our way homeward and
are Well tuff & Hearty

    Well good by sis for this time
    From your Husband

Guy. C. Taylor

    One ½ mile from the Rebs Capitol in Fair vew of the Sity
    Will march threw it tomorrow morning at 8 oc AM

∽

May 14th 1865
Camped 10 miles from Washington

My Dear Wife

    I once more will try to pen you a few words to let you know that I am
well and hope you are injoying the Same good blessing. Today is Sunday,
and we are a laying still in camp a resting. We have got somwheirs about
20 miles more to go to get to our plais of camp. We shell go into camp
between, Washington, and Baltimore. It seams as though we was most
home again. When we get threw it will make ous over 400 miles travel
since the 28 day March, but then we have not don so much tramping for
nothing we think that we have bin well paid for our travels this spring, and
that the prospects are fair for our being at home again before long. The
men are vary healthy considring the long march that we have had. Well sis
we have pass threw a good portion of Va. and it is one thing over again &
again, the sity of Richmon has somday bin quite a sity but it now a pile of
ruans all of the main part of the sity is distroied rite threw the hart of the
sity it has sweep a road 80 rods wide and a mile long slick & clean, the fire
did not leave anything that wood burn, then all out around town the main
buildings are burnt down . . . take what is left it wood make a sity about ⅔
as large as Madison, and about ⅔ of the town was burnt if not more. We
pass threw Fredicksburg two that is or has bin quite a town but the buildings are all full of holes wheir the shells have pass threw them, that is the
town wheir we bared nealy 5 thousand men and had 15 thousand wounded
that was in the days of little Mack raign[1] but he will not be apt to send anymore of our men up to the mouth of the canons to be cut down. We rather
think now that we will start again tomorrow morning to finish our tramping

Richmond, Virginia, ruined buildings in the burned district, April–June 1865 (courtesy Library of Congress Prints and Photographs Division)

it will take 2 days for we will be close to the sity and we will go slow and in good order so to look well their is a good deal of stile in the armey, it is allrite now I am in favor of the reg. to make as good a show as they can I like stile in surtain plaises, but this puting on stile in the field dos not pay for it makes the men twise as much marching to do but then the marching is over so their is no use to say anything about it. The boys are now fixing up for inspection they are talking and singing and the ringe of their ram rods all combined, it makes splendid music now I tell you. This letter is scribled so you cannot read it I guess, but then you may not get it to read for I do not know when I can send it out but I will as soon as their is a chance now you may be ashuared. But I must close so good By for this time

   From Your Hussey

Guy C. Taylor

   Write Soon

NOTE

   1. Taylor was mistaken about which general was in charge in Fredericksburg, Virginia. George B. McClellan was replaced by Ambrose E. Burnside before the first battle of Fredericksburg was fought on December 13, 1862. Maj Gen Joseph Hooker was in command at the time of the May 3–4, 1863, second battle of Fredericksburg (Faust, *Historical Times Illustrated Encyclopedia of the Civil War*, 287–88).

CHAPTER 8

Homeward Bound

May 16 to July 9, 1865

After returning to camp near Washington, D.C., Guy Taylor focused on going home. He watched regiment after regiment receive their discharge papers as he waited for his turn to come. Before any regiment left, however, there was one last Grand Review of the Army of the Potomac and the Army of the Tennessee. Taylor vividly chronicled this final, glorious march of the Union armies as they paraded through the streets of Washington and were cheered by the citizens of a grateful nation.

Taylor also continued to be more open with Sarah concerning the dangers he had experienced. In one of his letters he stated, "I was in frunt of rebels balls wheir I did not know what minuit that I mite be hit by a ball or be blown into a thousand peases by a shell." Previously, he had spared her such details, but now that he was safe, he was more open about those times he had nearly lost his life.

Eventually, the Thirty-Sixth Wisconsin Regiment received orders to pack up, get on a train bound for Parkersburg, West Virginia, and then board the steamship *Delaware*, which would take them down the Ohio River to Jeffersonville, Indiana. True to form, Taylor presented a detailed summary of his journey.

At Jeffersonville, the final paperwork and records were finalized, and the soldiers were discharged. Finally, they boarded a train for Madison, Wisconsin. After an extremely eventful sixteen months, the surviving soldiers of the Thirty-Sixth Wisconsin Volunteer Regiment were homeward bound.

In Camp 5 miles from Washington
May 16th, 1865

My Dear Wife

    I received your letter yesterday and was glad to hear from home again, but was sorrew to hear that our little boy has got hurt, but am glad it is not worse then what it is . . . When your letter reached me I was with the reg. and we was on the road a marching, so I don gust as you told me to do, (that is) I did not stop to read the letter but red it as I walk along but we have stoped now and we are not at home yet and we do not know when we will go home neather, but it is the genral opinion that we will not lay around hear vary long for it is to much of a expence upon the Govament to keep so meny men when their is nothing for them to do . . . that mounts to anything. Well Sis we have had a long tegeas march, but thank the good Lord we have got threw with it. Since the 25 day of March we have traveld 380 miles besides doing all the fiteing that we have and have come into camp with the small lost of 30 men and their is no acount of onley 4 of them being ded the rest will rejoin ous soon or be sent home. I call that doing pretty well for a reg. that Numbers 400 men but we was vary luckey, while we was after Lee, we was on the flank and the rebs wood not stand at all they did not try to make but one reglar stand and they got back in (short order) that was at long bridge[1] across the Adamadic river they set fire to the railroad bridge, and to the wagon bridge but we was so clost up to them that we put out the fire, and as we form a line to rush across the bridge the rebs com down towards ous with a heavy line of Battle but our big Bull dogs had got in persision and before the rebs got in musket shot of our skurmish line the dogs began to bark and it was fun for ous to see them gig back again but their was a good meny of the poor retches that never left the ground wheir they was we lost sevral men by the rebs skurmishers, but we cross the bridge and went on our way rejoising . . . Well as the war is over I do not know as their is any use in talking about warfair but now it becomes our duty to try to surpoit sivil sosiety, and I am vary glad to hear that the temprance sosiety is doing so well as it is in our state and espesley in our naborhood. I do hope that the people of the town of Bristole will try to be one of the leading town in the county. Well Sis their is no nuse to write, for you hear all the war nuse before we do, but it was chearing nuse to the Soldiers to hear of the capture of Jeff Davis, and his crew and the Soldiers wood like to see him a swinging in the air.[2] Well sis I will close this for I do not know what to write but I hope that we will know befor meny day wheather we will go rite home or wheather we have got to stay hear for 3 or 4 months yet but I will stop so good By

From Your Husband

Guy C. Taylor

NOTES
1. The long bridge was actually called the High Bridge.
2. Jefferson Davis was captured near Irwinville, Georgia, May 10, 1865.

In Camp Near Washington Va.
May the 20th 1865

My Dear Wife

I once more take up the pen to let you know that I am well, and am waiting as pasiantly as I can for som order, but what that order will be is more then we can tell but all hope it will be to go home before long. They have bin finding out how meny of the officers wants to stay in the Surfice. Their is about one third of our reg. officers wants to stay and they are thoes that has not bin up with the reg onley a short time and som of them do not know how a gun sounds when it is fiard. Well sis you say that you do not know what to write about if it bothers you any more then it dos me I pity you, for it is the hardest work that I can do, to try to write when I have nothing to write about. Well their is one thing that is we are agoine to try to kill somwheirs about 500 men. The fiteing is over with and their is to meny men left so they have put their wits to work to contrive som perlite way to kill a lot of them, and they have desided upon one plan, that is to have a (so called) grand revew on Tuasday & Wenday next. We have got to march in sollard Column threw the sity and back to camp again it will make ous 20 miles marching to do in one day in close order our armey are to march on Tuasday and Shurmans armey on Wensday no matter how hot it is, no matter if the streats will be lined with sun stricken men, the eyes of a few forren ministers, must behold the *splendid American armey* the Cry of the Soldier is let ous go home if you have no more work for ous to do and if the forren nation wants to know the streath of our armeys let them try ous on for a few battles, but we do not like to be lead around (like wild beasts) for a mear show . . . but never mind it will not be allwais that a mans tongue will be tied, or his body be subject to orders that is abusive, and a shame upon the people you may think that I am crasey or more foolish then ever but if so I am not the onley one it is the talk of evry soldier that I have talked to about it . . . well their is a little show for our being at home to help about harvesting allthough the men will not feal like doing much at first when they get home and their is a good meny that will not do anything untill they are ablidge to get somthing to live on, and of coars you well know that I will be one of that stamp or worst if anything for a man can be worse then being lazy . . . Well our camp it is situated upon a side hill in versinity of Buncins Hills.[1] The hill has a gentle slope to the south east it was once nicely covard with the blosoms of red clover, but it is now pretty well covard with the white canvas wheir the Boys of blue sheald themself from the heat of the southern sun, and the drenthing showers. At the foot of the slope their is a spring that surplies our brigade with vary nice drink the best that we have seen in old Va . . . and allso a little brook that surves ous as a famley washing tub, but I must close for it will not do to take another sheat to write folley upon so good By for this time. I hope that I shell have som nuse next time to write about

From yours Guy C. Taylor

NOTE

1. The Thirty-Sixth Wisconsin was camped on Munson's Hill, located in Fairfax County, Virginia. The 370-foot hill is now an important commercial area named Seven Corners, and the summit is covered with single-family dwellings.

☙

In Camp Near Washington D.C.
May the 24th 1865

My Dear Wife

I received your welcome letter yesterday and was glad to hear from home and to know that you are as comfrabale as you are. You say that Charley cannot walk yet . . . it must be that he is prety bad off . . . you say that you are a looking for me at home. Let me say that it is time to look for me when

Washington, D.C., the grand review of the Army, Gen Andrew A. Humphreys, staff and units of Second Corps passing on Pennsylvania Avenue, May 1865 (courtesy Library of Congress Prints and Photographs Division; Matthew B. Brady, photographer)

you see me a coming. We do not know when we will leave hear but it is most likely that we will get home somtime this summer. Well the great revew[1] of our armey com off yesterday the weather was vary fine for such a day it rained on Sunday & Monday, and Tuasday morning it com off vary fair and the wind blue up fresh and cool from the Northwest. The road is a high turnpike so it was good walking. We started at 7 am and got back to camp at 6 pm it was a splendid site to see. The sity was fix up in grand stile, but the soldier that marched in the ranks did not have a chance to see much

of anything as it hapen I got permit to go wheir I had a mind to, but I had
to run my own resk of being taken up, but that was the least of my fears so
I went and com wheirever I pleased so I had a fair vew of the sity and of the
troops, but then no one can discribe the site that was in the sity yesterday
and today I expect is the same for Shurman armey are on a revew today.
The sity of Washington never saw so meny soldiers togeather before and it
is a great doubt wheather they will ever see so meny togeather again. They
will not get togeather again to fite the Southern States for they know full
well the harvest of war. Va. is one genral buaring ground from the North to
the south and from the east to the west the whole state (that is eastern Va.)
is a purfect waist. The houses have bin reduce to a great amount but not
much if anymore then what the people have bin . . . I have seen little children whiped untill they was meak and willing to surmit to any order but
then I never see anything compair to the willingness & meakingness of the
people of old Va . . . and the boys of Shurmans says that it is the same
wheirever they have bin, of late . . . Well all they have got to do is to mind
their own buisiness and try to fix up their homes once more, but som of
them will not want to plow up their land for it is all redy thrown up into
ridges for them to plant on. The worst trubble will be that the ridges are
prety high for planting. You say that you do not want to write so to have a
mess of letters com back to pay postage on . . . Well it is not best to write to
meny but if I cood get two a week from home it wood satify me vary well as
for letters goine back you nead not look for that yet for it now looks as
though we wood have to stay somwheirs around hear untill the latter part
of June and maybe longer but Shurmans armey will go home before we do
and it will take along time to ship so meny men over one road for they have
all got to go to Baltermore and their is onley one road from Washington
their that is, that the govament can make youse of but then their is one
thing about it we have not got to go wheir balls fly (like hail in a storm) anymore even if we have got to stay out our time, but then the govarment dos
not want ous, so we expect to be at home this sommer but anough for this
time so good By

    From your Husband

Guy C. Taylor

    Write soon so will I
    5 miles from Washington. You will find a rebble invelop and in the
invelop is the list of the lost men in Co. F

Take good cair of yourself & little Boy Be of Good Chear for all is well that ends well

NOTE

1. The Grand Review, a celebration of the Union victory, was held in Washington, D.C. On May 23, Gen Meade led 80,000 men along the Pennsylvania Avenue parade route; and on May 24, Gen Sherman's army, 65,000 men strong, followed the same route. The review was ordered by the War Department (Garrison, *Webb Garrison's Civil War Dictionary*, 128).

❧

Camped Near Washington D.C.
May the 30th 1865

My Dear Wife

I received your kind letter day before yesterday and was glad to hear once more that our little famley was all well. I shood have answered it before but I had gust sent out one as I got yours, so I thought that I wood wait a day or two. Well Sis you nead not be scarred to death, but Docter Woodard has got his discharge and it is most likely that he will be at home by the time that you get this letter for he expects to start tomorrow nite or the next morning, and if he has good luck he will be at home by Saterday.[1] Well, as for our other Docter he seams to be a first rate fellow if evrything goes smooth but he is a purfet fire brand, but then he seys that he well knows that he is flashey but he is as quick over it. Docter W. has gorn to Washington today. He is at work geting straiten up with the govarment but then he has kept evrything prety strait the most bother is with the things that Docter Miller disposed of. Docter Miller was a fine man and a good Docter but a misrable Buisness man. He let evrything run at loos ends never thinking that their was a day of settlement, and his being ded it makes a bad job of it. It is most likely that their will be as much as $150 dollars stopt from his pay and if the docters hear had not don som prety good talking he wood had som 3 hundred dollars stopt but Woodard or Bunnell[2] are men that keeps Buisness matters strate wheather they do anything elces or not. You sed in your last letter that you thought that we was on our way home, so did I and I think so now but I see that you have bin disapointed but then you of coars do not know how much work it is to disband a armey. I thought that we wood not stop hear more then 2 or 3 weeks but I thought when we first got hear that we wood be the first armey to be disbanded but a few days settled that for we soon was told that Shurmans armey was to be the first to go home and it seams now that we will be the last to get out that is of thoes that go home this Sommer, it looks now as though we wood not be at home before the last of July but then we do not know we may be on the way within 3 weeks and may not for 3 months but their is one thing that is surtain that is we will have a vary easy time of it while we do stay we do not have anything to do but to keep ourself all strate and that is somthing now I can tell you, and if the men lay hear for a few months they will get so they will not cair for anybody or thing. They grow more reckless evryday they now say that they have don their duty now they want to go home and as for being snub around by the officers they say that has plaid out, and the officers well understand that to they begin to think that they are not anything but men, and that one man has rites as well as another. Well Sis I am trying som more beans and I shell look out for the wood pile this time for it dos not pay to get mad evrytime that I want a dish of Beans. Well I will close for this time but let me say that a few stamps wood not come in miss but for money I do not want any So Good By

From Your Husband

A Soldier Guy C. Taylor

NOTES

1. Dr. Woodward resigned May 27, 1865 (Aubery, *Thirty-Sixth Wisconsin Volunteer Infantry*, 293).

2. Lafayette H. Bunnell, La Crosse, Wisconsin, first assistant surgeon, Thirty-Sixth Wisconsin Infantry (ibid.).

༄

Camp Near Washington D.C.
May the 30th 1865 [Note: Taylor dated two letters May 30.]

My Dear Wife,

As the Docter has gorn out on a revew with the reg., and I have a chance to write a few lines more. Their is a revew of the 2ed Corps today, By Genral Hancock, our old commander the boys do not cair much about theas revews now. They are geting so that they do not want to do anything. Their is a good meny of our boys Sick I guess that their is 20 in our reg. that are poisened with poisen ShewMake.[1] They did not know the wood so they brot up alot and burnt it to cook by, and by handleing it and by the steam of it a burning it give the boys fits. Well I hope that we will be wheir their is not quite so much poisen before long but then we cannot tell. The weather hear is vary fine now and it bids fair now for a spell of dry weather, not onley dry but hot allso. I expect that you will run to see the docter as soon as he gets home thinking that he will tell you when I am a coming but let me tell you what he will say that is, (I do not know anymore about it then you do) and that is the truath for he dos not know anymore about the mooveing of the armey then a nuween Child. When we get orders to pack up we think that we are agoine to go somwheirs but it is all guess work they are dischargeing men prety fast now within a weeks time our bregade will not have more then two full reg. in it. It has now 8 reg. but they are not full by no means and the orders are to discharge the 62 men[2] and the one year men[3] and that takes a heap of them, and the biggest potion of them will be at home or on their way within a weeks time. Well it will com our turn one of theas days and then we will have a chance to hurah and sing we are goine home. Our Corps has turn in all of their surply train so all the wagons that are on hand now is thoes that draws the stuff of the diffrence reg., So it will not take no time to dispose of them and the officers of each Co. are at work straitening up the books so they can make out the final Satement in a short time when the order coms for that, but then that will not be yet. It takes time this is a large checker board to play on. Andrew Nickels[4] discharge papers are made out he is the fifer in our Co. he has bin detailed to the Hospitol so he was one of the luckey ones if luck you cood call it. Well you nead not greas my old Boots unless you want to for I shell have a pair of U.S. gunboats[5] to wair for awhile when I get home but you may have one thing redy for me to poot on that is a Shurt that is not covard with grayback Lise. When I go home I shell take a Span of them fellows home with me if I can get tranpertation for them they grow so large hear that one of them wood do for a plow team but I do not think that they wood do so well up North a span wood be a (Strong team). You sed in your last that you wanted me to write to you twise a week. I presume if I stay hear long I shell write more then that and if I do and write two sheats two a time and have nothing in the letter then but nonsence you will be glad to tell me not to write so much. Well this sheat is covard with scribles and I will have to stop or take the 3 sheat and it wood be foley to waist another sheat so I will close by biding you good By

From yours, G.C. Taylor

NOTES

1. *Poison sumac* is a woody shrub or small tree that contains a resin that causes skin and mucous membrane irritation. When burned, inhalation of the smoke may bring about a rash on the linings of the lungs and lead to extreme pain and possibly fatal respiratory difficulty.

2. By 1862 Union troop enlistments were for three years, so men who had enlisted in 1862 were the first soldiers to be discharged.

3. Men who had enlisted for a one-year term during the winter of 1864–65.

4. Andrew Nichols, age 33, blacksmith, town of Burke, Dane County, Wisconsin, mustered out at Munsun's Hill, Virginia, June 6, 1865 (*Roster, 36th Wisconsin Infantry Regiment of Volunteers and Draftees*, 137).

5. *Gunboats* is a nickname for army boots.

In Camp Near Washington D.C.
June 1th, 1865

My Dear Wife,

I once more take up my pen to write you a few lines to let you know that I am rite in prime of health. The 2ed Corps has had a grand revew they was revewed by Gen. Hancock . . . they made a fine show it was a fine day for it, and they had a fine plais to march on I did not go out with them I have seen more revews then I wish I had. They are a vary fine thing for the looker on but death to the Soldier they are a devine red nikerchefs but the soldier dos not have a great deal to do anyway now the war is over. Their is one thing they wood like to do that is to go home, but then we have got to wait untill our time coms around. We had a wide awake prosession hear last nite their was somwheirs about 250 men that got in line with their guns and each gun had a lit candle in the musel of it and the lite shining on their bayonets made a splendid site, as they moved along two & frow they look like a brite line of fire and as they mooved on diffrance flanking it made a splendid site . . . at one moment they look to be in purfit confution then all at once they seam to fly into a reglar line then you mite hear by the words, by the rite of Co. to the rear into columns then you cood see the lites whirl appearntly into evry derrection, but soon they wood be as meny lines of lites as their was Co. in batalion. Then this morning we was call up to bid adew to the 19th main they started for home this morning and the air was filled with chear as they went marching by. They have bin men that has don good survice they have met with heavy losses they take back 284 men to their state the rest has becom victoms of war, but thanks to him that has brot ous out of this war with as meny lives saved as their is, not onley to the saveing the life of men but the life of our Nation. The South sucseded in killing the leader of our Nation, but they was greatley merstaken when they thought that his death wood be the death of the nation . . . Well Sis their is

all maner of repoarts are aflote . . . they have now got up a vary fine stoary
they say that they are a trying to discharge the officers and keep the men in
the surfese. Big stoarms now days, but then they will soon blow over, but
then their is som truath in this story that is Colonel Holmstid[1] has sent
in such a recommend to the war department, but then it will not mount
to a row of old rusty pins. This Colonel has charge of our brig. He has
shown himself a purfect Coward and a misrable scamp at high Bridge
while we was after Lees armey. Our men was out on the skurmish line and
he wood not send out the rest of the breg. to surpoart them, I say wood not
he did not that is surtain, so Genral Smith[2] took his Breg. 2ed and went
down and surpoarted our men on the Skurmish line and charge on the rebs
wheir our skurmishers cood not stand the fire and the genral was killed but
he showed himself a man & a officer and died at his post of duty, but it
becom his duty by our Breg. Comander srinking from his duty, he ort to be
stuck up on a pole somwheirs for a show but then their is no use in talking
about the poor puppy, if he shood get hold of this letter it wood be a bad job
for me but then no fear so Good By for this time

From Your Husband

G. C. Taylor

NOTES

1. William Olmstead commanded the First Brigade, Second Division, Second Army
Corps during the Appomattox Campaign.

2. Thomas A. Smyth commanded the Third Brigade, Second Division, Second Army
Corps. He died April 9, 1865, and was the last Union general killed in the war.

In Camp Near Washington
June the 4th 1865

My Dear Wife,

As it is Sunday and a vary hot day I thought that I wood stay in my tent
and write a little to pass away the time, and I stay in my tent more then what
I shood, if it did not hurt me to travile. I went down to the stream and went
in swiming and their was a purfet crowd in the water, and we got a fooling
trying to duck one another, and in our fooling I struck my tow against a
stone and today my foot is a fat one but then it is nothing but a little sprant
in the *Big Tow*. Well Sis you say that you have let Father Thompson have
som more money that is allrite, it is not probable that I shell want money

Union soldiers bathing and swimming, Virginia, May 1864 (courtesy Library of Congress Prints and Photographs Division)

before next fall for it will be so fur along in the sommer that I shood not want to go away anywheirs not untill after harvisting then I shell most likely want evry sent that I can get and a good deal more but then a purson cannot get all their wants surplyed with, and I expect that will be my case on the money line. I told you that you had better keep your money to yourself but then I told you in such a way that I recon that you wood take the hint and it seams as though you did, but the reason that I wrote as I did was so surtain ones wood not be a runing to you for 10 or 20 dollars or any amount, for I new that if you wood once say that it was my order to have the money keep while if you made any other excuses they wood keep trying to get som, but a short answer wood put a end to it.

June 5th

I will try to finish my letter now I thought when I commenced to write that I wood write it in a few minuits, but as I sat a writeing in com a lot of the 1st Minasota boys so I put a way my paper and before they went away I was Sick without any fooling about it, but I feal prety well this morning again. That swim that I took proved a dear job to me. You see it was a hot day and I was prety warm when I went into the watter, and the watter was prety cold well all I have got to say it has learnt me somthing but it com vary near Capsizeing me, and it will be somtime before I give the watter another such a chance. I wrote to you somtime ago about the allotment money and you wrote to me about it, but I have forgot wheather you sed you had got it or had not so I wish you wood write again and let me know wheather you have received any or not and the amount. The other boys that had money taken out of their pay have bin notifide of it by the State but I have not hurd a word about my 10 dollars onley what you wrote about it, and I am such a fool that I foregot all about what you sed about it. Well their is no nuse to write, it is all one thing that is sending off men the men are goine home at wholesale now but it seams that we have got to be near the late end so much the better for ous on som acounts. You say that it makes you mad when you think of the 1 years men acoming home so soon. Well all I can say will not make any odds, But I am sorrow that you will get mad at any such thing as that when I inlisted I inlisted to see fiteing don and to have a hand in the pooden with the rest, theas men that went out for one year they do not know anymore about Soldiering then they did when they was at home (that is that went to the west) thoes that com down hear have seen som fiteing this spring and a good deal of tramping but then their is a large amount of men that did not get hear untill we had got back to Washington and most likely a large amount of them will go home and tell what blody sites they have seen, and how they have bin rite up to the canons mouth & (no doubt but what they have bin) but no load in it nor no rebs near it . . . Well I am in hopes that the 1 year men will injoy themself first rate when they get home. I think that I can injoy myself when I get home that is if you do not get so mad at theas 1 years men that their will be no such thing as living with you but now I guess when you look at the thing gust as it is and take the history of 64 & 65 and study it you will not feal quite so mad. Now when you write gust let me know wheather you get over that madiness any or not. Well I do not cair how mad you get if you will be shure to get over it by the time that I get home. Well Sis I expect that it is pretty warm weather wheir you are now days but it is not hear But it is most pesty *hot* and the hot weather is a pileing up a good meny of the boys. Their is a good meny boys that never will see home againe. The boys as a genral thing do not take cair of themself they are so homesick now they keep up a purfet cry about goine home and the officers are vary easy with them trying to keep them from geting out of patiants. Our Colonel will talk to the boys in such a cool way that they do not want to refuse doing anything that he wants don, and he will not ask to have anything don unless he thinks it is better for the men to do it. The Breg. Comander gave orders to drill 4 hours a day and the boys set up a purfet howl and sed that they wood not go out at all, so the Colonel had them all fall in and repoart at his headquarters so they com down pell mell and formed in a Circle and the Colonel steps out of his tent and ses to the boys that the order is to drill 4 hours a day but he dos not think that it is rite to do so much but that it wood be better for the men to drill ½ hour in the morning and ½ hour towards nite each day, and that he wood like to have them do the best they cood on drill and allso to try and keep the camp as clean as possable, then he ses "that is all" you had ort to sean the caps flying in the air and hurd the Chears that rosed from that line of the men for the Colonel, the Colonel will do all he can for the boys and the boys are redy to do anything for him but they are down on the Breg. Comander, evrytime they see him a rideing along som of the boys will begin to hollow out at him som slang or other. Well I do not think of anything more to write so I will close By Biding you Good By From Your Husband Guy C. Taylor

June the 6th 1865

Well I did not mail this yesterday so I will say one thing that is I am well once more onley I have got poisen a little and that we have gust got orders to go to Leauisville, Kentuca so you had not better send me any stamps for it is doutfull wheather I get your letters or not. We do not know yet when we will start but most likely in 2 or 3 days, and we do not know what we are agoine their for, but it is the genral opinion that we will muster out of the survice their if so I wish we was to start today but then som thinks that we will have to stay in the armey for somtime yet but let that be as it may we will get rid of so much white gloves opperration and I hope get in a healther plais then what we are now in. Well good by the next time I write I may not be in Va. I hope not write soon. From your husband

Guy C. Taylor in Va.

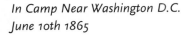

In Camp Near Washington D.C.
June 10th 1865

My Dear Wife,

I once more sit down to pen you a few words to let you know that I am well & hope you & yours the same we are expecting to moove to George-town eather tonight or in the morning and wait their for a few days, for transpertation from their or from Washington. We expect to go to Louis-ville Kentucky, and from their I hope home but it is my opinion that we have got to be at Milawakey to tend to that great fair but don the fair,[1] I say if they do not want ous in the surviss why do they not let ous go home and not take ous all over the Country showing ous like so meny Baboones, but stile and vary fine vew for thoes that can sit in the shade and look on, but if the umbriled folks meant to see soldiers why did they not go south wheir they cood see yankee soldiers and reb soldiers both, but the truath of it is their is a good meny that had reather see the Yankees on perrade then to see the rebs in their frunt in line of battle. I do not want you to think that we call evrybody cowards that has not bin in the armey, not by no means but their is a pile of such men in evry sity, and for our being led around for them to gaze at we think is about plaid out or ort to be at any rate. You nead not take it to granted that we are agoine rite home for we may not go home for a long time yet you can guess how much we know what we are agoine to do. Some says that we are goine to be put into the reglar armey to surve out our time others say we have got to go along the Mississippi river to do garrison duty, others says that we have got to go to Salt Lake to take cair of the Mormons and others are agoine to send ous to fite Indians but they do not know anything about it not a bit more then a nursing baby we are not surpose to know what we are agoine to do . . . so all we can do is to growl & fret and wourrey ourself to death or make up our minds that we can stand it if the govament can and take no thought of the morrow and I have never had any truble yet when I wood let the morrow look out for itself. Well I will send you Jeff Dream[2] be vary carful with it and not get it broke that is the paper. Well I will close By Biding you good By. I will let you pay for this letter for I have no stamps.

From Your Huzzy

Guy C. Taylor

NOTES
1. Wisconsin State Fair.
2. "Jeff's Dream" was a song written by Bernard Covert. It was released on November 21, 1862.

༄

In Camp Near Washington
June the 12th 1865

My Dear Wife,

I received your kind letter day before yesterday and wood had writen yesterday but I was about sick and to tell the truath I have not felt first rate since I took the swim but I have bin as contry as a hog (guss as usal) and wood not take anything, but I was so yesterday that I was vary glad to take medison the Docter sed he thought that I wood com to turms after awhile. Today I feal a good deal better and fair show of fealing better still. We have not left hear yet and do not expect to untill the last of this week now. The reason we have not mooved before is we cood not get transpartation and we are not shure when we will go now but it is most likely that we will go by the first of next week anyhow and we cannot go any two soon to suit the boys . . . they are discharging alot of the men in our reg. but let them go the more the better thoes that are not fit for duty have bin sent to the genral hospitol, and from their they will go home but they do not get this Child to the genral Hospitol, as long as he can keep from them I know what they are to well to be fooled by any fair talk about geting my discharge, they have got to stay in the Hos. For sevral days anyway and be in a room wheir they may be all kinds of dezeases and when they do get their papers (*discharged for Disability*) I do not want no such papers as that now. I have stood the test untill the war is over and pease once more raigns over our land, and now to have a discharge that says that I am not fit for a soldier, I do not want, nor will I have as long as I can do what duty is asined to me, for it is most probaley that we will be at home anyway somtime this sommer and I had reather stay 3 months longer and go out with the reg then to go out on a sick discharge. Well you ask me how I wood like som bake Chicken, I wood like it first rate but I will ask you how wood you like to be hear to take supper with me tonite. I will give you the bill of fair for Drink, Tea & Coffee, with Can milk & Brown & White shuger in it, for food potatoes Bread & Butter onions & pickels, and a good large Bake bread Pooding, now you

may think that we cannot have a pooding that is fit to eat hear in the field
but if you cood onley get a good big dish of it to taist of I am afraid that you
wood see the bottom of the Dish befor you wood set it down. Oh well we
must thank the Sanitary Commissioners for our good living now. Well sis
I do not know of anything new to write about so I will close By Biding you
good By. Write soon

From your Husband

Guy C. Taylor

In Camp Near Washington
June the 15th 1865

My Dear Wife,

I once more take up my pen to write you a few lines to let you know that
I am well once more, and I rather think that I shell be a little carfull how I
expose myself to the air & watter after this. I received a letter from you last
nite and was glad to hear that you are as well as you are but I see you are
geting so you think their is vary little hopes in our geting home vary soon.
You say that you are homesick that (is great) ha ha ha geting homesick now
are you, for the war is over and I suppose that you begin to think that I will
get out of the armey alive. So you are *homesick*. Well their I will give it up,
you never sed a word about such a thing while I was in frunt of rebels balls
wheir I did not know what minuit that I mite be hit by a ball or be blown
into a thousand peases by a shell. Well I guess that I will gust inquire into
this thing a little, it may be that you will find it hard work to get red of this
cooney much harder then you may think you spoke about a pedler the other
day, now I do not know about theas pedlers runing around town. I did
think that it was allrite, but then their was not so much show for our geting
home as their is now, and I see the more show for my geting home the
more homesick you get. Well I will not say anymore for fear you will get to
mad, and I do not want you to hurt anyone, but be carful how you talk with
the streat pedlers. Well Sis we have not got to K. Y. yet and we do not know
when we will get their we are waiting for orders & we will get orders gust
as soon as they can get transpertation for ous, the cars are runing off men

gust as fast as they can, and it is most probley that we will get started in a
vary few days I hope so anyway. You say that you have seen the docter did
you see his white boy and how do you like his looks. I do not thank the
docter any for seting you crasey about me but then it makes no diffrance to
me for I had my mind made up long ago what to do, but for my geting out
of the armey I will never make any false statements to get out, *no*, I will
leave my bones in the south before I will do that. Their is somthings that a
man can do and it may look allrite to the eyes of most of men, but for me
it wood be worse then a honerable death. This armey has bin the ruan of
meny men, and meny that you nor no one elces wood think that it had
affected, unless they knew them, I cood tell you of a good meny things that
have bin don in the armey that you wood say that you wood die before
you wood do the like, and I have bin adviced to do the same thing, and go
home but armey or no armey an oath is the same thing their has bin som
of the bigest swairing I ever hurd by men don hear and they seam to think
it allrite for it is in the armey. A few dollars will hire most anyone to, Swair
in their favor and to make shure of them gust show them a canteen of
whiskey. Well I do not know of anything to write so I will close so good By
    From Your Husband

Guy C. Taylor

～

June the 20th 1865
On Board the Delawair

My Dear Wife,

    I will try to pensel you a few lines to let you know that I am well and allso
let you know wheir I am. Well I am on a fine vessel the Name of the Boat
is Delawair.[1] We are now sailing along the shore of Ohio on the Ohio river,
the weather is fine and the seanary is allso fine. All along the shore the
ladyes are swinging the white handchief and the little Stars and Stripes,
and chear after chear rises from our little craft. We have got our reg. and all
of the Baggage that belongs to it so we have plenty of room for evrything.
We expect to get to our plais of desternation tomorrow nite that is at Louis-
ville K.Y. and how long we will stay their I cannot tell but we all hope not
long, but let me say that we had a vary nice time on the cars from Washington to the river. We was on the cars 3 days and we will be on the watter

3 days surtain. I do not know wheir I shell mail this but to som plais in Ohio I guess at anyway at the first plais the boat stops. The boat rocks so I cannot write but I guess you can pick out a little of it. Well I will write again as soon as we stop so good By

From your Husband

Guy C. Taylor

June 22th 1865

Well Sis as I did not get a chance to mail my letter, I will write a few lines more. We have got to our new home and it is a fine plais to, but we have bin disapointed in our home, we expected to be at Louisville K.Y. but thank God we are once more on sorrell that no band of trators ever trod. We are in the state of Indeanny across the river from Lousiville K.Y. Well I cannot tell you any nues about coming home, but we have bin in luck once, if we had got hear 3 days sooner we wood had to gon down to Arkansass, but we was not hear quick anough, so they had send another division, and they say now that their is fair prospects of our staying hear untill we get our discharge, but then I am afraid that we will not get out as soon as I thought but then we will not have to stay such a orfull while anyway todays paper states that they will discharge all of the armey except 100 thousand by the first of January, and we will stand a good show of geting out in less then 2 months and I shood not be at all surprised if we was out in 4 weeks but then we may not be out as quick as I think for but then I mean to make the best of it anyway, if we get our pay hear in the field I shell try to get a furlow and be at home in the middle of July or the first of Augest, but I now expect to be at home by that time but not on furlow but with a pease of paper that says (to all whom it consurns) and so fourth. Well I will close so good By

Guy C. Taylor

NOTE

1. The USS *Delaware*, which transported the Thirty-Sixth Wisconsin from Parkersburg, West Virginia, to Jeffersonville, Indiana, was a sidewheel steamer built in 1861. During the Civil War the ship served as a gunboat and transport. The *Delaware* was decommissioned at the Washington Naval Yard on August 5, 1865, and sold to the Treasury Department September 12, 1865 (Naval History and Heritage Command, "Dictionary of American Naval Fighting Ships," http://www.history.navy.mil/danfs/d/Delaware.htm).

❧

In Camp at Jeffersonville, Indiana
June the 25th 1865

My Dear Wife,

I once more take up my pen to let you know that I am well and hopeing that you are allso. I have not got any letter yet since we got hear but then I expect to get a lot of them one of theas days, that is if the mail is not lost. I wrote to you awhile ago, asking you if you had got that 10 dollars installment that was took out of my last payment. I know you wrote to me once about it but I have forgot what you sed about it and as the state has not notifyed me of it, so I want somthing to show that it has not bin drawn for their is som show for our geting som money before meny days now and I want evry sent that the govament agreed to pay me, but I am in hopes that the govament will not pay me a great while longer, for I wood like to be my own boss for awhile anyway, but then I expect to have to stay as long as the reg. dos unless I am taken sick and I shell try and avored Sickness the best that I can. I have had all the Sickness I want to have in the armey and I think that I have had my shair but then I have no reason to complain for I have lived threw it so far and have a chance yet, while hundreds of others has gon home but not to their earthley one wheir they can see thoes that they left behind, but have gorn to their everlasting home. Well Sis, I want you to get over being homesick and take the world easy until I get home, for I inlisted for 3 years or sooner discharged or the war and if the govament dos not think proper to let ous go home before next fall they will keep ous and I do not know as we have any reason to find falt, but then I well know that we will find falt whether we have any reason to or not, for it is gust as our Colonel ses that is (tis natural for Soldiers) to find falt and he says if they have not got the rite to he wood like to know who had but then I cannot see the point of our staying hear until fall, but their is a good meny that think so, but if we do not get home within 6 weeks I shell be orfull fooled in my vews of the matter. It is a vary easy matter to get out of the armey now all a man has got to do is leave and he will be discharged without any pay and have the name of deserting they do not try to cetch them now and their is hundreds of them going home now evryday they are willing to loose their pay and repertation to get home and a good meny of them will want to beg for a living when they do get home well evryone to their own fancy but I shell try to get home som other way before I shell desurt but then their is not much show for geting out now unless a purson is good at playing up sick and a good meny do try it and it proove to be a dear job to them for goine out and exposeing themself so much they get sick in good earnest and a heap of them die. Well I must close so good By write often.

From your Husband

Guy C. Taylor

∽

June 26th 1865

Well Sis,

As it is Sunday and a nice cool day I will try to write you a few lines to let you know a little about our trip. Well we got onto the cars at Washington and started out with fair prospects of runing over the taretory at a rapid rate but we did not run onley a short ways before we was stoped by a train of cars that had got smashed up by a tree falling across the track so we had to lay over 3 hours after that we had no truble on our train, but we run vary slow for fear of brake up their was 6 trains of cars caring our troops one rite close up to the other the boys wood run from one train to another evrytime they stop. Well as for our car we had a vary good one we had 8 sick ones to take cair of and then their was 3 or 4 offercers stuck themself in their. They thought that they cood live a little better and they new the Docter wood not turn them out, so it made quite a car load of ous in all 17 besides all of the Hospitol Storage and we had a good load of Senatory Provisions, we gust feed the boys that was sick on evrything that was good to eat & drink at any rate we used up one box of lemons one box of oranges ½ barel of crackers 8 bottles of Blackbary wine 10 cans of tomatoes 12 cans of cranbareys 6 lbs. tea 8 cans milk 5 lbs. white shuger and Lord onley knows how much brown sugar beside a large amount of new bread that was got on the road. This is what the boys was fed on that was sick after we got onto the boat we had a nice cool plais the docter own frunt corner of the boat for the sick and we cood keep it clean and neat for the boys. We took the boat at Parkersburg Va.[1] on the Ohio river we stoped at Cincinnatti and we got a large amount of dryed & smoked meat and I cared a reglar mule load of warm Bread on board the ship. We lived like pigs in the clover and we do now but I have got red of seeing to so meny we do not have onley 3 to look out for now except our own crew and they are geting better fast, but such a nite as we had last nite their was 3 men fairley Screaming with pain in their Bowals, and one of them was our Colonel he went downtown and rode around in the heat all day (and it was orfull hot) and he got prety hungry and eat a vary harty Supper and about midnite he began to grow sick and he was a sick man now I tell you. He is Better this morning I have gust took him a cup of tea and som crackers, he looks as white as a sheat but he feals vary well onley weak. I had a good laugh at him a good Templer & Colonel of a reg. cood not go to town without geting sick it looks Bad. But then their is no one hear thinks that he drank anything and I for mear talk declair that he (did) for his breath smelt of whiskey (not much).[2] Well we had the joek on him anyway this time he got the joek onto me once and he run it good & stout so I thought that I wood run him prety well if he was sick but he says its allrite go on is his onley reply on the goine to town. Well good By

From your Husband

Guy C. Taylor

Co. F 36 Reg. Wis. Vol. Jeffersonville Indiana

NOTES
1. Parkersburg, West Virginia.
2. Aubery discussed the visit to Cincinnati and stated that many of the officers saw the sites and enjoyed themselves (*Thirty-Sixth Wisconsin Volunteer Infantry*, 251).

June 30th 1865
In Camp Jeffersonville

My Dear Wife,

I have received two letters from you since we got hear they both went to Washington first I am in hopes that we will get mail more reglar in a few days. You sed in your last letter that you had the blews well I am sorrow that you feal so downharted. But I do not know how I can help it I thought that I had tryed to make it as pleasent as I cood for you, and if I cood have don anymore then what I have I am not to blaim, for the Lorde has not made me a being to do anymore then what I know you may think that I mite get my Discharge and com home so I mite, but if I know anything at all I know that it wood be the worst thing that I cood do for myself my wife & child, and you will say so to somday. You do not realice the diffrance between a discharge of disability and muster out and it is not to be wondered at but their is one thing that I have thought a good deal of, that is, I thought that you had lived with me long anough to know that I wood do what I thought was for our intrest not mearly for my own benifit but for yours as well as for my own what is for one is for the other, but of late you seam to think that I mite gust as well com home as not and evrything looks to you to be a vary fine thing but I cannot see it in that lite. Well sis we mustard today for 2 months more pay I think we have made our last muster in the field but then I cannot say they keep to work as fast as they can a sending the men home, and our time will com somtime and it will not be a vary long time neather allthough we may not get out before it gets to be cool weather again but it is most probaly that the winter will not find a reg. in the survice except the U.S. troops them will of coarse stay their time out and they expect to and want to and the black Scamps are better off in the armey then anywheir elces, they are trying for furlows now and their is a good meny that have gorn today from our reg. I tryed but I cood not get one this time the officers had som choosen ones they wanted to go but they found out that I was not to be bluffed much as soon as I found out how the thing was a runing I went to the Colonel and told him gust what I thought about it and he says I can go next time. Well Sis we have got a lot of Seneatory Stuff now, last nite the Docter went and got a armey wagon load he gave it out to the men this morning he gave me one pair of drawrs that was all that I was in want of . . . the Docter gave me two heavy blankets to sleap on while I am hear, so it makes me the vary best kind of a bed. Well old gal, you had better be a little Shy with the pedlers that stroals around the Country for pedlers are not men that Bare vary good reputation as a genral thing, but as for the one that sells postage Stamps you may be better prepaired to gage then what I am . . . but let me say that you had better get the old lady to keep still and go a telling the Pedlers that the Boy that is a runing around Belongs to you . . . Well it is gust as I expected for I did not believe that Sarah wood let Ira run around much well never mind I will be let out of Camp one of theas days. Well I do not know as their is anything new to write about so I will close by warning you to *bewair* of *Pedlers*

So good By

Yours Guy C. Taylor

∿

In Camp near Jeffersonville Indiana
July 2ed 1865

My Dear Wife,

I received your letter of the 11th last nite and nite before last I got one of the 17th so you can see how I get your letters but then that cannot be helped. Well Sis I do not see but what you will have to spend the 4th without my being with you. How I shell spend the 4th I do not yet know if I had a plenty of money I wood go to town and go to the big show that they are agoine to have their but as I have no money I think that I will go a black-barring I have bin two days and had good luck. If I onley had som way to bake I wood have a fine mess of pies for the 4th but if I have any I will have to get somone out in the Country to Bake them for me. As for my health it is first rate, but the hot weather has taken off som of my flesh I now way 150 I am on the gad all the time most and mean to be as long as I stay in the camp, for the more I run around the better I feal and the better it is for me. I shell try to be at home somtime the last of this month or the 1st of next that is if the reg. dos not go home they now say that we will not get anymore pay untill we get to Madison how that is I do not know nor do I cair about the pay. Well Sis I wish you wood send me som money I want to by a book and som other things but do not take it out of your state money but take it out that I have sent you. Well sis I do not know of anything new to tell you so I will have to close By Biding you good By

Your Husband

Guy Taylor

∿

Jeffersonville Indiana
July the 5 1865

My Dear Wife,

I received one letter from you day before yesterday and one last nite. You say that you was not hardly able to sit up. I do not know but I have got a ide that you have bin at work for the last year that you had not ort to have don for you well know how you have bin for a long time, but I know the reason of your doing as you have don, you have bin deturmand to save evry sent that you cood. It is a good thing to be saveing but then health is before money but then you must be your own juge. You ask me if you had don rite about the money, of coars you have, for you have kept it all at one plais and if he wants anymore let him have it but you cannot have much more if any now but if we shood get paid off before we get home you will have som but keep anough so you will have somthing to go to in case you want money for anything. Their is not much show now for our geting our pay untill we settle up with the govament for good. They are sending off men from hear as fast as they can and their is not any of them that are paid off hear they have to wait untill they get the eagle discharge[1] in their pockets as the Boys say, then they get their money and go home. I wish I cood get my eagle befor harvisting time but I am afraid that they will not work fast anough so to let ous get home to harvest for it will take awhile to get so any one of ous cood work after we get home. We are now 2 miles from the town but we will eather moove tonite or in the morning rite up to town our reg. will do gard duty in the sity we take the plais of the 7th Reg. Michigan Vet Vol they are musterd out today and start tomorrow for home. They are a mad set of boys for they have got to go home befor they can get a sent of money. They will be at home this week. Well I am glad to see the boys on their way home, and I will be still more glad when we get our papers so we can go. You wanted me to write to you what I wood have to do to get my Discharge I shood have to swair falces, or swair to a purfet lie, if I had stayed in the ranks and took a gun I cood got my papers before this time but I cood not before last winter and I am at a dout wheather I ever wood had sean last winter or not if I had tryed to carred a gun I rather think My bones wood be laying in the sand befor winter sat in but now I think that we all will be at home before a great while and be able to injoy life once more. Maybe you wood like to know what kind of weather we are a having hear it is so hot you cannot hardly stur. Well the 4th has passed and gorn. I went to a picknick and it was a fine afair their was about 40 blew boys their and they was treated with greatest respect. When the table was spread, the Soldiers was the first ones that had to take part in provition line and we don ample justes to the tables to, for nicer tables I never see spread, then they took great delite to make it chearfull for the boys, it was somthing new for ous this is the first time we have had the pleasure of siting down with the Sitersons and protake of the bounteis of life. Well I must close so good By

From Your Husband

Guy C. Taylor

I went at Blackberring this fordnoon and got about 2 quarts so we have Black B sauce for dinner & anough for Supper may you wish you had som with good white shugar on them.

NOTE
   1. The *Eagle Discharge* was a nickname for an honorable discharge paper. The nickname came from the eagle on the mast of the paper.

∿

In Camp near Jeffersonville
July 6th 1865

Dear Wife,

   I wrote you yesterday but as evrything looks diffrance from what they did yesterday I thought I wood write again today. I wrote to you a few days ago to send me som money but I do not want it now, so if you have not sent it do not, for it may be such a thing as our being on a moove before it will get hear and then it will be likely to be lost. I suppose that you wood like to know wheir we are agoine to, well I do not know as it is best to tell you for fear that it will be sad nuse to you but then I will ventur to say that our muster out roals have got hear and the offercers are at work on them as fast as they can and the road will be redy for ous somtime next week, and I will allso say that we now expect to see Madison in less then 3 weeks and their we expect to have a nice time when we get their. Well Sis I wrote to you that I shood try to be at home on a furlow I now think that our furlows will have the Spread eagle on it which honerably Discharged from the survace of the U.S. Survice. Well the sooner we get started the better but we cannot say how long it will be before we get started it is a good deal of work to get the papers made out, but the genral was on hand to send the papers to ous and offercers are hard at work in fixing them so it looks as though we wood be in our own state by the last of this or the first of next month. Well I have nothing more to write about that will interrest you as I know of so I will close.

   By Biding you good By

   Now do not make up your mind that I will be at home in one or 2 weeks for it may be sevral weeks before I get home.

   From Your Husband

Guy C. Taylor

Be carfull of yourself
Health is the happerness of life.

❧

Co. F 36 Reg. Wis. Vol. 1st Brig. Morrow Div.
July 9th 1865
Jeffersonville

My Dear Wife,

I once more pick up my pen to let you know that I am well and am in hopes that theas few lines will find you the same. Well Sis I rather think that this is the last time that I shell write to you, for we expect to be in Madison the last of this week, but then we cannot tell for their is so meny to go and then the cars maybe stopt by som cause or other but then we are agoine home in a few days at the longest but how long we have got to stay in Madison we do not know and for my part it dos not make no great odds for if they keep me over one nite they will do well for I think that I have not forgot the road to Bristoll yet. Well Sis you will not have a great while longer to wait to see me but suppose I shood get home and shood happen to find that Stamp peddler their then what do you think wood be the (quincequance) well anough of this but what to write I do not know, onley to say that I am agoine Home. You may think that you will see me next Sunday but do not be to shure of it, but if evrything goes rite I will be in Bristol next Sunday we do not know but what we will start Tuasday, if not most likely we will Wendsday, and good fortune wood take ous home Fryday nite if so Satterday will take me to Bristol. I have writen this to Jane but I will not derrect it to hur for fear she will not get it if she is up to Leeds, if she is up their, I wish you wood see that she is at home, by the 15th of July for it is not likely that I can get out for more then 24 or 36 hours at first when we get to camp. Well I will close By Biding you good By
   From yours

Guy C. Taylor

Epilogue

In Taylor's final service letter of July 9, 1865, he wrote, "Well Sis I rather think that this is the last time that I shell write to you, for we expect to be in Madison the last of this week."

What a joyous reunion it must have been for the young family. Throughout the war, Guy and Sarah Taylor offered each other their love and support. Each faced a difficult task, Guy as a soldier and Sarah as a single parent left alone to raise their son Charley. Their separation created a painful physical and emotional strain as was indicated in the following passage from Taylor's June 16, 1864, letter: "I wish that I cood see you and little Charley. When I get losome I go out under a tree and set and read in the testerment, and once and a while look at yours & Charleys picture, and it seams as so you was rite with me." Responding to one of Sarah's letters, Guy wrote in his June 22, 1864, letter: "You said in your last letter that you did not know as you ever would see me again, that may be the case, but I hope not. [. . .] If it shood be the case I am in hopes that we may meat hearafter wheir their is no war."

Fortunately, Guy and Sarah Taylor did not have to wait for the hereafter to celebrate their reunion. Many other war couples were not so lucky. For example, losses for Taylor's unit, the Thirty-Sixth Wisconsin, included 157 who were killed or died of wounds and 185 who died from disease with 102 of those dying in Rebel prisons. All in all, the Thirty-Sixth had 578 casualties out of 1,014 men enrolled.[1] The percentage of those killed in battle ranked sixteenth of all the regiments in the Union armies.[2] In less than a year at the front, the Thirty-Sixth had been involved to some degree in eighteen battles.

Soon after returning from the war in July of 1865, Guy, Sarah, and Charley moved to the town of Clinton, Vernon County, Wisconsin. Guy's brother George, along with his wife and family, had settled there in 1864. Guy established a farm, which neighbored the one George owned. According to a warranty deed dated November 25, 1865, Guy C. Taylor purchased 40 acres of land in the town of Clinton in Vernon County, Wisconsin, from Moses Mossey and Lydia Mossey.[3] Perhaps the Mossey mentioned in Taylor's June 16, 1864, letter, and Lydia, whose surname was never given in the letters, were husband and wife.

In 1866, Sarah gave birth to her second son, who they named John. Two years later their third son George was born and was followed by daughters Jane in 1870 and Elizabeth in 1873 and by son Marshall in 1876.

On March 19, 1884, their son John died at the age of seventeen. Sarah passed away August 17, 1888. She had lived to be only forty-four. At the time of her death, her oldest child Charley was twenty-two, and her youngest was eight-year-old Marshall.

On December 12, 1889, Guy Taylor married Electa L. Hurd. In 1893 Guy, Electa, and family moved from the farm into the nearby village of Cashton. There Guy became an insurance agent. In that same year, he also became justice of the peace. From a document I found in the archives of the Cashton Village office, I discovered Guy Taylor and C. M. Culver each received thirty-seven votes in the election. The result was then determined by candidates drawing lots, which resulted in the selection of G. C. Taylor. Taylor held the office of justice of the peace continually until the spring of 1902 at which time he felt he could no longer attend to the duties of the office. Taylor was also elected four times to represent the village of Cashton on the Monroe County Board of Supervisors.[4]

On December 7, 1902, at the age of sixty-two, Guy Taylor died in his home in Cashton. He had taken ill six weeks previously, and after failing considerably, he succumbed to pneumonia. From his obituary, which I located at the Monroe County Historical Museum, I quote,

> He had endeared himself to the people of this village and to all he became acquainted. . . . As a man he was above reproach, always kind to all and ready to help anyone in need, and never was a needy person turned from his door empty handed. His advice was sought and it was always safe to accept his guidance. He was a peacemaker and many can testify of his ability to help in clearing up difficulties without resorting to law. . . . He will long be missed by

the people of Cashton and vicinity but they will ever cherish the memory of his earnest life of toil and may strive to imitate his virtues.[5]

Guy Taylor was laid to rest next to his first wife Sarah and son John in the picturesque Clinton Ridge Cemetery on land Guy sold for use as a burial ground.

Coincidentally, the day after Taylor's funeral, his mother, Axchsa, age 99, passed away at her daughter's home in Winona, Minnesota. Her body was returned to Cashton for her funeral and burial. The bearers who carried her remains had acted as bearers at her son's funeral, and the choir also sang the same songs. She was buried in Clinton Ridge Cemetery next to her husband George who had passed away in 1880 at the age of 82.

Charley, the little boy in Taylor's letters, lived a full life. At the time of his father's death he was living in Peoria, Illinois, but he made it back for the funerals. By 1910, he was living in Tennessee, and he was still there at the time of the 1930 census.

Patsy and I have often visited the Clinton Ridge Cemetery and left flowers at Guy's and Sarah's graves. We feel that through Guy's letters, and our research, we came to know them well.

NOTES

1. Aubery, *Thirty-Sixth Wisconsin Volunteer Infantry*, 260.

2. Ibid., 272.

3. *Warranty Deed*, Vernon County, Wisconsin, Register of Deeds (Chicago: Culver, Page, and Hoyne), 8:560.

4. "Official Records," village of Cashton, Wisconsin, accessed September 2010.

5. Obituary, "Guy C. Taylor," *The Cashton Record*, December 1902, Monroe County Historical Museum, Sparta, Wisconsin, accessed September 2010.

The graves of Guy and Sarah Taylor, Clinton Ridge Cemetery, Vernon County, Wisconsin (photo by Patsy Alderson)

Roster of the Officers of the Thirty-Sixth Wisconsin Regiment

ROSTER

THIRTY-SIXTH WISCONSIN INFANTRY.

FIELD AND STAFF.

NAME.	RESIDENCE.	DATE.	REMARKS.
OFFICERS.			
Colonels.		*Rank from.*	
Frank A. Haskell.....	Madison	Feb. 9, '64...	From 1st Lieut. Co. D, 6th Wis. Inf.; killed in action June 3, '64, Cold Harbor, Va.
John A. Savage, Jr...	Milwaukee.....	June 11, '64...	Lieut. Col., Feb. 9, '64; wnd. June 18, '64, Petersburg, Va.; died July 4, '64, Washington, D. C., wnds.
Harvey M. Brown...	Columbus.......	July 15, '64...	From 1st Lieut. Co. I, 31st Wis. Inf.; Major, Feb. 9, '64; Lieut. Col., June 11, '64; wnd. June 18, '64, Petersburg, Va.; disch. Oct. 27, '64, wnds.
Lieutenant Colonel.			
Clement E. Warner..	Windsor.........	July 15, '64...	From Capt. Co. B; Major, June 11, '64; Col., May 7, '65, not mustered; wnd. Aug. 14, '64, Deep Bottom, Va.; left arm amp.; M. O. July 12, '65.
Major.			
Wm. H. Hamilton....	Spring Green...	July 15, '64...	From Capt. Co. A: Lieut. Col., May 7, '65, not mustered; wnd. Aug. 14, '64, Deep Bottom, Va.; M. O. July 12, '65.
Adjutant.			
Benjamin F. Atwell..	Madison.........	Feb. 24, '64...	From Sergt. Major 1st U. S. S. S.; wnd. June 3, '64, Cold Harbor, Va.; pris. Ream's Station, Va.; M. O. July 12, '65.
Quartermasters.			
Charles B. Peck........	Edgerton........	Feb. 15, '64...	Resigned Oct. 4, '64, disability.
Frederick S. Capron	Chippewa F'ls	Oct. 19, '64...	From Q. M. Sergt.; M. O. July 12, '65.
Surgeons.			
Clarkson Miller........	Geneva.....	Feb. 11, '65...	Pris. Ream's Station, Va.; died Dec. 20, '64, Geneva, Wis., disease.
Elijah A. Woodward	Sun Prairie.....	Jan. 6, '65...	2d Asst. Surgeon., Apr. 1, '64; 1st Asst. Surg., July 29, '64; pris. Ream's Station, Va.; res. May 27, '65.
First Asst. Surgeons.			
Geo. D. Winch...........	Otsego.....	Feb. 20, '64...	Prom. Surg. 42d Wis. Inf. July 29, '64.
Lafayette H. Bunnell	La Crosse.......	Feb. 21, '65...	From Co. B, 2d Wis. Cav.; Surg., July 11, '65, not mustered; M. O. July 12, '65.
Chaplain.			
Peter S. VanNest......	Geneva...........	July 22, '64...	Disch. Jan. 6, '65.
NON-COMMISSIONED OFFICERS.			
Sergeant Majors.		*Appointed.*	
Manly T. Matthews	Gale................	April 1, '64...	From Co. I; returned to Co. as 1st Sergt., July 1, '64.
James M. Aubery.....	Milwaukee.....	Sept. 1, '64...	From Co. G; appointed Quartermaster Sergt., Nov. 1, '64.
Andrew J. Markham	Oshkosh.........	Nov. 1, '64...	From Sergt. Co. B; Brevet Capt., Apr. 2, '65; M. O. July 12, '65.

NAME.	RESIDENCE.	DATE.	REMARKS.
Quarterm'er Serg'ts.			
John J. Gibbs............	Ixonia............	Apr. 1, '64...	From Co. A; disch. Sept. 15, '64.
Frederick S. Capron.	Chippewa F'ls	Sept.15, '64...	From Co. K; prom. Quartermaster, Oct. 19, '64.
James M. Aubery.....	Milwaukee.....	Nov. 1, '64...	From Sergt. Maj.; 2nd Lieut. Co. G, June 15, '65, not mustered; M. O. July 12, '65.
Commissary Sergt.			
Joseph N. Clemmer...	Juda	Apr. 1, '64...	From Co. D; M. O. July 12, '65.
Hospital Steward.			
Alanson Miller.........	Geneva...........	Apr. 1, '64...	From Co. A; M. O. July 12, '65.
Principal Musicians.			
Louis Coulong.........	Waterford......	Apr. 1, '64...	From Co. G. 35th Wis. Inf.; disch. Feb. 1, '65, disability.
Jerome B. Forsyth...	Green Bay......	Feb. 1, '65...	From Co. G; M. O. July 12, '65.
Milo Jones.	Sparta...........	May 1, '65...	From Co. C; M. O. July 12, '65.

Roster of Company F of the Thirty-Sixth Wisconsin Regiment

ROSTER OF COMPANY "F."

NAME.	RESIDENCE.	DATE.	REMARKS.
OFFICERS.			
Captains.		*Rank from.*	
Prescott B. Burwell,	Sun Prairie....	Mar. 9, '64...	Wnd. and pris. June 1, '64, Cold Harbor; died June 28, '64, Richmond, Va., wnds.
Oliver N. Russell.......	Princeton	Oct. 18, '64...	1st Lieut., Mar. 9, '64; wnd. Aug. 25, '64, Ream's Station; M. O. July 12, '65.
First Lieutenants.			
George E. Albee........	Madison..........	Oct. 18, '64...	From 3rd Wis. Battery; 2nd Lieut., Feb. 11, '64; pris. Ream's Station; on det. service, David's Island, N. Y., from Dec. 12, '64, to May 22, '65; M. O. July 12, '65
Second Lieutenant.			
George E. Albee........	Madison	Feb. 11, '64...	Promoted.
Ferdinand A. Wilde...	Princeton	July 15, '65...	From 1st Sergt., not mustered.
Brev't Captain.			
Wm. F. Dantz..........	Dayton............	Aug. 25, '64...	From Private.
Richard Donovan.....	New Holstein.	June 3, '64...	From Corp.
F. H. Holloway	Dayton............	July 1, '64...	From Corp.
Brev't First Lieut.			
D. M. Kanouse.........	Lowell.............	June 2, '63...	From Sergt.
Hyram McIntyre.....	Princeton	July 12, '64...	From Sergt.
Robt. McIlroy..........	Brighton	Oct. 24, '64...	From Private.
ENLISTED MEN.		*Enlisted.*	
Akins, Marshall J.....	Manchester....	Mar. 18, '64...	Corp.; M. O. July 12, '65.
Atkins, DeWitt C	Sun Prairie....	Mar. 14, '64...	Wnd. June 1, '64, Cold Harbor; died Aug. 1, '64, Sun Prairie, Wis., wnds.
Beaumont, William..	St. Marie.... ...	Feb. 26, '64...	Wnd. May 27, '64; left wrist amp.; disch. Dec. 8, '64. wnds.
Bowerman, Nelson...	Vienna............	Mar. 7, '64...	M. O. July 12, '65.
Bowerman, Ernest...	St. Marie........	Feb. 15, '64...	M. O. Sept. 20, '65.
Brazee, Martin.........	Lowell............	Feb. 25, '64...	Pris. Ream's Station; died Nov. 24, '64, Salisbury, N. C., disease.
Brazee, Allen	Lowell.....	Feb. 25, '64...	Corp.; wnd. June 1, '64, Cold Harbor; M. O. July 12, '65.
Carr, Patrick	Manchester....	Feb. 25, '64...	M. O. June 27, '65.
Carr, Patrick, Jr......	Pewaukee.......	Mar. 31, '64...	Corp.; M. O. July 12, '65.
Cassidy, Frank	Princeton	Feb. 25, '64...	Killed in action June 3, '64, Cold Harbor, Va.
Chapin, Marvin J.....	Lowell............	Feb. 28, '64...	Pris. Ream's Station; died Mar. 31, '65, Leeds, Wis., disease.
Cleveland, David L..	Milwaukee.....	Mar. 8, '64...	Disch. Feb. 3, '65, disability.
Cope, Charles H.	Leeds..............	Feb. 22, '64...	Wnd. June 18, '64, near Petersburg; M. O. June 1, '65.
Crampton, Nath. A..	Dekorra..........	Feb. 29, '64...	M. O. May 10, '65.
Crawford, Robert R.	St. Marie........	Feb. 25, '64...	M. O. June 17, '65.
Dailey, Joseph L.......	Leeds..............	Feb. 23, '64...	Sergt.; died Aug. 10, '64, Washington, D. C., disease.
Dantz, William W	Dayton...........	Feb. 29, '64...	Wnd. Ream's Station; Bvt. Capt. Aug. 25, '64; right leg amp.; disch. Jan. 6, '66, wnds.
Donosan, Richard	New Holstein.	Feb. 26, '64...	Corp.; wnd. June 1, '64; Bvt. Capt., June 3, '64; M. O. July 12, '65.
Dore, Edwin L.........	Princeton	Feb. 25, '64...	Corp.; M. O. June 19, '65.
Eggabroad, Albert...	Manchester	Mar. 18, '64...	Wnd. June 18, '64, near Petersburg; pris. Ream's Station; M. O. May 23, '65.
Eichner, Mike........	Milwaukee.....	Feb. 27, '64...	Corp.; wnd. Aug. 16, '64, Deep Bottom, Va.; M. O. July 12, '65.
Foster, John E.........	Leeds..............	Feb. 29, '64...	Died Mar. 28, '64, Madison, Wis., disease.
Frank, Charles H.....	Princeton	Feb. 26, '64...	Corp.; pris. June 1, '64, Cold Harbor; died July 25, '64, Richmond, Va., wnds.
Fuller, John J	Milwaukee.....	Mar. 9, '64...	Corp.; wnd. Aug. 14, '64, Deep Bottom, Va.; M. O. June 1, '65.
Gaston, Vincent C....	Sun Prairie.....	Mar. 14, '64...	Corp.; M. O. July 12, '65.

NAME.	RESIDENCE	DATE.	REMARKS.
Gray, Peter.............	St. Marie........	Feb. 25, '64...	Wnd. June 1, '64, Cold Harbor; M. O. July 12, '65.
Green, Franklin........	Saybrook	Feb. 29, '64...	Pris. June 1, '64, Cold Harbor; absent sick at M. O.
Hackmeister, Henry.	Arlington	Feb. 23, '64...	Vet. Vol.; pris. June 1, '64, Cold Harbor; M. O. July 12, '65.
Hall, William	Lowell............	Mar. 4, '64...	Deserted Apr. 6, '64.
Halleck, George B	Dayton............	Feb. 29, '64...	M. O. July 12, '65.
Hamer, George T	Manchester	Feb. 15, '64...	Vet. Vol.; Sept.; M. O. July 12, '65.
Hewitt, John L	Princeton	Feb. 29, '64...	Wnd. June 13, '64, near Petersburg; M. O. May 12, '65.
Holloway, Jay	Princeton	Feb. 29, '64...	Pris. Ream's Station; M. O. May 21, '65.
Holloway, Frank. H	Dayton............	Feb. 29, '64...	Corp.; wnd. and pris. Cold Harbor; right leg amp.; Bvt. Capt., July 1, '64; M. O. June 1, '65.
Howard, Jay D	Manchester	Feb. 25, '64...	Sergt.; M. O. July 12, '65.
Hughes, Richard M..	Sun Prairie.....	Feb. 29, '64...	Wnd. June 1, '64, Cold Harbor; .M. O. June 1, '65.
Johnson, Leonard H	Dayton............	Feb. 29, '64...	Wnd. June 1, '64, Cold Harbor; died July 8, '64, Dayton, Wis., wnds.
Kanouse, David M...	Lowell............	Feb. 25, '64...	Corp., Sergt.; pris. June 1, '64, Cold Harbor; Bvt. 1st Lieut., June 2, '64; M. O. July 12, '65.
Kellogg, Newton J ...	St. Marie.......	Feb. 25, '64...	Vet. Vol.; Corp., Sergt., 1st Sergt.; prom. 2nd Lieut. Co. C. Oct. 31, '64.
Kirwin, John..........	Manchester	Feb. 17, '64...	M. O. July 12, '65.
Knapp, Jefferson D..	Manchester	Mar. 19, '64...	Corp.; M. O. July 12, 65.
Laymon, Samuel P..	Bovina...........	Feb. 27, '64...	Wnd. June 1, '64, Cold Harbor; disch. Dec. 15, '64, disability.
Lounsbury, James H	St. Marie.......	Feb. 25, '64...	M. O. July 12, '65.
Magill, William.......	Princeton	Feb. 26, '64...	Corp., Sergt.; M. O. July 12, '65.
Main, Henry	Dayton.........	Feb. 29, '64...	Pris. June 1, '64, Cold Harbor; died Oct. 26, '64, Andersonville, Ga., disease.
Marr, John B	Bristol...........	Mar. 11, '64...	Died Oct. 29, '64, Philadelphia, Pa., disease
McCormick, Peter ...	Princeton	Feb. 26, '64...	M. O. May 10, '65.
McElroy, James	Brighton	Feb. 15, '64...	Vet. Vol.; wnd. June 22, '64, near Petersburg; M. O. Aug. 10, '65.
McElroy, Robert......	Brighton	Feb. 26, '64...	Bvt. 1st Lieut., Oct. 24, '64; M. O. July 12, '65.
McIntyre, Hiram	Princeton	Feb. 26, '64...	Corp., Sergt.; wnd. June 18, '64; Bvt. 1st Lieut., June 18, '64; M. O. July 12, '64.
McIntyre, Warren N	Manchester	Feb. 26, '64...	Musician; trans. to V. R. C., Oct. 22, '64; M. O. July 31, '65.
Moe, Abraham D.....	St. Marie........	Feb. 15, '65...	M. O. July 12, '65.
Moe, James G........	Manchester	Mar. 18, '64...	M. O. May 16, '65.
Moore, Isaac..........	Sun Prairie.....	Feb. 29, '64...	Vet. Vol.; Corp.; pris. Oct. 27, '64, Hatcher's Run; M. O. May 27, '65.
Nichols, Myron C.....	Milwaukee	Mar. 8, '64...	Wnd. Aug. 14, '64, Deep Bottom; left arm amp.; disch. Jan. 14, '65, wnds.
Nichols, Andrew.......	Burke	Feb. 27, '64...	Vet. Vol ; Musician; wnd. July 21, '64; M. O. June 7, '65.
O'Neil, Terrence........	Arcadia	Feb. 27, '64...	Wnd. June 18, '64, near Petersburg; M. O. July 31, '65.
Palmer, Lucius........	Manchester	Mar. 18, '64...	Disch. Feb. 29, '65, disability.
Parker, James..........	Manchester	Feb. 25, '64...	M. O. June 1, '65.
Parker, James J.......	Princeton	Mar. 30, '64...	M. O. July 12, '65.
Parkhurst, Chas. G..	Princeton	Feb. 27, '64...	M. O. July 12, '65.
Parsons, Eraseus M.	Manchester	Feb. 27, '64...	Musician; M. O. July 12, ,65.
Perry, George W......	Leeds.............	Feb. 23, '64...	Deserted Apr. 26, '64.
Perry, John..........	Milwaukee	Feb. 25, '64...	Deserted Apr. 26, '64.
Pierce, Emilius W.....	Manchester	Feb. 29, '64...	Pris. Ream's Station; M. O. July 3, '65.
Pillsbury, Granville.	Pewaukee.......	Mar. 30, '64...	Pris Ream's Station; died Dec. 25, '64, Salisbury, N. C., disease.
Pixley, Ira B............	Germantown.	Feb. 27, '64...	Wnd. June 23, '64, near Petersburg; M. O. May 25, '65.
Pohl, William...........	Brighton	Feb. 24, '64...	Vet. Vol ; wnd. June 1; '64, Cold Harbor; M. O. July 12, '65.
Pooler, James...........	Sun Prairie.....	Feb. 25, '64...	Wnd. June 1, '64, Cold Harbor; M. O. July 12, '65.
Rice, Luther.............	St. Marie........	Feb. 25, '64...	Wnd. June 1, '64, Cold Harbor; M. O. July 12, '65.
Russell, Marion C....	St. Marie........	Feb. 15, '65...	M. O. July 12, '65.
Scoville, Luman.......	St. Marie........	Feb. 25, '64...	Pris. Ream's Station; M. O. July 12, '65.
See, John B.............	Dayton............	Feb. 29, '64...	Wnd. June 3, '64, Cold Harbor; M. O. June 10, '65.
Shingler, William.....	St. Marie........	Feb. 25, '64...	Corp.; wnd. June 18, '64, near Petersburg; M. O. July 12, '65.
Slater, Edgar...........	Princeton	Feb. 26, '64...	M. O. July 12, '65.

NAME.	RESIDENCE.	DATE.	REMARKS.
Slingerland, John G..	Brighton	Feb. 29, '64...	Pris. Ream's Station; absent sick at M. O. of Regt.
Soper, Sherman H....	St. Marie........	Feb. 26, '64...	Pris. Ream's Station; died Nov. 19, '64, Salisbury, N. C., disease.
Soule, Henry C.........	St. Marie........	Feb. 16, '64...	Wnd. June 1, '64, Cold Harbor; M. O. July 12, '65.
Switzer, Allen T........	Leeds..............	Feb. 26, '64...	Wnd. June 1, '64, Cold Harbor; disch. Feb. 1, '65, wnds.
Taylor, Guy C..........	Bristol............	Mar. 21, '64...	M. O. July 12, '66.
Trickey, Clement.......	Germantown..	Feb. 25, '64...	Wnd. June 1, '64, Cold Harbor; M. O. July 12, '65.
Tucker, Frank..........	Sun Prairie.....	Apr. 25, '64...	Wnd. June 1, '64, Cold Harbor; disch. Jan. 4, '65.
Tucker, Joel..............	Manchester	Feb. 25, '64...	Disch. Jan. 4, '65.
Twining, Phineas E.	Milwaukee......	Feb. 26, '64...	1st Sergt.; wnd. June 1, '64, Cold Harbor; died Oct. 16, '64, Philadelphia, Pa., wnds.
Van Auken, Francis.	Dayton..........	Feb. 29, '64...	Wnd. June 1, '64, Cold Harbor; M. O. July 12, 65.
Van Voorhees, L.......	Leeds.........	Feb. 29, '64...	Corp.; wnd. June 18, '64, near Petersburg; M. O. July 12, '65.
Vroman, Henry.......	Dayton...........	Feb. 25, '64...	Wagoner; M. O. July 12, '65.
Weldon, Benjamin....	Brighton	Feb. 22, '64...	M. O. May 22, '65.
Whiting, Welcome W	St. Marie........	Feb. 25, '64...	M. O. June 13, '65.
Whitney, Selden H...	Union	Feb. 19, '64...	M. O. June 10, '65.
Wicks, Clarence........	Manchester	Mar. 18, '64...	Vet. Vol.; wnd. and pris. June 1, '64, Cold Harbor; died July 15, '64, Richmond, Va., wnds.
Wilde, Ferdinand A..	Princeton	Feb. 25, '64...	Sergt., 1st Sergt.; 2d Lieutenant.. July 15, '65, not mustered; pris. June 1, '64, Cold Harbor; prom. 2d Lieut., 101st U. S. C. T., Oct. 9, '65.
Wilson, Charles G....	Lowell............	Mar. 4, '64...	Deserted Apr. 6, '64.
Wolf, Daniel G..........	Brighton	Feb. 29, '64...	Wnd. June 1, '64, Cold Harbor; M. O. July 12, '65.

Guy Taylor's December 1, 1864, Letter

Dear wife as I did not
send out the letter to day
that I have writen I thought that
I mite write a few lines more this even
as whitney is laying in bed I am a
siting up and a writing to you & to
mother Taylor as I got a letter from
her to nite I do not now but what
you wood like to now what kind
of a chance I have got for writing well
it is a very good one to write for a
table I have got a pease of a barel
that has bin cut into to make a
tub of that is turnd botom side
up and then I have got a lanton
that I borrowed of one of the sutlers
and for a seat I have the hold
of a handfull of strow on the ground
so you can give som little idy of my
chance for writing but I will have

a letter plais in a day or to
for we have got our house pretty
well a long and if it is fair to
morrow I think that we will finish
yet and then for a table and
a stand to write on after we get
our new house don and get it fixing
I will gust send you a invition to
com and see me and I shall expect
that you will com for it is only a
short distance you say that their is
som trubl th lodge it is a sham
if the boys and girls to, can not get
to geather and a gree well to tell
the truath it is a shame to let a
sosiety like that be broke
up by one or two pursons and I
can not hardely think that it
will be broke up at least I
hope not for I expect to be back
their a gain in the coarse of time

and I want to see that lodge
and all of the lodges in good
runing order what dos Brother Flint
say a bout it or is he a fraid that
he may get sombody vext if he says
a great deal he is a man that
ort to take hold of it in good
earnist and not onley him but
evry Brother & Sister ort to try
and help the thing a long now
is the time for the people to work
at home if they ~~want to have good~~
~~society~~ for they will have a good
deal more to con ten with as soon
as the boys gets back from the
armey and in case they go home
and find that their is a good society
and most of the folks around their
homes belongs to it a great meny
will take rite hold and help them
a long while if their is no inflivme

P 4

to throw a round them only what
is to draw them in to som grog shop
you may expect to see a sorafull
time of it. for their is a large
amount of the boys that will act
like so meny mad men when they
onc get loose if you had seen
what I have by men drinking
licker you wood not think estrange
of my wanting eny body to work
for the caus I temp'ance and if
a man tell me he is a trying to
live a christain life and throws
one ston in the way of any saiety
that is working for the cais of
temp'ance I set him down as a
purfett hipocrick and a pursson
not fit to live in a civilice community
but ort to be kick out of all
civilize community for he is not

P 5

a purson fit to live in
theas times you tell the lodge
members that I say if they let
the lodge go down I shall think
that they are not worthey to be
trusted with any thing for they are
pledge to work for the order and
if they work as they out to the
thing will com out all rite and
the old saying is all is well that
ends well I hosed that
the lodge was well and I want
to see it end well but if it
goes up in any such a way as that
it dos not look to me as so it
wood end well but I can not
believe yet but the thing will
com out all rite after all I
hope so at any rate and the Lodge
haves my best wishes and may god help
them

you will See that I am crasy
or foolish for I have made
orfull blunder when I had got
two pages writen I see that I
had got to sheats to geather and
I though that I wood not throo
one of them a way but I wood
write on both and you can see
by the number of the pages how
they go for I do not expect you
can pick out sence of it any way
so you cood not tell by that
you said that you wanted me to
send to you for what I wanted
I shood have don so if Chipman
had paid you but as he has
not paid you what I want I
meant to make him pay it it
is all the same for all what I
can see but you have got a
Ide that I am in need of things

7

and dont want you to now it
it is not so I am in good health
health and have a plenty to eat
and to wair and good a nough plain
to sleap so their is not any thing
except som clothing that I have
bin in mead of and I have got them
now becaus I am a soldiering you
must not get it into your mind that
I am out of the world & in som body
melon patch for I am not and
I do not expect to go as long as I
can help it their is one thing that
I wood like to have you send
to me that is a buget of tea
that is som thing that we can not
bye hear at any rate what evry
the girls wrote to me and I was
vary glad to get a letter from them
and I wood try and answer them to
rite but I have bin at work

8

all day and I have writen one letter
to write to Mother Taylor and it is
now nearly 11 oc and it is time that
I was at bed But I will write to
the girls in a day or two I began
to write a letter to them gust before
we made our last movve and I have
not finished it yet well I must
close so I will Bid you Good
By

From your Husband Guy Taylor
Take good cair of Charley

But do not make to
much of a pet of him
for if you do he will get
so he will try to be
boss in a little
while

Guy Taylor's December 1, 1864, Letter Rewritten in Sarah's Hand

to be read in the Lodge
Mrs Lewis was very much
pleased with
it

Dec 5 1864

My Dear Wife

As I did not send the letter out today that
I had written I thought that I would
write some tonight, Henry
is in bed and I am writing to you and
Mattie as I got a letter from her tonight
I do not know but you would like to
know what kind of a chance I have for
writing. well it is a very good one to
night, for a table I have got a piece of
a barrel that has been cut in two to
make it. of it in its round bottom
side up and then I have a lantern that I
borrowed of one of the Sutters and for a
seat I have the whole of one handful of straw
on the ground, so you can give some little
idea of my chance for writing but I will
have a better place in a day or two for we
have got our new house pretty well along,
and if it is fair tomorrow I think that

we will finish it, and then get a table
or stand to write on, and after we get our
new house done and get it furnished I
will just send you an invitation to come
and see us, and I shall expect that you
will come for it is only a short distance
you say that there is some trouble in
the Lodge, it is a shame if the boys
and girls too cannot get together and
agree, well to tell the truth it is a
shame to let a society like that be
broken up by one or two persons and
I cannot hardly think that it will be
broken up at least I hope not for I
expect to be back there again in the
course of time and I want to see that
Lodge and all of the Lodges is good
running order, What does Brother
Flint say about it; he is the man that
aught to take hold of it in good earnest
and not only him but every Brother and
Sister aught to try and help the thing
along. Now is the time for the people

to work at home if they want to
have good society to ~~there~~ live in for
they will have a good deal more to contend
with as soon as the boys get back from the
army, for in case they go home and find a
good society and most of the folks belong
to it a great many will take right hold
and ~~helps~~ help them along while if there
is no influence to throw around them
only what is to draw them to the ~~grog~~
grogshop you may expect to see a
sorrowful time of it for there is a large
amount of ~~them~~ the boys that will act
like madmen when they get loose
if you had seen what I have by men drinking
liquor you would not think strange of
my wanting everybody to work for the
cause of Temperance and if a man tells
one he is trying to live a Christian life
and throws obstacles in the way of any
Temperance society I set him down as
a perfect hypocrite and a person not
fit to live in a civilized community

but ought to be kicked out of the society for he is not a person fit to live in these times, you tell the Lodge members that I say if they let the Lodge go down I shall think that they are not worthy to be trusted with any thing, for they are pledged to work for the Order and if they work as they ought to it will come out all right and the old saying is "all is well that ends well" and I have supposed that the Lodge was well and I want to see it end well but if it goes up in any such a way as that it does not look to me as if it did end well But I cannot believe yet but the thing will come out all right after all I hope so at any rate and the Lodge has my best wishes and may God help them, and let me say to the the members of the Lodge stand fast to your work and by the help of Divine Grace you can run a profitable society

But I must close by bidding you

Good Bye from your husband

G. C. Taylor

P.S. Write often and be of good cheer for cheerfulness is what makes life pleasant

(All is well that ends well)

Bibliography

Alderson, Eldred "Red." *The World beyond the Ridge*. N.p., 1995.

Ambrose, Stephen E., ed. *A Wisconsin Boy in Dixie: Civil War Letters of James K. Newton*. Madison: University of Wisconsin Press, 1961.

Aubery, James M. *The Thirty-Sixth Wisconsin Volunteer Infantry*. Milwaukee: Milwaukee Evening Wisconsin Company, 1900.

Bevin, Alexander. *Robert E. Lee's Civil War*. Avon, MA: Adams Media, 1998.

Catton, Bruce. *Grant Takes Command, 1863–1865*. Boston: Little, Brown, 1969.

———. *A Stillness at Appomattox*. Garden City, NY: Doubleday, 1953.

Faust, Drew Gilpin. *This Republic of Suffering: Death and the American Civil War*. New York: Alfred A. Knopf, 2008.

Faust, Patricia, ed. *Historical Times Illustrated Encyclopedia of the Civil War*. New York: Harper Perennial, 1991.

Fox, William F. *Regimental Losses in the American Civil War, 1861–1865*. Albany, NY: Albany, 1889.

Garrison, Webb, Sr. *Webb Garrison's Civil War Dictionary: An Illustrated Guide to the Everyday Language of Soldiers and Civilians*. With contributions by Cheryl Garrison. Nashville: Cumberland House, 2008.

Grant, Ulysses S. *Personal Memoirs of U. S. Grant*. Edited with notes by E. B. Lang. New York: Da Capo, 1982.

Klein, Peter Michael. *Sun Prairie's People, Part 1: Shadows and Dreams*. Sun Prairie, WI: Sun Prairie Historical Society and Museum, 1993.

Klement, Frank L. *Wisconsin and the Civil War*. Madison: State Historical Society of Wisconsin Civil War Centennial Commission, 1963.

Kreiser, Lawrence A., Jr. *Defeating Lee: A History of the Second Corps Army of the Potomac*. Bloomington: Indiana University Press, 2011.

Paar, Jerry, and Mickie Paar. *Vernon County Wisconsin Tombstone Inscriptions*. Vernon County, WI: Vernon County Historical Society, 2003.

Quiner, E. B. *The Military History of Wisconsin: A Record of the Civil and Military Patriot-ism of the State in the War for the Union.* Chicago: Clark, 1866.

Roster, 36th Wisconsin Infantry Regiment of Volunteers and Draftees. N.p.: Wisconsin Historical Society, [2003?].

Trudeau, Noah Andre. *Bloody Roads South: The Wilderness to Cold Harbor, May–June 1864.* Baton Rouge: Louisiana State University Press, 2000.

———. *The Last Citadel: Petersburg, Virginia, June 1864–April 1865.* Boston: Little, Brown, 1991.

———. *Out of the Storm: The End of the Civil War, April–June 1865.* Baton Rouge: Louisiana State University Press, 1995.

Warner, Clement Edson, Elizabeth Marshall Warner, Judith Mayer Risser, E. B. [Edwin Bentley] Quiner. *The Letters of Colonel Clement Edson Warner, While Serving in the Thirty-Sixth Wisconsin Volunteer Infantry Regiment during the American Civil War, 1864–1865.* Milwaukee, WI, 2004.

Index

Note: *page numbers in italics indicate illustrations.*